Book by Book

Book by Book

An Annotated Guide to Young People's Literature with Peacemaking and Conflict Resolution Themes

Carol Spiegel

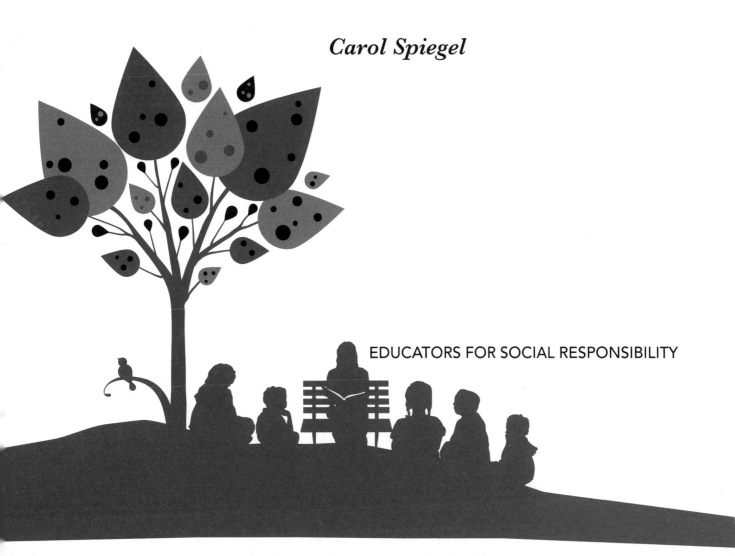

EDUCATORS FOR SOCIAL RESPONSIBILITY

Book by Book: An Annotated Guide to Young People's Literature
for Conflict Resolution and Peacemaking

By Carol Spiegel
© 2010 Educators for Social Responsibility

esr

EDUCATORS FOR SOCIAL RESPONSIBILITY

Educators for Social Responsibility, Inc.
23 Garden Street
Cambridge, MA 02138
www.esrnational.org

Interior design by Publication Services, Inc.
Cover design by Four Eyes Design

Printed in the United States of America

ISBN: 978-0-9423-49-931

This book is dedicated to
my mother Bea
whose storytelling led me to the wonderful world of children's literature,
and to the authors and illustrators
who created the rich collection of books which are annotated in these pages.

Contents

Acknowledgments

I am grateful to all who made this book possible:

❐ the faculty, staff, and administrators at the St. Paul and Minneapolis schools where I served (Trinity, Risen Christ, New Visions, Minnesota Transitions, San Miguel, St. Peter Claver, and St. Matthew's), and especially those people who recommended books to include or suggested improvements to make in this publication;

❐ those who shared resources that enriched this book, or helped me in developing it, especially Joyce Stemper, OSF; Mary Healey, BVM; Jim Radde, SJ; Betty Maas Bennett; Jane Harrison; Ray Ogden; Jean Donahue; Barbara Tadin; the staffs at St. Paul Hayden Heights and Chicago Roosevelt Branch Libraries; Karen Kolb Peterson, Nancy Guertin, and the other librarians at St. Paul Central Library;

❐ William Kreidler (1952–2000), author of the ESR publication, *Teaching Conflict Resolution through Children's Literature*, and Rachel Poliner, whose workshop introduced me to that book and its approach; Jeff Perkins who was the first person at ESR to seriously consider my proposal, Audra Longert who continued the journey, and Denise Wolk whose enthusiasm and patience helped bring this book to completion;

❐ and all who encouraged me throughout the writing of this book, especially my family; Mary Maas; and my BVM sisters, whose unfailing support led me to the ministry of peacemaking and conflict resolution.

Notes to Teachers and Parents

Stories can gently steal into the lives of young people and show the way to peace and conflict resolution. Children's literature is rich with such tales.

As an example picture this. Annie struggles with her anger, and then she hears about Sophie who gets just as angry. Annie is heartened when she learns how Sophie copes. Had someone tried to talk directly with Annie about ways to deal with anger, Annie may have been defensive. This posture was unnecessary when Sophie was being featured.

For eight years I used many of these books in K-8 classrooms. As new books are published, you will find additional stories with the themes addressed here. You might also want to expand the collection to include your favorites or more books of a certain type, say fantasy or adventure, than are listed here. Consider this a "starter kit."

Some of the themes in this collection are closely related. Here are some distinctions that may help you:

- ❏ "Community Building" (under "Making Connections") refers to the creation of community within a group; "Community in Action" (under "Cultural Competence and Social Responsibility") indicates a situation where the members of a community take a stand or reach out to those in need.

- ❏ In the category "Emotional Literacy," "Coping" refers to ongoing or daily challenges, while "Overcoming Obstacles" indicates more intense trials.

- ❏ "Diversity of Individuals" (under "Cultural Competence and Social Responsibility") includes Family Diversity.

- ❏ "Responsible Decision Making" (under "Conflict Management and Responsible Decision Making") includes cases where an individual needs to resist peer pressure.

Here are a few comments about technical details. In the bibliographical data, the most recent printing date is given and, if it is different, the copyright date. Picture books are assumed to have 32 pages. So, the number of pages is not listed unless the book has noticeably more than 32.

Writing this book has been a joy from the beginning. It was a group of third-grade students who initiated this project, when they excitedly reported, "This week Sister Joyce read us a story about Point of View!" I am grateful to the individuals all along the way who contributed to the collection.

Now, may you the reader find treasures that will help you promote peacemaking and conflict resolution, book by book. Carry on, Peacemakers!

Carol Spiegel

Picture Books

All the Colors of the Earth

Sheila Hamanaka
Illustrated by: Sheila Hamanaka
New York: Morrow Junior Books, 2000, ©1994
Grade Level: K-3
Themes: Diversity of Cultures
Other: Audio, Video
Beautiful drawings show a variety of colors of children, their skin and their hair.

All the Colors We Are: The Story of How We Get Our Skin Color = Todos los colores de nuestra piel: la historia de por que tenemos diferentes colores de piel

Katie Kissinger
Photographs by: Wernher Krutein
St. Paul: Redleaf Press, ©1994
Grade Level: 1-4
Themes: Diversity of Cultures
The three sources of our color are explained: ancestors, sun, and melanin. Many pictures of people and some exercises are included.

Allison

Allen Say
Illustrated by: Allen Say
Boston: Houghton Mifflin, 1998, ©1997
Grade Level: P-3
Themes: Diversity of Cultures, Inclusion or Exclusion
When Allison realizes that she looks more like her Asian doll than her parents she feels rejected, until a stray cat finds a home with her family.

The Alphabet War: A Story about Dyslexia

Diane Burton Robb
Illustrated by: Gail Piazza
Morton Grove, IL: Albert Whitman & Company, ©2004
Grade Level: 1-3
Themes: Diversity of Individuals, Overcoming Obstacles
Although Adam loves stories and is gifted in several ways, he meets failure in school. In kindergarten he learns only a few letters of the alphabet. In first and second grades he acts out, trying to cover the fact that he cannot learn to read. Then, in third grade, Adam is tested and a special teacher, Mrs. Wood, helps him overcome his dyslexia. (A Note for Parents and Teachers gives background on learning disabilities.)

Am I a Color Too?

Heidi Cole and Nancy Vogl
Illustrated by: Gerald Purnell
Bellevue, WA: Illumination Arts Publishing, ©2005
Grade Level: K-3
Themes: Diversity of Cultures
Tyler, a biracial boy, asks what color he is if his mother is white and his father black. He goes on to tell all the ways color is a part of our lives: beauty, music, thinking, dreams, love. Then he says, "… am I a color too? No, my name is Tyler. I'm a person just like you." The book is written in poetry.

A to Z: Do You Ever Feel Like Me?: A Guessing Alphabet of Feelings, Words, and Other Cool Stuff

Bonnie Hausman
Photographs by: Sandi Fellman
Styling by: Megan Krieman
New York: Dutton, ©1999
Grade Level: K-2
Themes: Recognizing Emotions
A clever list of situations describes feelings that the reader must guess. (*C is for Curious: An A B C of Feelings* by Woodleigh Marx Hubbard (San Francisco: Scholastic, 2002, ©1990) uses drawings of animals to depict feelings.) *L is for Loving: An ABC for the Way You Feel* by Ken Wilson-Max (New York: Scholastic, 2000, ©1999) uses feeling words and a context for each letter of the alphabet.)

The Accident

Carol Carrick
Illustrated by: Donald Carrick
New York: Clarion Books Books, 1991, ©1976
Grade Level: K-3
Themes: Anger, Apologizing or Forgiving, Coping
Other: Audio, Video
When Christopher's dog is run over, he recovers from his anger, gets a stone for the grave, and talks with his dad.

Alexander and the Terrible, Horrible, No Good, Very Bad Day

Judith Viorst
Illustrated by: Ray Cruz
New York: Atheneum Books for Young Readers, 2003, ©1972
Weekly Reader, 2005, ©1972
Grade Level: 2-4
Themes: Recognizing Emotions
Other: Audio, Video
After Alexander tells in great detail all the things that have gone wrong throughout the day, his mother tells him some days are like that.

Albert's Impossible Toothache

Barbara Williams
Illustrated by: Doug Cushman, 2003; Kay Chora, 1974
Cambridge, MA: Candlewick Press, 2003, ©1974
London: Walker, 2004, ©1974
Grade Level: P-3
Themes: Listening
No one will believe that Albert has a toothache; turtles don't have teeth. Then his grandmother asks Albert where he has the toothache and finds out a gopher had bitten Albert's left toe.

Alex Did It!

Udo Weigelt
Illustrated by: Cristina Kadmon
Translated by: J. Alison James
New York: North-South, ©2002
Grade Level: K-2
Themes: Honesty, Responsible Decision Making
Three little hares, Bouncer, Buster, and Baby, blame their mischief on "Alex." The next day they discover there really is a new hare, and his name is Alex. So, they introduce Alex to all those they had offended, and tell the truth.

Amber was Brave, Essie was Smart: The Story of Amber and Essie Told Here in POEMS and PICTURES

Vera B. Williams

Illustrated by: Vera B. Williams
New York: HarperCollins, 2004, ©2001
    Paw Prints, 2008, ©2001
Grade Level: 2-4
Themes: Coping, Responsible Decision
    Making
Other: Audio
Amber and Essie are two sisters whose father is in jail. They live in a poor high-rise and care for each other when their mother works.

An Angel Just Like Me

Mary Hoffman

Illustrated by: Mary Hoffman,
Cornelius Van Wright, and Ying-Hwa Hu
New York: Dial, 1998, ©1997
London: Frances Lincoln Children's Books,
    2007, ©1997
Grade Level: P-2
Themes: Inclusion or Exclusion
Young T.J. searches for an African American angel that looks like him.

And to Think that We Thought We'd Never be Friends

Mary Ann Hoberman

Illustrated by: Kevin Hawkes
Columbus, OH: McGraw-Hill, 2005, ©1999
Grade Level: K-3
Themes: Peacemaking
A neighborhood squabble becomes a parade that brings peace to the world.

Andrew's Angry Words

Dorothea Lachner

Illustrated by: Thé Tjong-Khing
New York: North-South, 1997, ©1995
Grade Level: K-3
Themes: Anger
Andrew's angry words go from person to person until they finally reach a woman in a market. She gives Andrew some kind words, and he replaces the chain of angry words with kind ones.

Angel Child, Dragon Child

Michele Surat

Illustrated by: Vo-Dinh Mai
Torrence, CA: Frank Schaffer Publications,
    1993, ©1983
Grade Level: 1-4
Themes: Empathy, Diversity of Cultures,
    Hurtful Words
This book tells the story of Ut, her father, and her siblings, who are from Vietnam. They experience many difficulties adjusting to school in the U.S. because a group of students, led by Raymond, the "red-headed boy," make fun of their language, clothes, and customs. Ut sometimes has to be a brave, fierce Dragon Child when she meets with the challenges of a new language or teasing. But she wants to be a happy Angel Child. When she and Raymond end up in the principal's office, the principal requires Raymond to listen to Ut's story and write it down. As a result, Raymond and Ut come to see and appreciate each other through new eyes. The students decide to hold a fund-raising fair in order to bring Ut's mother from Vietnam to be reunited with her family.

Angry Dragon

Thierry Robberecht

Illustrated by: Philippe Goossens
New York: Clarion Books, 2004, ©2003
Grade Level: P-1
Themes: Anger

A boy describes how his anger turns him into a dragon, and how he feels. He ends up crying so hard that his tears put out the fire. He is a little boy again, and his parents assure him they still love him.

Anna and Natalie

Barbara Cole

Illustrated by: Ronald Himler
New York: Star Bright Books, ©2007
Grade Level: K-2
Themes: Respect for Elderly or Disabled

Third-grader Anna, who is never chosen first for teams, writes a winning letter to her teacher Mrs. Randall and is chosen to be one of four students to lay a wreath at the Tomb of the Unknown Soldier in Arlington. Anna's essay is narrated by Natalie who had an ancestor in special services for World War II. Not until the end does the story reveal that Natalie is Anna's seeing-eye dog.

Annie's Gifts

Angela Medearis

Illustrated by: Anna Rich
Boston: Houghton Mifflin, 2001, ©1994
    Paw Prints, 2008, ©1994
Grade Level: 1-3
Themes: Accepting Limitations and Gifts

After being disappointed that she is not musically gifted like her siblings, Annie discovers that art is her gift.

Annie's Plan: Taking Charge of Schoolwork and Homework

Jeanne Kraus

Illustrated by: Charles Beyl
Washington, DC: Magination Press, 2007,
    ©2006
Grade Level: 2-5
Pages: 47
Themes: Problem Solving

Although Annie wants to learn, she finds it difficult to organize and focus. Mrs. Boyer helps Annie and her parents with a ten-point plan for organizing her school work (including organizational aids, cues, and a study buddy), and for carrying out her plan at home. (Endpapers give details on each ten-point plan.)

Antonio's Card = La tarjeta de Antonio

Rigoberto González

Illustrated by: Cecilia Concepción Álvarez
Translated by: Jorge Argueta
San Francisco: Children's Book Press, ©2005
Grade Level: 1-3
Themes: Gender Roles, Diversity of Individuals

Antonio lives happily with his mother Mami and her partner Leslie, until his classmates make fun of Leslie. He is then reluctant to show his handmade Mother's Day card in class, until he realizes how much Leslie means in his life. (*Molly's Family* by Nancy Garden (New York: Farrar, Straus and Giroux, ©2004) poses a similar dilemma.)

Armadillo Tattletale

Helen Ketteman

Illustrated by: Keith Graves
New York: Scholastic, 2003, ©2000
Grade Level: K-3
Themes: Listening, Hurtful Words

Armadillo's long ears helped him overhear other animals. However, when he told what the animals had said, he garbled their words. So, he got his ears clipped.

Armando and the Blue Tarp School

Edith Hope Fine and Judith Pinkerton Josephson

Illustrated by: Hernán Sosa
New York: Lee & Low Books, ©2007
Grade Level: 1-4
Themes: Community in Action, Overcoming
    Obstacles

This is the true story of David Lynch who, in 1980, began a school for children who lived near a city dump in Tijuana. Armando, a composite of the actual children who attended the school, gradually wins the support of his father so that he can stop working and attend the school. After a fire destroys the colony of houses, it is Armando's drawing in a newspaper that gains the support of a benefactor who helps build a school for the community. (The book includes a Glossary and Pronunciation Guide, as well as an author's note giving the historical background.)

Arnie and the Skateboard Gang

Nancy Carlson

Illustrated by: Nancy Carlson
New York: Puffin Books, 1997, ©1995
Grade Level: 1-3
Themes: Peer Pressure, Responsible Decision
    Making

Arnie does not take The Fly's challenge to take the skateboard down too steep a hill and the gang follows Arnie. In *Arnie and the New Kid* (1992, ©1990), Arnie meets a boy in a wheelchair. Arnie gets a lesson in honesty in *Arnie and the Stolen Markers* (1989, ©1987).

Arthur and the New Kid

Marc Tolon Brown

Illustrated by: Marc Tolon Brown
New York: Random House, ©2004
Grade Level: 2-3
Themes: Prejudice or Dislike
Arthur and his friends find that, contrary to first impressions, Norbert the new student is friendly, smart, and athletic.

Ask Me

Antje Damm

Illustrated by: Antje Damm
Translated by: Doris Orgel
Brookfield, CT: Roaring Book Press, 2003,
    ©2002
London: Frances Lincoln Children's Books,
    2008, ©2002
Grade Level: P-3
Pages: 220
Themes: Listening
This book contains over 100 questions about many aspects of life, each on a page facing an illustration or photo. This collection could be used as a resource for initiating class discussion.

Babar's Battle

Laurent de Brunhoff

Illustrated by: Laurent de Brunhoff
New York: Harry N. Abrams, Inc., 2002, ©1992
Grade Level: P-2
Themes: Peacemaking, Mediation or
    Negotiation, Nonviolent Response
Rataxes, the rhino king, is urged by rhino witch Macidexia to do away with Babar, the elephant king. In order to avoid battle, Babar convinces Rataxes to fight one-on-one, and then defeats Rataxes without hurting him.

Babu's Song

Stephanie Stuve-Bodeen
Illustrated by: Aaron Boyd
New York: Lee & Low, 2008, ©2003
Grade Level: P-3
Themes: Overcoming Obstacles, Honesty

In order to attend school in his Tanzanian village, Barnardi markets the toys made by his grandfather "Babu" who cannot speak because of a stroke. After Barnardi is tempted to buy a soccer ball with the money from a music box that plays a song sung by Babu, he ends up telling his grandfather. Babu uses the money for school and makes another music box.

A Bad Case of Stripes

David Shannon
Illustrated by: David Shannon
New York: Scholastic, 2007, ©1998
Grade Level: K-2
Themes: Peer Pressure
Other: Audio

Camilla Cream worries too much about what others think of her and tries desperately to please everyone. She's cured when she learns to relax and accept herself.

Ballerina Dreams: A True Story

Lauren Thompson
Photographs by: James Estrin
New York, NY: Holtzbrinck Publishers, ©2007
Grade Level: P-2
Themes: Overcoming Obstacles, Respect for
    Elderly or Disabled

This is a true story about five girls (Abbey, Monica, Nicole, Shekinah, and Veronica), ages three to seven, who attend ballet class given by Joanne Ferrara, a physical therapist in Queens, NY. Although four of the girls have cerebral palsy and one has Erb's palsy, Joanne and her teenage volunteers make it possible for the girls to fulfill their dreams of dancing on stage like their sisters and friends. Photographs and text give an account of that stage performance, the preparations for it, and the motivation and satisfaction it gives the young performers. Background notes are included.

Barack Obama: Son of Promise, Child of Hope

Nikki Grimes
Illustrator: Bryan Collier
New York: Simon & Schuster, ©2008
Grade Level: K-5
Pages:
Themes: Community Building, Diversity of
    Cultures, Overcoming Obstacles, Point of
    View

A mother tells her young son David the story of Barack Obama becoming a presidential candidate. As he hears the story, David identifies with many elements in Barack's life, including his own hopes of helping others live better lives, as well as the absence of his divorced father. Throughout the story, Hope guides Barack's life.

A Bargain for Frances

Russell Hoban
Illustrated by: Lillian Hoban
New York: HarperFestival, 2008, ©1970
Grade Level: 1-3
Themes: Friendship
Other: Audio

Frances, a lovable badger, outwits Thelma who has tried to made an unfair trade. They both decide it's better to be friends than to have to be careful of each other.

Baseball Saved Us

Ken Mochizuki
Illustrated by: Dom Lee
New York: Scholastic, 1996, ©1993
Pine Plains, NY: Live Oaks Media, 2004, ©1993
Grade Level: 2-4
Themes: Coping, Oppression
Other: Audio

In a World War II internment camp, Ken, a young Japanese-American boy and his father build a baseball diamond and form a league so that the internees will have something to look forward to—even if only for nine innings.

A Basket of Bangles: How a Business Begins

Ginger Howard
Illustrated by: Cheryl Kirk Noll
Brookfield, CT: The Millbrook Press, ©2002
Grade Level: 1-4
Themes: Cooperation, Community in Action
Five women in Bangladesh get loans from the Grameen Bank and begin businesses. Additional explanation on the Grameen Bank is included.

The Bat Boy & His Violin

Gavin Curtis
Illustrated by: Earl B. Lewis
New York: Aladdin Paperbacks, 2001, ©1998
Grade Level: 1-4
Themes: Accepting Limitations and Gifts, Gender Roles
Although his dad manages the Dukes who play baseball for the 1948 Negro National League, Reginald is devoted to his violin. Eventually, as bat boy, he uses his violin to help the players through a tough season. In the end, Reginald learns that his dad loves him no matter how limited his sports ability.

Bat in the Dining Room

Crescent Dragonwagon
Illustrated by: S. D. Schlinder
New York: Marshall Cavendish, 2003, ©1997
Grade Level: K-3
Themes: Point of View
Observant Melissa thinks about how a bat feels when it lands in the dining room of a hotel. While everyone else panics, she keeps her cool and leads the bat back into the night.

Be Gentle!

Virginia Miller
Cambridge, MA: Candlewick Press, 2002, ©1997
London: Walker, 2008, ©1997
Grade Level: K
Pages: 24
Themes: Respect in General
Bartholomew, a bear cub, does not understand how to be gentle with a little black kitten. When she hides from him, he gets the message and succeeds.

Beads on One String

Dennis Warner
Illustrated by: Alison Love Unzelman
St. Cloud, MN: MK Publishing, ©2004
Grade Level: K-4
Themes: Peacemaking
A song begins, *We're all Beads on One String*, and its lyrics form the text of the book. Full-page illustrations show people from around the world in a range of activities. The CD and sheet music are included with the book.

Beatrice's Goat

Page McBrier
Illustrated by: Lori Lohstoeter
New York: Aladdin, 2004, ©2000
    Spoken Arts, 2006, ©2000
Grade Level: K-3
Themes: Community in Action, Problem Solving
Other: Video
This is a true story about Beatrice, a nine-year-old Ugandan girl whose family receives a goat through Project Heifer. The goat provides steady income and the opportunity for Beatrice to attend school, and for her family to get the resources they need. The Afterword is written by Hillary Rodham Clinton.

Beautiful Blackbird

Ashley Bryan
Illustrated by: Ashley Bryan
New York: Atheneum, 2005, ©2003
Grade Level: K-2
Themes: Diversity of Cultures
Other: Audio
In this Zambian tale Blackbird, considered the most beautiful, shares black markings with the other birds.

Beauty, Her Basket

Sandra Belton
Illustrated by: Cozbi A. Cabrera
New York: Greenwillow, ©2004
Grade Level: 1-4
Themes: Diversity of Cultures
While a young girl stays with her Nana in the Sea Islands, she learns how to make a sea grass basket and hears of other legacies brought by her ancestors from Africa.

Becky the Brave: A Story about Epilepsy

Laurie Lears
Illustrated by: Gail Piazza
Morton Grove, IL: Whitman, ©2002
Grade Level: P-3
Themes: Inclusion or Exclusion, Respect for Elderly or Disabled
Other: Audio
Sarah tells about her big sister Becky who has epilepsy. After Becky has a seizure in school and does not want to return, Sarah explains to the class and they write notes of welcome to Becky.

Bein' With You This Way = La alegría de ser tú y yo

W. Nikola-Lisa
Illustrated by: Michael Bryant
Translated by: Yanitzia Canetti
Boston: Houghton Mifflin, 1997, ©1994
Pine Plains, NY: Live Oaks Media, 1999, ©1994
Grade Level: K-2
Themes: Alike and Different, Diversity of Cultures
Other: Audio
Rhythmic verses celebrate lots of differences: "Different—Mm-mmm, but the same, Ah-ha!"

Being Friends

Karen Beaumont
Illustrated by: Joy Allen
New York: Dial, ©2002
Grade Level: P-K
Themes: Alike and Different
Two girls celebrate their friendship and the ways they are alike and different.

The Berenstain Bears' New Neighbors

Stan Berenstain and Jan Berenstain
Illustrated by: Stan Berenstain and Jan Berenstain
New York: Random House, ©1994
Level: K-3
Themes: Prejudice or Dislike
Father Bear is worried about the Panda family who moves in, because they are "different." (The Berenstain Bears books address themes in several categories.)

Best Best Friends

Margaret Chodos-Irvine

Illustrated by: Margaret Chodos-Irvine
Orlando, FL: Harcourt, ©2006
Grade Level: P-1
Themes: Conflict Escalator, Friendship, Jealousy

Mary and Clare are best friends. When the preschool celebrates Mary's birthday, Clare gets so jealous that she starts a fight that escalates, but the two friends make up before the day is over.

The Best Eid Ever

Asma Mobin-Uddin

Illustrated by: Laura Jacobsen
Honesdale, PA: Boyds Mills Press, ©2007
Grade Level: 1-4
Themes: Coping, Diversity of Cultures, Sharing

It is Eid, and Aneesa is missing her parents who have left United States for the Hajj Pilgrimage in Saudi Arabia. Her grandmother Nonni gives Aneesa three new outfits for the Eid holiday. At Eid prayers, Aneesa meets young Zayneb and her sister Mariam whose family has recently arrived, having left all their possessions behind. Aneesa and Nonni live out the lessons of their Eid holiday by sharing food and clothes with the new family.

Best Friends

Miriam Cohen

Illustrated by: Lillian Hoban
New York: Aladdin Paperbacks, 2007, ©1971
Grade Level: K-3
Themes: Friendship

After some misunderstandings about friendship, Jim and Paul learn that they really are best friends.

Best Friends

Steven Kellogg

Illustrated by: Steven Kellogg
New York: Puffin Books, 1992, ©1986
Grade Level: K-3
Themes: Sharing, Jealousy

Kathy and Louise are inseparable until Louise's aunt and uncle arrive to take Louise camping for the summer. Prior to Louise's adventurous trip, the two girls did everything together, and while Louise is away, her friend Kathy continually feels lonely and sorry for herself. When Kathy receives a postcard from her friend informing her about the fun she is having and the new friends she is making, Kathy becomes extremely jealous. Kathy is hesitant and acts rather strangely upon Louise's return. A surprise ending helps Kathy realize that she is loved and valued by her best friend after all.

The Best Friends Club: A Lizzie and Harold Story

Elizabeth Winthrop

Illustrated by: Martha Weston
Orlando, FL: Harcourt Brace, 1996, ©1989
Grade Level: K-2
Themes: Inclusion or Exclusion

Lizzie and Harold create an exclusive club, but the club is not any fun until it is open to others.

Best Friends for Frances

Russell Hoban

Illustrated by: Lillian Hoban
New York: HarperTrophy, 2009, ©1969
Grade Level: K-3
Themes: Inclusion or Exclusion
Other: Audio

Frances befriends her sister Gloria and teaches Albert to include girls in his activities.

The Best Kind of Gift

Kathi Appelt
Illustrated by: Paul Brett Johnson
New York: HarperCollins, ©2003
Grade Level: K-2
Themes: Community Building, Sharing
When the congregation has a pounding (each person brings a pound of something) to welcome Brother Harper to the community, Jory Timmons feels bad that he cannot give gifts like those from his family (milk, pie, eggs, etc.). In the end, Jory gives a gift from his heart—a bag of skipping stones.

The Best Part of Me

Wendy Ewald
Illustrated by: Wendy Ewald
Boston: Little, Brown, ©2002
Grade Level: 1-4
Themes: Accepting Limitations and Gifts
Photos show children in 3rd through 5th grades who tell their favorite features.

Big Al and Shrimpy

Andrew Clements
Illustrated by: Yoshi
New York: Aladdin, 2005, ©2002
Grade Level: P-2
Themes: Cooperation
Other: Audio, Video
When Big Al gets caught in the Big Deep of the ocean, a tiny fish coordinates his rescue. This is a sequel to *Big Al* (1998, ©1988), which involves acceptance of gifts and limitations.

The Big Bad Rumor

Jonathan Meres
Illustrated by: Jacqueline East
New York: Orchard, ©2000
London: Red Fox, 2002, ©2000
Grade Level: K-2
Themes: Rumors or Suspicion
The goose says a big bad wolf is coming, and the message gets garbled throughout. At the end there is a little sad wolf—and his dad.

The Biggest Nose

Kathy Caple
Illustrated by: Kathy Caple
Boston: Houghton Mifflin, 1988, ©1985
Grade Level: K-2
Themes: Accepting Limitations and Gifts
Eleanor the elephant is teased about her big nose. She ties it in a knot and, when she finally gets the knot out, she is grateful for her nose. [Class discussion may be needed regarding the way Eleanor calls attention to unattractive features of the other animal students.]

The Biggest Soap

Carole Lexa Schaefer
Illustrated by: Stacey Dressen-McQueen
New York: Farrar, Straus and Giroux, ©2004
Grade Level: P-3
Themes: Sharing
When Kessy, a young boy on a South Pacific Island, gets a big bar of soap for his mother's laundry, he returns with a delightful story of how he has already shared the soap.

The Biggest Test in the Universe

Nancy Poydar

Illustrated by: Nancy Poydar
New York: Holiday House, 2005, ©2004
Grade Level: 1-3
Themes: Fear or Worry, Rumors or Suspicion
Other: Video

Because of all he has heard, Sam worries about the big test on Friday. After the test is over, Sam feels better because he has survived the big test. Yet, Sam and his classmates perpetuate the rumors to the other students.

Bikes for Rent!

Isaac Olaleye

Illustrated by: Chris Demarest
New York: Orchard, ©2001
Grade Level: K-2
Themes: Honesty, Responsible Decision
  Making

After saving his money, Lateef, a village boy in Nigeria, rents a bike. He accepts a dare and damages the bike. Babatunde, the owner, allows Lateef to work in order to pay for the damages, and then to earn enough to buy his own bike.

The Birdman

Veronika Martenova Charles

Illustrated by: Annouchka Gravel Galouchko
  and Stéphan Daigle
Platsburgh, NY: Tundra Books, ©2006
Grade Level: 2-5
Themes: Emotions, Point of View, Sharing

This is the true story of Noor Nobi, a Calcutta tailor who reached out after the accident which claimed his three children. Nobi, deep in grief, was able to imagine the pain of illegally caged birds. So, he earned money in order to purchase and free the birds, building a new life for himself and others.

A Birthday for Frances

Russell Hoban

Illustrated by: Lillian Hoban
New York: HarperCollins, 1995, ©1968
London: Red Fox, 2002, ©1968
Grade Level: K-3
Themes: Sharing
Other: Audio

Frances tries to be generous when her little sister Gloria has a birthday.

Blabber Mouse

True Kelley

Illustrated by: True Kelley
New York: Scholastic, 2003, ©2001
Grade Level: 1-3
Themes: Social Skills
Other: Audio

Blabber Mouse constantly blurts out and cannot keep a secret. At a surprise party, his friends help him by giving him a diary for his secrets.

Black All Around!

Patricia Hubbell

Illustrated by: Don Tate
New York: Lee & Low, ©2004
Grade Level: P-3
Themes: Diversity of Cultures

A young girl celebrates as she finds the color black in all areas of life. (*Shades of Black: A Celebration of our Children* by Sandra Pinkney (New York: Scholastic, 2006, ©2000) gives colorful descriptions of black children's skin and eye color and hair texture.)

Black is Brown is Tan

Arnold Adoff

Illustrated by: Emily Arnold McCully
New York: Harper Collins, 2002, ©1973
   Paw Prints, 2008, ©1973
Grade Level: 1-3
Themes: Diversity of Cultures
A poem tells the story of an interracial family celebrating their diversity. (In *Hope* by Isabell Monk (Minneapolis: Carolrhoda Books, 2000, ©1998) a young girl learns about her biracial heritage from her aunt.)

Blackberry Stew

Isabell Monk

Illustrated by: Janice Lee Porter
Minneapolis: Lerner, 2006, ©2005
Grade Level: K-3
Themes: Fear or Worry, Coping
When Hope hesitates to go to Grandpa Jack's funeral, her Aunt Poogee shows Hope how to see Grandpa Jack in her mind's eye. Hope recalls blackberry picking and Grandpa Jack helping her overcome her fear of garden snakes. A recipe for Blackberry Stew is included.

The Blind Hunter

Kristina Rodanas

Illustrated by: Kristina Rodanas
New York: Marshall Cavendish, ©2003
Grade Level: K-3
Themes: Respect for Elderly or Disabled,
   Apologizing or Forgiving
Chirobo is a wise African man who is blind. When they go hunting, Chirobo teaches Muteye about his many ways of observing, and about how to forgive and see with the heart.

Block Party Today

Marilyn Singer

Illustrated by: Stephanie Roth
New York: Knopf, ©2004
Grade Level: K-3
Themes: Cooperation
After Yasmin and Sue do not let her have the first turn in Double Dutch, Lola refuses to help prepare the Block Party. However, the two girls manage to help Lola get over her mood and join in the party.

The Blue Ribbon Day

Katie Couric

Illustrated by: Marjorie Priceman
New York: Doubleday, ©2004
Grade Level: K-2
Themes: Accepting Limitations and Gifts
Carrie O'Toole is distraught when her friend Ellen McSnelly makes the soccer team and she does not. After her mother encourages her to find out what she is good at, Carrie and her lab partner Lazlo's crystal project wins first place in the science fair. Then Carrie cheers Ellie in a soccer victory.

Boundless Grace

Mary Hoffman

Illustrated by: Caroline Binch
New York: Puffin Books, 2000, ©1995
   Paw Prints, 2008, ©1995
Grade Level: K-3
Themes: Community Building, Diversity of
   Individuals
Other: Audio
Grace learns to accept her family as it is when she and her Nana go to Africa to visit Grace's father and his family. This is a sequel to *Amazing Grace* (New York: Puffin Books, 2000, ©1991) which addresses gender roles.

The Boxer and the Princess

Helme Heine
Illustrated by: Helme Heine
New York: Margaret K. McElderry, ©1998
Grade Level: K-3
Themes: Recognizing Emotions
Max, a sensitive rhinoceros, wears armor that protects him, but it also hides his feelings. When he meets a princess, he no longer needs the armor.

Boxes for Katje

Candace Fleming
Illustrated by: Stacey Dressen-McQueen
New York: Farrar, Straus and Giroux, ©2003
Grade Level: 1-4
Themes: Community Building, Sharing, Basic
     Emotional Needs
Other: Audio, Video
This true story begins after World War II, when Rosie Johnson from Mayfield, IN, sends a box to Katje Van Stegeran in Olst, Holland. Katje shares the chocolate with the Postman Kleinhoonte and sends a thank you to Rosie. This begins a series of boxes sent by Rosie and her neighbors to Katje's community during a winter of hardship. The story ends with the Hollanders sending tulips to Indiana.

Boy, You're Amazing!

Virginia Kroll
Illustrated by: Sachiko Yoshikawa
Morton Grove, IL: Whitman, ©2004
Grade Level: P-2
Themes: Gender Roles
This book celebrates many talents and qualities of a young boy. (*Girl, You're Amazing!* (©2001), for grades K-4, also addresses gender roles.)

The Bracelet

Yoshiko Uchida
Illustrated by: Joanna Yardley
Evanston, IL: Dougal Littell, 1997, ©1993
Grade Level: 2-5
Themes: Friendship, Oppression
Other: Video
In 1942, Emi and her family are sent to a Japanese internment camp. When she loses the gift bracelet from her friend Laurie, Emi learns that she does not need a reminder to remember her friend.

The Brand New Kid

Katie Couric
Illustrated by: Marjorie Priceman
New York: Scholastic, 2001, ©2000
Grade Level: P-3
Themes: Inclusion or Exclusion, Diversity of
     Individuals
Lazlo is excluded and sad, until Elly McSnelly reaches out to him and gets to know him.

Bravery Soup

Maryann Cocca-Leffler
Illustrated by: Maryann Cocca-Leffler
Morton Grove, IL: Whitman, ©2002
Grade Level: P-2
Themes: Fear or Worry
Big Bear sends Carlin, a fearful raccoon, to a scary cave to get an ingredient for Bravery Soup. Carlin discovers that he has bravery inside himself.

Bravo, Mildred & Ed!

Karen Wagner
Illustrated by: Janet Pedersen
New York: Walker, ©2000
Grade Level: P-3
Themes: Problem Solving
When Mildred's violin concert conflicts with Ed's button art show, the two old friends find a way to stay friends and to do things separately. (In *Heron & Turtle* by Valeri Gorbachev (New York: Philomel Books, ©2006), two friends find clever ways to accommodate their differing needs.)

Broken Cat

Lynne Rae Perkins
Illustrated by: Lynne Rae Perkins
New York: Greenwillow, ©2002
Grade Level: P-2
Themes: Fear or Worry
While Andy waits at the vet's with his cat Frank, Andy's mother and grandmother tell the story of his mother breaking her wrist when she was a girl.

Brothers and Sisters

Laura Dwight
Photographs by: Laura Dwight
New York: Star Bright Books, ©2005
Grade Level: K-3
Themes: Respect for Elderly or Disabled
Multicultural children with six disabilities (Asperger Syndrome and autism, cerebral palsy, congenital amputation, Down Syndrome, hearing and visual impairments) are described by their siblings. Photos show them engaged in activities. Resources in U.S., UK, and Canada for general disabilities as well as for each of the six featured are listed. (*We Can Do It!* (1998, ©1992) also features children with disabilities.)

Brothers in Hope: The Story of the Lost Boys of Sudan

Mary Williams
Illustrated by: R. Gregory Christie
New York: Lee & Low, 2007, ©2005
Grade Level: 1-5
Pages: 40
Themes: Cooperation, Overcoming Obstacles, Community in Action
In the 1980s, eight-year-old Garang Deng was tending calves when his Sudanese village was attacked, leaving many young boys like himself, ages 5 to 15. They banded together, older ones adopting younger and traveled over 1,000 miles to Ethiopia and then, when war broke out again, to Kenya. Some attended school during the day and others foraged for food. In the evening they shared their food and lessons with each other. When Garang was 21, Tom who had been in an Ethiopian refugee camp, returned and helped several of the boys get to the United States.

The Bully Blockers Club

Teresa Bateman
Illustrated by: Jackie Urbanovic
Morton Grove, IL: Whitman, ©2004
Grade Level: P-2
Themes: Bullying, Nonviolent Response
After Lotty Raccoon tries several ways of dealing with Grant Grizzly's bullying, she successfully enlists the aid of her classmates.

But Mom, Everybody Else Does

Kay Winters
Illustrated by: Doug Cushman
New York: Dutton, ©2002
Grade Level: P-2
Themes: Peer Pressure
A girl's statements to her mother are illustrated literally, showing their exaggeration. In the end, her mom tells her that "EVERYBODY gets a good-night kiss, and NOBODY goes to bed without a hug."

The Butter Battle Book

Dr. Seuss
Illustrated by: Dr. Seuss
New York: Random House, ©1984
Grade Level: 2-5
Pages: 56
Themes: Conflict Escalator
Other: Audio, Video

The Yooks and Zooks have an increasingly intense battle about whether to butter their bread on the top or the bottom. A Yook grandfather relates the history to the narrator. In the end, Grandpa and a Zook meet on the wall dividing them, each holding the ultimate weapon and deliberating on whether to use it.

Butterflies for Kiri

Cathryn Falwell
Illustrated by: Cathryn Falwell
New York: Lee & Low, 2008, ©2003
Grade Level: K-3
Themes: Coping

After repeated tries, Kiri learns to fold an origami butterfly. She uses it to complete the artwork that she had thought was ruined by a smudge.

By My Brother's Side

Tiki Barber and Ronde Barber with Robert Burleigh
Illustrated by: Barry Root
New York: Scholastic, 2005, ©2004
Grade Level: 1-5
Themes: Cooperation

This is a true story about Tiki and Ronde Barber, who played sports together until a bike injury kept Tiki in a cast. Ronde cheered him on and they continued their playing together. In 1997 Ronde joined the Tampa Bay Buccaneers and Tiki, the New York Giants.

Callie Cat, Ice Skater

Eileen Spinelli
Illustrated by: Anne Kennedy
Morton Grove, IL: Albert Whitman, ©2007
Grade Level: K-2
Themes: Accepting Limitations and Gifts, Competition

Callie Cat feels a "melting sweetness" whenever she skates. When the Honeybrook Ice Skating Contest is announced, Callie's friends and family convince her she would be a "banana" if she didn't enter. She endures the stress of practice and competing, enjoys and executes a flawless performance, and loses to another skater. Although her friends think she would be a "banana" not to feel awful for losing, she feels fine. After the contest, she returns to the rink without pressure and once again feels the "melting sweetness."

Can You Hear a Rainbow?
The Story of a Deaf Boy Named Chris

Jamee Riggio Heelan
Illustrated by: Nicola Simmonds
Atlanta: Peachtree, ©2002
Grade Level: K-3
Themes: Respect for Elderly or Disabled

Chris describes his daily life: in class his interpreter signs for him, at soccer his mother signs the coach's directions, and when he and Samantha are in a play someone interprets their signs to the audience. The title is derived from Chris's statement that his hearing friend Dominic told him a rainbow is silent for everyone, hearing or not.

Caps for Sale

Esphyr Slobodkina

Illustrated by: Esphyr Slobodkina
New York: HarperFestival. 2008, ©1940
Grade Level: K-3
Themes: Anger, Listening, Nonviolent
   Response
Other: Audio, Video

Monkeys take a peddler's caps and wear them. After realizing that the monkeys are imitating everything he does, the peddler gets his caps back by throwing his own cap on the ground.

A Castle on Viola Street

DyAnne DiSalvo-Ryan

Illustrated by: DyAnne DiSalvo-Ryan
New York: HarperCollins, ©2001
Grade Level: P-3
Themes: Community in Action

Andy tells the story of his family helping build Habitat for Humanity houses in the neighborhood and then getting their own house.

The Cats in Krasinski Square

Karen Hesse

Illustrated by: Wendy Watson
New York: Scholastic, ©2004
London: Frances Lincoln Children's Books,
   2007, ©2004
Grade Level: 3-5
Themes: Community in Action, Oppression,
   Problem Solving

During the early 1940s in Nazi-occupied Poland, the young narrator passes as a Polish girl. She and her older sister Mira smuggle food to people in the Warsaw Ghetto. They hear that the Gestapo plan to take dogs and stop the passengers on a certain train from smuggling more food. So the locals gather up homeless cats and create chaos, allowing food distribution to continue.

Cecil's Garden

Holly Keller

Illustrated by: Holly Keller
New York: Scholastic, 2003, ©2002
Grade Level: P-K
Themes: Conflict Nature, Win-Win Solutions
Other: Audio

When Cecil, Jake, and Posey cannot agree which vegetables to plant, the garden is empty—until Cecil comes up with a solution.

The Cello of Mr. O

Jane Cutler

Illustrated by: Greg Couch
New York: Puffin Books, 2008, ©1999
Grade Level: 1-4
Themes: Community Building, Fear or Worry,
   Overcoming Obstacles

In this touching story, a courageous old man shares his music with a village that has been bombed.

Chachaji's Cup

Uma Krishnaswami

Illustrated by: Soumya Sitaraman
San Francisco: Children's Book Press, ©2003
Grade Level: K-3
Themes: Coping, Problem Solving

Neel tells of his storytelling uncle Chachaji, who always drinks tea from the cup his mother carried from Pakistan in 1947, the time of the partition of India. Neel accidentally breaks the cup, but finds a way that it can still hold memories.

A Chair for My Mother

Vera B. Williams

Illustrated by: Vera B. Williams
New York: Morrow Junior Books, 1998, ©1982
Grade Level: K-3
Themes: Sharing, Community in Action
Other: Audio, Video

Rosa, her mother, and her grandmother lose all of their belonging when a fire destroys their apartment. The family saves their coins in a big jar to purchase the chair they've always dreamed of. It takes a long time, but as a result of their efforts they can finally afford to buy the chair. The neighborhood community also comes to their aid and donates furnishings to help them begin a new life in a new apartment. (*Cherries and Cherry Pits* (New York: Mulberry, 1991, ©1986) also depicts a caring community.)

Champions on the Bench

Carole Boston Weatherford

Illustrated by: Leonard Jenkins
New York: Dial, ©2007
Grade Level: 2-5
Themes: Discrimination
Other: Historical Note

Young Cleveland becomes a member of the 1955 Cannon Street YMCA Little League All-Stars, the only African American little league in South Carolina. When the other teams, all white, refuse to play and the Cannon Street team wins by default, they are invited to attend the national playoffs but are not allowed to play because they had won by forfeit. This is based on a true story; in 2002 the original players received official recognition.

Chester's Way

Kevin Henkes

Illustrated by: Kevin Henkes
New York: Greenwillow, 2004, ©1988
Grade Level: P-3
Themes: Sharing, Friendship, Diversity of
    Individuals
Other: Audio

Chester and Wilson, two mice, are very much alike and very comfortable with their set routines. When Lilly moves into the neighborhood, they are put off at first by her outrageous behaviors. That is, until they are bullied and she rescues them. Then they begin to realize what fun differences can be.

Chestnut Cove

Tim Egan

Illustrated by: Tim Egan
Boston: Houghton Mifflin, ©1995
Grade Level: K-2
Themes: Competition

King Milford offers his kingdom to the one who grows the largest and juiciest watermelon. The people start to compete and lose their community spirit, until they start helping each other.

Chicken Chickens

Valeri Gorbachev

Illustrated by: Valeri Gorbachev
New York: North-South, ©2001
Grade Level: P-1
Themes: Inclusion or Exclusion, Peacemaking

Unlike his companions who tease the little chickens for being scared of the slide, Beaver helps them go down.

Chicken Joy on Redbean Road: A Bayou Country Romp

Jacqueline Briggs Martin
Illustrated by: Melissa Sweet
Boston: Houghton Mifflin, 2007, ©2006
Grade Level: P-2
Themes: Win-Win Solutions

When the blue-headed rooster gets chicken measles and loses his voice, Mrs. Miser Vidrine decides to make rooster soup. Miss Cleoma, the brown hen, goes to fetch Joe Beebee who can play music that will heal the "blue-headed roo." On her way to get the ax, Mrs. Miser keeps discovering vegetables that she should put into the soup; by the time she is ready for the rooster, a crowd has come with Joe Beebee. Mrs. Miser sells bowls of vegetable soup to the crowd as they dance, and the animals find a safer place to live.

Chicken Sunday

Patricia Polacco
Illustrated by: Patricia Polacco
New York: Paper Star, 1998, ©1992
Grade Level: 1-3
Themes: Community Building, Responsible
    Decision Making
Other: Audio, Video

Patricia and her friends make Pysanky eggs for Mr. Kodinski who thinks they had thrown eggs at his store. He invites them to sell eggs and they earn money for a hat for Miss Eula who fixes Sunday dinners for them.

The Christmas Menorahs: How a Town Fought Hate

Janice Cohn
Illustrated by: Bill Farnsworth
Morton Grove, IL: Whitman, ©1995
Grade Level: 2-5
Themes: Community in Action, Racism

A rock is thrown through Isaac Schnitzer's home because of the menorah in his bedroom window. Inspired by the story of how the people in Denmark wore stars in order to support the Jewish people from the Nazis, Isaac's friend Teresa Hanley and her family join many people in Billings, MT, by putting pictures of menorahs in their windows. Eventually, the hate crimes diminished. This is based on a true story and has an introduction giving historical background. (In *The Trees of the Dancing Goats* by Patricia Polacco (New York: Aladdin, 2000, ©1996) a Jewish family distributes trees decorated with Hanukkah toys, and, on the eighth day of Hanukkah, the Christian neighbors reciprocate.)

Chrysanthemum

Kevin Henkes
Illustrated by: Kevin Henkes
New York: Greenwillow, 2007, ©1991
Grade Level: P-2
Themes: Hurtful Words
Other: Audio, Video

Chrysanthemum is proud of her musical name until she goes to kindergarten and is tormented by others. The popular music teacher, who has an unusual name herself, Delphinium, tells her students she plans to name her expected baby the prettiest name she has heard, Chrysanthemum.

Cinder Edna

Ellen Jackson
Illustrated by: Kevin O'Malley
New York: Mulberry, 1999, ©1994
Grade Level: K-3
Themes: Accepting Limitations and Gifts
Other: Video

Edna and Ella have different values, and different degrees of happiness.

Circle Unbroken: The Story of a Basket and Its People

Margot Theis Raven
Illustrated by: Earl B. Lewis
New York: Farrar, Straus and Giroux, ©2004
New York: Square Fish, 2008, ©2004
Grade Level: K-5
Themes: Diversity of Cultures
As a grandmother teaches her granddaughter to weave a coiled basket, she tells the origins of the weaving in Africa before the time of slavery.

Circles of Hope

Karen Lynn Williams
Illustrated by: Linda Saport
Grand Rapids, MI: Eerdmans, ©2005
Grade Level: K-2
Themes: Overcoming Obstacles
Facile, who has his own mango tree, wants to give a gift to his baby sister Lucia. When all of Facile's seeds fail to grow in the Haitian countryside, Tonton tells Facile he needs to have hope. Then Facile makes a circle of stones to protect his seed and grows a mango tree for Lucia. Eventually other trees are also growing in circles of stones.

Circus Girl

Tomek Bogacki
Illustrated by: Tomek Bogacki
New York: Farrar, Straus and Giroux, ©2001
Grade Level: K-3
Themes: Inclusion or Exclusion
A circus girl helps the narrator discover a friend in the boy he was excluding.

City Green

DyAnne DiSalvo-Ryan
Illustrated by: DyAnne DiSalvo-Ryan
Boston: Houghton Mifflin, 2003, ©1994
Grade Level: K-3
Themes: Community Building, Cooperation
Other: Audio
Young Marcie tells how she and her neighbors began a city garden in a vacant lot. Information is given on the American Community Gardening Association.

Clancy's Coat

Eve Bunting
Illustrated by: Lorinda Bryan Cauley
New York: Frederick Warne, ©1984
Grade Level: P-3
Pages: 48
Themes: Conflict Nature, Apologizing or
    Forgiving
When Clancy takes his coat to Tippitt the tailor, the two old friends get a chance to mend their friendship after a longstanding conflict.

Color of Home

Mary Hoffman
Illustrated by: Karin Littlewood
New York: Phyllis Fogelman Books, ©2002
Grade Level: K-2
Themes: Coping, Diversity of Cultures
Through art, Hassan deals with her sad memories of being driven out of her home in Somalia and paints a brighter picture of her present home.

The Colors of Us

Karen Katz
Illustrated by: Karen Katz
New York: Henry Holt, 2007, ©1999
Grade Level: P-2
Themes: Diversity of Cultures
Seven-year-old Lena has an artistic mother who teaches her that skin colors are like many familiar shades from our daily lives: cinnamon, autumn leaves, pizza crust, etc.

Come Here, Little Hedgehog

Tilde Michels
Illustrated by: Sara Bell
Nashville: Abington Press, ©1988
Grade Level: P-3
Themes: Empathy
Lee Anna learns how unhappy her pet hedgehog is when her grandfather tells the story of a family of hedgehogs who kept a little girl.

Company's Coming

Arthur Yorinks
Illustrated by: David Small
New York: Hyperion, 2000, ©1987
Grade Level: 2-4
Themes: Point of View, Rumors or Suspicion
Other: Audio, Video
When two small visitors from outer space visit Shelly and her husband Moe, the two humans have quite different ways of seeing their visitors.

Cool Cat, Hot Dog

Sandy Turner
Illustrated by: Sandy Turner
New York: Atheneum, ©2005
Grade Level: P-2
Themes: Alike and Different
In each pair of pages, a cat and a dog tell their differing qualities and ways of acting.

A Cool Drink of Water

Barbara Kerley
Illustrated by: Melissa G. Ryan, Editor
Washington, DC: National Geographic Society, 2006, ©2002
Grade Level: P-2
Themes: Community Building, Diversity of Cultures
Full-page photographs from all over the world show people drawing, storing, and drinking water. An endnote explains the shortage of drinking water and the importance of water conservation.

Cooper's Lesson

Sun Yung Shin
Illustrated by: Kim Cogan
San Francisco: Children's Book Press, ©2004
Grade Level: 3-5
Themes: Inclusion or Exclusion, Honesty, Empathy
Cooper, who is Korean American, is frustrated because he does not have enough allowance money to buy his mother a hairbrush. In addition, he thinks the store owner Mr. Lee is laughing at him for not being able to speak Korean; so, Cooper steals a hairbrush and gets caught. However, Mr. Lee gives Cooper a chance to clean the store in retribution. In the end, Cooper and Mr. Lee develop a friendship and understanding of each other.

Courage

Bernard Waber
Illustrated by: Bernard Waber
Boston: Houghton Mifflin, ©2002
Grade Level: P-3
Themes: Fear or Worry
Situations requiring courage are shown. The wide range of examples shows that courage can be found everywhere, and many of the scenarios demonstrate that courage is an effective means of peacemaking.

The Cow That Went Oink

Bernard Most
Illustrated by: Bernard Most
San Diego: Harcourt Brace, 2003, ©1990
Grade Level: P-1
Themes: Cooperation
Other: Audio
A cow that oinks and a pig that moos are taunted, until they teach each other and become the only bilingual animals on the farm.

The Crab Man

Patricia Van West

Illustrated by: Cedric Lucas
New York: Turtle Books, ©1998
Grade Level: 1-4
Themes: Respect in General
Other: Video
Neville collects crabs and sells them to a man who holds crab races for the tourists in Jamaica. When Neville discovers how the crabs are treated, he frees them.

The Crayon Box that Talked

Shane De Rolf

Illustrated by: Michael Letzig
New York: Scholastic, 1998, ©1997
Grade Level: P-2
Themes: Diversity of Cultures
An artist creates a picture with a group of crayons which had been squabbling. When they see each other in the artwork, they begin to get along.

Crocodile Smile: 10 Songs of the Earth as the Animals See It

Sarah Weeks

Illustrated by: Lois Ehlert
New York: HarperCollins, 2003, ©1994
Grade Level: P-4
Themes: Point of View, Diversity of Cultures,
   Respect in General
Other: Audio
Ten songs observe creation from different points of view. One song describes animal characteristics of humans, one is a plea against extinction, and another questions the myth that dragons eat princesses.

Crow Boy

Taro Yashima

Illustrated by: Taro Yashima
New York: Scholastic, 1990, ©1955
Grade Level: 1-4
Themes: Hurtful Words
Other: Audio, Video
Chibi's classmates think he is stupid. After six years of study, when he imitates crows at a talent show, his classmates recognize Chibi's gifts.

Dad, Jackie, and Me

Myron Uhlberg

Illustrated by: Colin Bootman
Atlanta: Peachtree, 2006, ©2005
Grade Level: 2-5
Themes: Discrimination, Nonviolent Response
In this fictional story partly based on truth, the narrator tells of his deaf father's devotion to Jackie Robinson. The author describes some of the 1947 games when Robinson responded nonviolently to abuse.

The Dancing Deer and the Foolish Hunter

Elisa Kleven

Illustrated by: Elisa Kleven
New York: Dutton, ©2002
Grade Level: K-3
Themes: Community in Action
When a hunter tries to remove a dancing deer from the forest and put it into a circus, he finds that all of nature is interconnected.

Danitra Brown, Class Clown

Nikki Grimes
Illustrated by: Earl B. Lewis
New York: HarperCollins, ©2005
Grade Level: 3-5
Themes: Friendship, Accepting Limitations
  and Gifts
Zuri Jackson worries about her classes and her
own abilities, but her best friend, Danitra Brown,
is always there to encourage and support her.

The Day I Saw My Father Cry

Bill Cosby
Illustrated by: Varnette P. Honeywood
Introduction by: Alvin F. Poussaint
New York: Scholastic, ©2000
Grade Level: 1-4
Themes: Anger, Conflict Escalator
When Alan Mills died, Little Bill's dad cried. Alan
had taught Little Bill and his brother Bobby to
say, "Merry Christmas!" to de-escalate fights.
(Several "Little Bill" books address the themes.)

A Day's Work

Eve Bunting
Illustrated by: Ronald Himler
New York: Clarion Books, 2004, ©1997
Grade Level: K-3
Themes: Honesty
Other: Audio, Video
On Francisco's recommendation, his grandfather
Abuelo (who speaks no English) is hired for the
day by Benjamin's Gardening. Unfortunately,
Francisco and Abuelo pull out the plants and
leave the weeds. When Abuelo discovers that
Francisco has misrepresented his gardening
abilities, he offers to replant the area. Ben
appreciates the elderly man's honesty; he
is willing to keep Abuelo on and teach him
gardening, because he already knows "the
important things."

Dear Ichiro

Jean Davies Okimoto
Illustrated by: Doug Keith
Seattle, WA: Kumagai Press, ©2002
Grade Level: K-3
Themes: Apologizing or Forgiving
After Oliver and Henry have a fight, Grampa
Charlie takes Henry to a baseball game where
Ichiro Suzuki and Kazuhiro Sasaki play. When
Grampa explains that this is remarkable because
of World War II, Henry decides that he and
Oliver can again be friends.

Dear Mr. Henshaw

Beverly Cleary
Illustrated by: Paul O. Zelinsky
New York: Scholastic, 2003, ©1963
    Paw Prints, 2008, ©1963
Fitzgerald, 2007, ©1963
Grade Level: 4+
Other: Audio, Video
A boy's personal letters and private diary show
his feelings about his parents' divorce and his
growth in maturity.

Dear Mr. Rosenwald

Carole Boston Weatherford
Illustrated by: R. Gregory Christie
New York: Scholastic Press, ©2006
Grade Level: 2-5
Themes: Community in Action, Prejudice or
    Dislike, Sharing
Young Ovella tells how her community matched
funds in 1921 with Julius Rosenwald, president
of Sears, Roebuck, and Co., to build an African
American school. This is based on a true story
noted in an historical note.

Dear Willie Rudd

Libba Moore Gray

Illustrated by: Peter M. Fiore
New York: Aladdin, 2000, ©1993
Grade Level: 3-6
Themes: Discrimination
Miss Elizabeth writes a letter to the African American woman who cared for her. She pictures how different their relationship would be now.

Did You Hear about Jake?

Louise Vitellaro Tidd

Photographs by: Dorothy Handelman
Brookfield, CT: Millbrook Press, ©1999
Grade Level: K-2
Themes: Rumors or Suspicion
A message gets garbled because of noisy conditions.

Do Unto Otters: A Book About Manners

Laurie Keller

Illustrated by: Laurie Keller
New York, NY: Henry Holt, ©2007
Grade Level: 1-3
Themes: Social Skills
Other: Audio, Video
A rabbit learns how to treat his new neighbors, the otters, by thinking of the ways he would like them to treat him.

Dolores Meets Her Match

Barbara Samuel

New York: Farrar, Straus and Giroux, ©2007
Grade Level: P-2
Themes: Competition, Jealousy
Dolores is the official advisor on cats, until Hillary joins the class. Hillary and her Siamese kitten Harold enter into many classroom competitions with Dolores and her overweight cat Duncan. After Duncan inadvertently rescues Harold from Hillary's Egyptian maze, Dolores and Hillary become partners in the business of giving advice on cats.

Don't Call Me Names

Joanna Cole

Illustrated by: Lynn Munsinger
New York: Random House, ©1990
Grade Level: P-2
Themes: Hurtful Words
Mike and Joe make fun of Nell, the frog, until she forgets her shyness and defends her friend Nicky.

Don't let the PEAS TOUCH! and Other Stories

Deborah Blumenthal

Illustrated by: Timothy Basil Ering
New York: Scholastic, 2005, ©2004
Grade Level: K-2
Themes: Cooperation, Problem Solving
Three stories are told about Annie and her little sister Sophie. In one story, Annie uses a compartmentalized dish to solve Sophie's problem. In another, Annie helps Sophie plant a seed and see the new life.

Don't Need Friends

Carolyn Crimi

Illustrated by: Lynn Munsinger
New York: Dragonfly, 2002, ©1999
Grade Level: K-3
Themes: Social Skills
After Rat's best friend Possum moves away, Rat decides he does not need friends. The other animals get the message and stop inviting Rat. Then Dog moves in and, after much protesting that he does not need friends either, a winter storm brings the two together.

Don't Say Ain't

Irene Smalls
Illustrated by: Colin Bootman
Watertown, MA: Charlesbridge, 2004, ©2003
Grade Level: 2-4
Themes: Accepting Limitations and Gifts,
    Diversity of Cultures
Dana learns to reconcile her academic gifts and
her need to speak formal English with the Black
English of her godmother and friends.

Dragon Soup

Arlene Williams
Illustrated by: Sally J. Smith
Tiburon, CA: H.J. Kramer, ©1996
Grade Level: K-3
Themes: Win-Win Solutions
A girl finds a clever way to solve a conflict
between two dragons.

Duck & Goose

Tad Hills
Illustrated by: Tad Hills
New York: Schwartz & Wade Books, 2009,
    ©2006
Grade Level: P-2
Themes: Conflict Escalator, Sharing
Duck and Goose quarrel about who owns the
"egg." As they both keep it warm by sitting on
it, they begin to talk of "our baby." Finally, a
blue bird informs them that they are sitting on a
beach ball, and they both play with it.

Dumpling Soup

Jama Rattigan
Illustrated by: Lillian Hsu-Flanders
Boston: Little, Brown, 2001, ©1992
    Paw Prints, 2008, ©1992
Grade Level: K-3
Themes: Accepting Limitations and Gifts,
    Diversity of Cultures
Seven-year-old Marisa, a Korean girl who lives
in Hawaii, gets to help make the dumplings
for their New Year's Eve celebration. Even her
funny-looking dumplings are delicious.

Earth Mother

Ellen Jackson
Illustrated by: Leo Dillon and Diane Dillon
New York: Walker, ©2005
Grade Level: 1-3
Themes: Peacemaking
Earth Mother is a beautiful black woman who
visits her creatures. Man, Frog, and Mosquito
are interrelated; each complains of one and
praises the other.

Eddie, Harold's Little Brother

Ed Koch and Pat Koch Thaler
Illustrated by: James Warhola
New York: Putnam, ©2004
Grade Level: K-3
Themes: Accepting Limitations and Gifts
Eddie cannot play baseball as well as his big
brother Harold, who teaches Eddie to use his
gift of speaking. Eddie grows up and becomes
mayor of New York City.

Eddie Longpants

Mireille Levert

Illustrated by: Mireille Levert
Berkeley, CA: Groundwood Books, ©2005
Grade Level: K-1
Themes: Diversity of Individuals, Hurtful Words
Pete and the other kids make fun of Eddie Longpants who is extremely tall. When Pete climbs a tree and cannot get down, Eddie helps rescue him, and Eddie's good heart earns Pete's appreciation.

Eddie's Kingdom

D. B. Johnson

Illustrated by: D. B. Johnson
Boston: Houghton Mifflin, ©2005
Grade Level: P-3
Themes: Peacemaking, Mediation or
   Negotiation
Eddie draws a picture of each of the people in his apartment building and mediates solutions for their complaints about each other. In the end, his completed picture portrays each neighbor as one of the animals in the Peaceable Kingdom, adding peace to the spirit of the apartment.

Eddy's Dream

Miriam Cohen

Photographs by: Adam Cohen
New York: Star Bright Books, ©2000
Grade Level: K-2
Themes: Community in Action
When first grade puts on a play about their dreams, Eddy is the last to join in. Trisha reveals Eddy's longtime dream to visit his grandma in Puerto Rico, and the class helps him act out that dream.

Edgar Badger's Fishing Day

Monica Kulling

Illustrated by: Neecy Twinem
Greenvale, NY: Mondo Publishing, ©1999
Grade Level: 1-3
Pages: 47
Themes: Conflict Nature
Edgar and his friend Duncan go fishing and have a quarrel that lasts for two weeks, until they make up.

Edna's Tale

Lisze Bechtold

Illustrated by: Lisze Bechtold
Boston: Houghton Mifflin, ©2001
Grade Level: K-2
Themes: Competition, Accepting Limitations
   and Gifts
When Edna learns that the new cat Ivan might have a nicer tail than she, she preens her tail with disastrous results, and then learns that there are more important qualities than outer beauty.

Edwardo: The Horriblest Boy in the Whole Wide World

John Burningham

Illustrated by: John Burningham
New York: Alfred A. Knopf, 2007, ©2006
Grade Level: P-3
Themes: Hurtful Words
Edwardo unintentionally causes harm. He is consistently told how awful he is, and his actions continue to spiral downward. Then, after a series of events where his actions prove helpful to others, he is complimented and lives up to his new reputation.

Eeyore Has a Birthday

A. A. Milne
Adapted by: Stephen Krensky
Decorations by: Ernest H. Shepard
New York: Dutton, 2003, ©1926
Grade Level: 1-3
Themes: Sharing
Other: Audio
Although Pooh and Piglet give him imperfect gifts for his birthday, Eeyore is happy.

Eggbert: The Slightly Cracked Egg

Tom Ross
Illustrated by: Rex Barron
New York: Putnam, 1997, ©1994
Grade Level: K-6
Themes: Accepting Limitations and Gifts,
    Diversity of Individuals
Eggbert tries to hide his cracked shell. Evicted from the refrigerator, he travels and discovers many great cracked things in the world.

Elana's Ears or How I Became the Best Big Sister in the World

Gloria Ruth Lowell
Illustrated by: Karen Stormer Brooks
Washington, DC: Magination Press, ©2000
Grade Level: K-3
Themes: Respect for Elderly or Disabled
Lacey the dog tells the story of becoming a hearing dog for Elana who was born deaf.

Elliot's Noisy Night

Andrea Beck
Illustrated by: Andrea Beck
Tonawanda, NY: Kids Can Press, ©2002
Grade Level: P-2
Themes: Fear or Worry
Elliot, a toy moose, hears sounds in the night, and the next morning he tells his fears to his friends. That night Beaverton helps Elliot identify the sources of the sounds: the refrigerator, furnace, shutters. After Elliot is asleep, his scared friends create new sounds when they come to spend the night with him.

Elmer and the Kangaroo

David McKee
Illustrated by: David McKee
New York: Scholastic, 2002, ©2000
Grade Level: P-1
Themes: Cooperation
A kangaroo can only bounce, but Elmer teaches him that he can jump and win the contest. Strangers become friends. (In *Elmer* (New York: HarperCollinsPublishers, 2004, ©1968) the elephant feels left out because he is plaid. When he tries to look like the other elephants, they miss him.)

Empty Pot

Demi
Illustrated by: Demi
New York: Henry Holt, 2007, ©1990
Grade Level: K-3
Themes: Honesty
Other: Audio, Video
Ping can usually grow anything. However, when the Emperor gives each child a flower seed to grow in order to determine his successor, Ping's seed does not grow. Ping is rewarded for his honesty about his results.

Enemy Pie

Derek Munson
Illustrated by: Tara Calahan King
San Francisco: Chronicle Books, ©2000
Grade Level: K-3
Themes: Jealousy, Conflict Nature
Other: Video
Jeremy Ross becomes an enemy when he moves next door to the narrator's best friend. The narrator's wise dad shows how to make a pie that turns an enemy into a friend.

Erandi's Braids

Antonio Hernandez Madrigal
Illustrated by: Tomie dePaola
New York: Puffin Books, 2001, ©1999
Grade Level: K-3
Themes: Community Building, Sharing
In this touching story, Erandi sells her hair to help pay the family bills.

Ernest and the BIG Itch

Laura T. Barnes
Illustrated by: Carol A. Camburn
Sergeantsville, NJ: Barnesyard Books, ©2002
Grade Level: P
Themes: Win-Win Solutions
Ernest, a little donkey, rubs against the pole holding up Chipper the bluebird's house; together they figure out a way that both Chipper's and Ernest's needs are met.

Especially Heroes

Virginia Kroll
Illustrated by: Tim Ladwig
Grand Rapids, MI: Eerdmans, ©2003
Grade Level: 3-6
Themes: Racism, Nonviolent Response
Fourth-grader Ginny tells how her father, in 1962, confronted some young men who were harassing their black neighbor Mrs. Hall. Ginny realized that her father was a real hero.

Estela's Swap

Alexis O'Neill
Illustrated by: Enrique O. Sanchez
New York: Lee & Low, 2004, ©2002
Grade Level: P-2
Themes: Sharing
At a swap meet, when Estela gives her music box to a woman selling flowers, she loses her chance to earn money for dancing lessons. In gratitude, the flower lady gives Estela a skirt for her dancing.

Everybody Cooks Rice

Norah Dooley
Illustrated by: Peter J. Thornton
Minneapolis: First Avenue Editions, 1997, ©1991
Grade Level: K-3
Themes: Diversity of Cultures
Other: Video
Carrie searches the neighborhood for her little brother Anthony. In following his trail, she observes people from all over the world who are cooking rice. Recipes are included.

Evie & Margie

Bernard Waber
Illustrated by: Bernard Waber
Boston: Houghton Mifflin, ©2003
Grade Level: P-3
Themes: Jealousy
Other: Audio
When her best friend Margie gets the part of Cinderella, Evie feels jealous. After substituting for Margie who is sick, Evie acknowledges her feelings.

Father Bear's Special Day

Else Holmelund Minarik
Illustrated by: Teri Lee
New York: HarperCollins, ©2003
Grade Level: K-2
Themes: Accepting Limitations and Gifts,
   Jealousy

Little Bear has a hard time finding a special gift for Father's Day. When they go fishing, Emily and Duck join them, leaving Little Bear feeling left out. Although Duck finds worms (after Little Bear had forgotten to bring some) and Emily catches the fish for Father Bear, Little Bear is assured by his father that the best gift is having Little Bear as his son.

Father's Day

Anne Rockwell
Illustrated by: Lizzy Rockwell
New York: HarperCollins, ©2005
Grade Level: P-2
Themes: Diversity of Individuals

In the diverse classroom also featured in *Mother's Day* (©2004), each child writes a book about his or her father and gives it to him for Father's Day.

The Feel Good Book

Todd Parr
Illustrated by: Todd Parr
Boston: Little, Brown, ©2002
Grade Level: P-2
Themes: Sharing, Basic Emotional Needs

There is a wide variety of ways in which we can feel good. (Parr also wrote *The Feelings Book* (2001, ©2000).)

The Fire

Annette Griessman
Illustrated by: Leonid Gore
New York: Putnam, ©2005
Grade Level: K-3
Themes: Coping

Mama, Maria, and little Pepito are a family. Although a fire destroys their home, young Maria learns that they have not lost everything because they have each other.

First Day in Grapes

L. King Pérez
Illustrated by: Robert Casilla
Markham, Ontario: Fitzhenry & Whiteside,
   2004, ©2002
Grade Level: 1-4
Themes: Overcoming Obstacles, Bullying

Chico, whose migrant family moves frequently, begins third grade with a teacher who recognizes his math ability. This helps Chico to stand up to Mike and Tony, two 4th graders who bully him.

First Grade Takes a Test

Miriam Cohen
Illustrated by: Lillian Hoban
New York: Star Bright Books, 2006, ©1980
Grade Level: K-3
Themes: Accepting Limitations and Gifts,
   Diversity of Individuals

When Anna Marie moves to another class because she did so well on a test, everyone learns that there are many ways to be smart.

First Pink Light

Eloise Greenfield

Illustrated by: Jan Spivey Gilchrist
New York: Black Butterfly Children's Books,
  1994, ©1976
Grade Level: P-1
Themes: Mediation or Negotiation
Tyree wants to stay up until his father returns,
but he and his mother negotiate a bed time.

Fishing Day

Andrea Davis Pinkney

Illustrated by: Shane Evans
New York: Hypernion, 2004, ©2003
Grade Level: K-4
Themes: Prejudice or Dislike
Reenie and her mother fish on one side of the
Jim Crow river, and Peter Troop and his dad fish
on the other side. However, Reenie and Peter
begin to overcome the barrier.

Fishing for Methuselah

Roger Roth

Illustrated by: Roger Roth
New York: HarperCollins, 1999, ©1998
Grade Level: K-2
Themes: Cooperation, Competition, Problem
  Solving
Ivan and Olaf, best friends, argue and compete
in everything—until the old fish Methuselah
causes them to cooperate in order to save their
lives. They continue working together and win
the ice sculpture contest.

Flying Jack

Kathye Fetsko Petrie

Illustrated by: Paula J. Mahoney
Foreword by: Reeve Lindbergh
Honesdale, PA: Boyds Mills Press, ©2003
Grade Level: K-3
Themes: Overcoming Obstacles
All his life Jack dreams of flying, but his concern
for others changes his plans. On his 60th birthday
his family throws a huge party, and his daughter
Harriet, named after the pilot Harriet Quimby,
gives Jack his first pilot lesson.

For Every Child: The UN Convention on the Rights of the Child in Words and Pictures

Caroline Castle, ed.

Illustrated by: John Burningham and others
New York: Phyllis Fogelman Books published
  in association with UNICEF, 2001, ©2000
London: Red Fox, 2002, ©2000
Grade Level: K-8
Themes: Diversity of Cultures, Respect in
  General
Human Rights are listed on pages drawn by
multicultural artists. The Foreword is written by
Desmond M. Tutu.

The Forever Dog

Bill Cochran

Illustrated by: Dan Andreasen
New York: HarperCollinsPublishers, ©2007
Grade Level: P-3
Themes: Emotions, Overcoming Obstacles
Mike makes a "Forever Plan" with his dog Corky:
they will be best friends and do everything
together forever. When Corky dies and Mike
is angry that the dog broke his promise, Mike's
mother teaches her that Corky will live forever
in Mike's heart.

A Father Like That

Charlotte Zolotow
Illustrated by: LeUyen Pham
New York: HarperCollinsPublishers, 2007,
    ©1971
Grade Level: P-2
Themes: Coping, Social Skills
Other: Video
The young African American narrator's father left before his son was born. Even so, the boy tells his mother what his father would be like if he were around. After the caring father is described in vivid detail, the mother assures her son that when he grows up he himself can be a father like that. (The 1971 edition features a Caucasian family.)

Four Feet, Two Sandals

Karen Lynn Williams and Khadra Mohammed
Illustrated by: Doug Chayka
Grand Rapids, MI: Eerdmas Books for Young
    Readers, ©2007
Grade Level: 2-5
Themes: Friendship, Sharing
In this touching story, Lina and Feroza are two young girls in a Pakistan refugee camp. When a supply of clothes is delivered, the girls each find one shoe that belongs to a pair. They work out a system where they wear the shoes on alternating days and then become close friends.

Four Legs Bad, Two Legs Good!

D. B. Johnson
Illustrated by: D. B. Johnson
Boston: Houghton Mifflin, ©2007
Grade Level: P-3
Themes: Cooperation, Discrimination
In an Animal Farm setting, Farmer Orvie, a pig, after learning to walk on two legs and then decreeing that two legs are better than four, rules over the other animals. After Orvie refuses to apply that principle and let Duck have a turn as the farmer, she drains the pond. Then, when Orvie gets stuck in the mud, the other animals pull him out, showing that 18 legs are the best.

Free to Be ... You and Me

Marlo Thomas and Friends, Edited by
Carole Hart
Illustrator: Peter H. Reynolds et al.
Philadelphia: Running Press Kids, 2008, ©1973
Grade Level: K-4
Pages: 129
Themes: Diversity of Individuals, Feelings,
    Friendship, Gender Roles, Stereotypes
Other: Audio, Video
This collection of poems, songs, and short stories celebrate the rights of children and grownups to be their best selves. The Special 35th Anniversary Edition includes sheet music for eight songs and a CD with four songs. [Proceeds from this edition are donated to the Free to Be Foundation.]

Franklin and the Hero

Paulette Bourgeois
Illustrated by: Brenda Clark
Towanda, Toronto: Kids Can Press, 2002,
    ©2000
Grade Level: P-2
Themes: Community Building, Sharing
Other: Audio
Franklin and Snail almost miss seeing their superhero Dynaroo because they help Mrs. Muskrat get into her locked house. After hearing their story, Dynaroo honors them as heroes. Several Franklin books address the themes.

Franklin Forgets

Paulette Bourgeois
Illustrated by: Brenda Clark
New York: Scholastic, ©2000
Grade Level: K-3
Themes: Honesty, Responsible Decision
    Making, Apologizing or Forgiving
Other: Audio
After promising to do chores while Mr. Mole is away, Franklin forgets about the garden which gets ruined. Franklin admits his neglect, and together they replant the garden. (*Franklin Says Sorry* (2001, ©1999) also deals with reconciliation.)

Freckleface Strawberry

Julianne Moore
Illustrated by: LeUyen Pham
New York: Scholastic, 2008, ©2007
Grade Level: P-2
Themes: Accepting Limitations and Gifts
A seven-year-old girl with red hair and freckles is tired of being called Freckleface Strawberry. She tries scrubbing away her freckles, covering them up, and hiding away before she accepts them and doesn't care as much about having freckles.

Fred Stays with Me!

Nancy Coffelt
Illustrated by: Tricia Tusa
New York: Little, Brown, 2007, ©2006
London: Little, Brown Children's, 2008, ©2006
Grade Level: K-3
Themes: Coping, Problem Solving
The young narrator says her dog Fred always goes with her, whether she stays with her father or her mother. When Fred causes problems in both households, the parents want to get rid of him, but the daughter convinces them how important it is that Fred stay with her, and they all manage to resolve the problems so that Fred can stay.

Freedom on the Menu: The Greensboro Sit-ins

Carole Boston Weatherford
Illustrated by: Jerome Lagarrigue
New York: Puffin Books, 2007, ©2005
Grade Level: K-4
Themes: Assertiveness, Discrimination
Eight-year-old Connie tells how she could not sit at a counter for a banana split. Then her siblings joined the 1960 boycott begun by the Greensboro Four and gained the right for blacks to sit at Woolworth's lunch counter. An historical note is included.

Friend on Freedom River

Gloria Whelan
Illustrated by: Gijsbert van Frankenhuyzen
Chelsea, MI: Sleeping Bear Press, ©2004
Grade Level: 3-5
Themes: Oppression, Responsible Decision
   Making
Young Louis is in charge of the farm while his dad is away. Sarah, whose husband was sold away in slavery, and her daughter Lucy and son Tyler arrive. Risking jail because of the "Fugitive Slave Law," Louis decides to row with Tyler and get the family across the freezing Detroit River to Canada. He safely returns home, knowing he has done what his father would have wanted.

Friends

Kim Lewis
Illustrated by: Kim Lewis
Boston: Walker, 1999, ©1997
Grade Level: P-1
Themes: Cooperation, Conflict Nature
Sam and Alice find an egg and then it breaks when they fight over it. Together they gather another.

From Me to You

Anthony France
Illustrated by: Tiphanie Beeke
Cambridge, MA: Candlewick Press, 2004,
   ©2003
Grade Level: P-2
Themes: Commuity Building, Recognizing
   Emotions, Social Skills
Rat is depressed until he gets a letter from a secret admirer. Then he continues the chain of kindness. (In *The Kiss that Missed* by David Melling (Hauppauge, NY: Barron's, 2007, ©2002) a king's goodnight kiss to his son misses, and a knight on horse is dispatched to catch the kiss that kindly affects all in its path.)

From Slave Ship to Freedom Road

Julius Lester

Illustrated by: Rod Brown
New York: Puffin Books, 2000, ©1998
   Paw Prints, 2008, ©1998
Grade Level: 5-9
Pages: 40
Themes: Empathy, Oppression
The historically correct artwork that accompanies the story inspired Lester to write about slavery. Lester describes the slave experience, beginning with transport aboard three-masted ships to the auction block, and on to the plantation fields. The text is written in such a way that readers "step into" the artwork and imagine themselves as slaves.

Geranium Morning

E. Sandy Powell

Illustrated by: Renée Graef
Minneapolis: Carolrhoda Books, ©1990
Grade Level: 1-3
Themes: Friendship, Empathy
Timothy Brandon Blair, Jr., whose father has died, meets Frannie, whose mother is dying. They share their grief.

Get Busy, Beaver!

Carolyn Crimi

Illustrated by: Janie Bynum
New York: Scholastic, 2005, ©2004
Grade Level: P-2
Themes: Competition, Diversity of Individuals
Other: Audio
While his family competes with the neighbors in building the bigger dam, Thelonious sees the beauty around him and builds a dam that is beautiful, leading the others to add beauty to their dams.

Getting' Through Thursday

Melrose Cooper

Illustrated by: Nneka Bennett
New York: Lee & Low, 2001, ©1998
Grade Level: 1-3
Themes: Coping, Community in Action,
   Problem Solving
Third-grader Andre dreads the day before his mother's paycheck comes. However, the family has ingenious and loving ways to solve the problems of scarcity.

A Gift for Sadia

Marie Fritz Perry

Illustrated by: Marie Fritz Perry
Northfield, MN: Buttonweed Press, ©2004
Grade Level: K-3
Themes: Coping, Diversity of Cultures
Sadia, recently immigrated from Somalia, takes ESL classes at her grade school and struggles to learn the alphabet. She feeds an injured Canada goose and then, when it is time to say her ABCs and she cannot remember "V," her goose leads the others in a V-formation near the classroom window.

The Gnats of Knotty Pine

Bill Peet

Illustrated by: Bill Peet
Boston: Houghton Mifflin, 1984, ©1975
Grade Level: K-3
Themes: Community Building, Cooperation
Some gnats work together to save the forest animals from hunters.

Go Away, Shelley Boo!

Phoebe Stone

Illustrated by: Phoebe Stone
Boston: Little, Brown, ©1999
Grade Level: 1-3
Themes: Fear or Worry, Rumors or Suspicion
When Emily Louise sees a new girl moving into the house next door she imagines all the horrid things that will happen because of that girl "who looks like a Shelley Boo." Then Emily meets the girl, Elizabeth, who is different from what she had imagined.

The Goat Lady

Jane Bregoli

Illustrated by: Jane Bregoli
Gardiner, ME: Tilbury House Publishers, 2008, ©2004
Grade Level: 2-4
Themes: Community Building, Diversity of Individuals
The townspeople are skeptical of Noelie, a mysterious old woman who raises goats and other animals. Then the narrator and her brother meet Noelie and discover her kindness. When their mother features Noelie in an art exhibit and people get to know her they begin to appreciate and respect her. The story is based on the life of Noelie Lemire Houle, who was born in Quebec in 1899. An historical note is included.

Goggles!

Ezra Jack Keats

Illustrated by: Ezra Jack Keats
New York: Scholastic, 2002, ©1969
Grade Level: K-3
Themes: Bullying
Other: Audio, Video
Some boys push Peter down in an inner city lot and his newly found pair of motorcycle goggles falls to the ground. Their dog Willie returns the goggles to Peter and his friend Archie, and then the two boys outwit the three older boys and escape them.

Goin' Someplace Special

Patricia. C. McKissack

Illustrated by: Jerry Pinkney
New York: Aladdin Paperbacks, 2009, ©2001
Grade Level: K-5
Themes: Inclusion or Exclusion, Discrimination
Based on the author's own experience in the 1950s, young Tricia Ann gets permission to go "someplace special." She meets up with the humiliation of Jim Crow laws on the bus and also at a hotel where a musical idol is staying. While she feels the humiliation of being excluded, Tricia Ann keeps remembering to keep her dignity as her grandmother Mama Frances has told her. Finally, Tricia Ann goes to the public library and feels welcome.

Going North

Janice N. Harrington

Illustrated by: Jerome Lagarrigue
New York: Melanie Kroupa Books, ©2004
Grade Level: 3-5
Themes: Community in Action, Discrimination, Responsible Decision Making
Other: Audio
Young Jessie and her African American family leave their home and family, deal with the limited number of restaurants and gas stations where they could be served, and arrive in Lincoln hoping for a better life. This story is based on the author's experience of moving from Vernon, AL, to Lincoln, NE, in 1964.

Goldie Is Mad

Margie Palatini

Illustrated by: Howard Fine
New York: Scholastic, 2002, ©2001
Grade Level: P-K
Themes: Anger, Conflict Nature
When Goldie's baby brother Nicholas licks her doll Veronica, Goldie wishes Nicholas would disappear. Then she realizes how she would miss him.

A Good Day

Kevin Henkes

Illustrated by: Kevin Henkes
New York: Greenwillow, ©2007
Grade Level: P
Themes: Overcoming Obstacles
The day begins with a problem for each of four animals. Little yellow bird loses a feather, little white dog tangles her leash, little orange fox can't find his mother, and little brown squirrel drops her nut. Each experiences an improved situation, and a little girl has a great day because she finds a yellow feather.

Grandma's Beach

Rosalind Beardshaw

Illustrated by: Rosalind Beardshaw
New York: Bloomsbury, 2004, ©2001
Grade Level: P-2
Themes: Problem Solving
When Emily's mother gets called to the office before they go to the beach, Emily's grandma makes a backyard beach.

Grandpa, Is Everything Black Bad?

Sandy Lynne Holman

Illustrated by: Lela Kometiani
Davis, CA: The Culture CO-OP, 1999, ©1995
Grade Level: 1-4
Themes: Stereotypes, Diversity of Cultures
Other: Audio
After seeing how often the color black has a negative connotation, Montsho, a young African American boy, asks his grandpa if everything black, including himself, is bad. Grandpa Rufus replies by telling Montsho of his rich African heritage.

Grandpa's Face

Eloise Greenfield

Illustrated by: Floyd Cooper
New York: Putnam, 1996, ©1988
Grade Level: P-2
Themes: Recognizing Emotions
Tamika loves her grandpa but is scared when he makes faces for the theatre rehearsal. She is reassured when he tells her he will only look at her with love.

The Great Kapok Tree: A Tale of the Amazon Rain Forest

Lynne Cherry

Illustrated by: Lynne Cherry
San Diego: Harcourt Brace, 2000, ©1990
Grade Level: K-3
Themes: Listening, Community in Action, Respect in General
Other: Audio, Video
A woodsman is visited by the local animals, birds, and people who tell what the Kapok tree means in their lives.

Gretchen Groundhog, It's Your Day!

Abby Levine

Illustrated by: Nancy Cote
New York: Scholastic, 2001, ©1998
    Paw Prints, 2008, ©1998
Grade Level: K-2
Themes: Fear or Worry
When Gretchen's Great-Uncle Gus is too old to search for his shadow, Gretchen is afraid to go out. Reading about her ancestors' fears gives her courage.

The Grouchy Ladybug

Eric Carle

Illustrated by: Eric Carle
New York: Scholastic, 2000, ©1977
Grade Level: K-1
Themes: Feelings
A grouchy ladybug, looking for a fight, challenges everyone she meets, regardless of their size. She finally learns good manners and how to respect others.

Growing Vegetable Soup

Lois Ehlert

Illustrated by: Lois Ehlert
San Diego: Harcourt Brace, 2008, ©1987
Grade Level: P-1
Themes: Cooperation
Other: Audio
A father and his child plant vegetables, harvest them, and make vegetable soup. (In *Soup* by Cathy Goldberg Fishman (New York: Children's Press, ©2002) a small boy tells how everyone in his family contributes when they make soup.)

Grumpy Bird

Jeremy Tankard

Illustrated by: Jeremy Tankard
New York: Scholastic Press, 2008, ©2007
Grade Level: P-K
Themes: Feelings
Bird wakes up grumpy. As he walks, the farm animals follow him and, eventually, Bird finds himself having fun. (In *I Love It When You Smile* by Sam McBratney (HarperCollinsPublishers, 2006, ©2005) Little Roo is coaxed out of a glum mood by his mother.)

Hair for Mama

Kelly Tinkham

Illustrated by: Amy June Bates
New York: Dial Books for Young Readers, ©2007
Grade Level: K-3
Themes: Sharing
When his mother loses her hair because of chemotherapy, 8-year-old Marcus Carter promises he will find her more hair. After Marcus discovers that his shorn hair cannot be used by his mother, she wears a gele (African headtie) in the family photo and also assures Marcus that her love for him will continue no matter what happens.

Hank and Fergus

Susin Nielsen-Fernlund

Illustrated by: Louise-Andrée Laliberté
Custer, WA: Orca, ©2003
Grade Level: P-2
Themes: Inclusion or Exclusion, Hurtful Words
Hank keeps his imaginary dog Fergus on a red string leash. When Cooper moves in next door and finds himself excluded because of Fergus, Cooper taunts Hank about his birthmark. After both boys feel lonely, they reconcile and become friends.

A Handful of Seeds

Monica Hughes

Illustrated by: Luis Garay
New York: Orchard Books, 1996, ©1993
Grade Level: 1-3
Themes: Sharing, Coping
When Concepcion's grandmother dies, Concepcion goes to a barrio and plants some of her grandmother's seeds, shares some of the seeds, and holds some back for planting.

Hands Can

Cheryl Willis Hudson
Photographs by: John-Francis Bourke
Cambridge, MA: Candlewick Press, 2007,
    ©2003
Grade Level: P
Themes: Peacemaking
Photos of children accompany a list of positive things that hands can do. (*I Call My Hand Gentle* by Amanda Haan (New York: Viking, ©2003) carries the message that we choose to use our hands as we wish, making peace and not hurting others.)

The Happy Lion and the Bear

Louise Fatio
Illustrated by: Roger Duvoisin
New York: Whittlesey House, ©1964
Grade Level: K-3
Themes: Fear or Worry
When a bear moves to the zoo, the Happy Lion decides he needs to keep control by roaring. As a result, the bear is friendly with everyone except the lion who scares him. When Francois the keeper's son is injured, the two forget their fears and work together. (*The Happy Lion* (New York: Knopf, 2006, ©1954) deals with the value of establishing boundaries.)

The Hard-Times Jar

Ethel Footman Smothers
Illustrated by: John Holyfield
New York: Farrar, Straus and Giroux, ©2003
Grade Level: K-4
Themes: Overcoming Obstacles, Honesty,
    Discrimination
Eight-year-old Emma Jane Turner, her two younger siblings, and their parents are African American migrant workers who have just moved to Pennsylvania. Emma loves to make her own books, with pencils and paper bags, and then she goes to 3rd grade where she discovers a library. After borrowing the books that were not to be taken home, Emma reports herself to her kind teacher. She then gets some coins from the hard-times jar to buy her own "store-bought" book. The story, set before the Civil Rights Act, is based on the author's own experiences.

The Harmonica

Tony Johnston
Illustrated by: Ron Mazellan
Watertown, MA: Charlesbridge, 2008, ©2004
Grade Level: 3-6
Themes: Community Building, Oppression
The Harmonica is the true story of Henryk Rosmaryn, a Polish Jew, who was sent to a concentration camp. When he was ordered to play Schubert on his harmonica for the commandant, he found his real inspiration from the other prisoners, who listened from a distance.

Harriet and the Garden

Nancy Carlson
Illustrated by: Nancy Carlson
Minneapolis: Carolrhoda Books, 2004, ©1982
Grade Level: K-3
Themes: Honesty, Apologizing or Forgiving
Other: Audio
After Harriet accidentally ruins Mrs. Hoozit's garden, nothing is right until she makes amends.

Harry's Pony

Barbara Ann Porte

Illustrated by: Yossi Abolafia
New York: HarperCollins, 2003, ©1997
Grade Level: 1-4
Themes: Sharing, Respect for Elderly or
    Disabled, Problem Solving
Harry wins a pony in the Jam Pops contest. After exploring several ways to keep the pony, he donates it to the Red Barn Pony Farm where children with disabilities learn to ride horses.

Harry's Smile

Kathy Caple

Illustrated by: Kathy Caple
Boston: Houghton Mifflin, ©1987
Grade Level: P-2
Themes: Accepting Limitations and Gifts
Other: Audio
Harry wants to impress his pen-pal Wilma, but, as he practices for his picture, he is not pleased with his smile.

Harvesting Hope: The Story of Cesar Chavez

Kathleen Krull

Illustrated by: Yuyi Morales
New York: Scholastic, 2004, ©2001
Grade Level: 3-6
Pages: 48
Themes: Overcoming Obstacles,
    Discrimination
Other: Audio
When Cesar Chavez was ten years old, drought forced his family to leave their ranch and move to California, where they became migrant workers who worked in terrible living conditions and were paid low wages. When Chavez became an adult, he worked for workers' rights and organized a nonviolent revolt, producing the first farm workers' union contract.

The Hating Book

Charlotte Zolotow

Illustrated by: Ben Shecter
New York: HarperTrophy, 1990, ©1969
Grade Level: K-3
Themes: Assertiveness, Conflict Nature
Other: Audio, Video
A misunderstanding between friends continues until one asks why the other is ignoring her. They discover that the first little girl thought the second had said she "looked like a freak" instead of "looked neat."

Henry and the Kite Dragon

Bruce Edward Hall

Illustrated by: William Low
New York: Philomel, ©2004
Grade Level: K-4
Pages: 40
Themes: Prejudice or Dislike, Win-Win
    Solutions, Mediation or Negotiation
In New York's Chinatown, Tony Guglione throws rocks at Grandfather Chin's elaborate kites. Young Henry and his friends learn the reason, and the whole group is able to negotiate a solution.

Hey, Little Ant

Phillip Hoose and Hannah Hoose

Illustrated by: Debbie Tilley
New York: Scholastic: 1999, ©1998
Grade Level: K-4
Themes: Point of View, Bullying
Other: Audio
A boy talks to an ant that he is about to crush. On the last page, the whole dialogue creates the lyrics to a song.

Home Now

Lesley Beake
Illustrated by: Karin Littlewood
Watertown, MA: Charlesbridge, 2007, ©2006
London: Frances Lincoln Children's Books,
    2008, ©2006
Grade Level: K-3
Themes: Coping, Emotions
After her parents die of AIDS, Sieta leaves her African village to live with her aunt at an orphanage. When Sieta and an orphaned baby elephant meet each other, some healing begins and Sieta responds to Aunty's attempts to make their living place more homelike.

Honest-to-Goodness Truth

Patricia C. McKissack
Illustrated by: Giselle Potter
New York: Aladdin, 2003, ©2000
Grade Level: K-3
Themes: Social Skills, Honesty
Other: Video
After deciding to never tell another lie, Libby gets into trouble for telling the unvarnished truth. When someone talks to her in like manner, Libby understands that the truth should be "sweetened with love."

Hooray for the Dandelion Warriors!

Bill Cosby
Illustrated by: Varnette P. Honeywood
New York: Scholastic, 2004, ©1999
Grade Level: K-3
Themes: Cooperation, Gender Roles, Win-Win
    Solutions
When Simone can play second base as well as Little Bill, he learns a lesson about being a real team. The team finds a gain-gain solution when they choose a name.

Hooway for Wodney Wat

Helen Lester
Illustrated by: Lynn Munsinger
New York: Scholastic, 2006, ©1999
Grade Level: P-3
Themes: Bullying, Hurtful Words
Other: Audio, Video
Rodney Rat is teased unmercifully because he cannot pronounce his r's. However, when Camilla Capybara joins the class and bullies Rodney and his classmates, Rodney regains control for the class.

Horace and Morris but mostly Dolores

James Howe
Illustrated by: Amy Walrod
New York: Aladdin, 2003, ©1999
Grade Level: K-3
Themes: Inclusion or Exclusion, Gender Roles
Other: Audio, Video
Boys' and Girls' Clubs exclude each other until some decide to break the rules.

Horton Hears a Who

Dr. Seuss
Illustrated by: Dr. Seuss
New York: Random House, 2008, ©1954
Grade Level: K-4
Themes: Cooperation, Respect in General
Other: Audio, Video
Horton the elephant saves a very tiny village because of his insistence on respecting every creature, no matter how small. Every single member of the village is needed for the village's survival.

Hot Day on Abbott Avenue

Karen English

Illustrated by: Javaka Steptoe
New York: Clarion Books, ©2004
Grade Level: K-3
Themes: Mediation or Negotiation
After Kishi buys the last blue ice pop, Renee avoids her until Miss Johnson gets the girls to talk and be friends again.

A House by the River

William Miller

Illustrated by: Cornelius Van Wright and Ying-Hwa Hu
New York: Lee & Low, ©1997
Grade Level: K-2
Themes: Fear or Worry, Coping
As Belinda and her widowed mother wait out a fierce storm in their house by the river, Belinda learns the strength that comes from her family.

A House Is not a Home

Anne Liersch

Illustrated by: Christa Unzner
Translated by: J. Alison James
New York: North-South, ©1999
Grade Level: K-4
Themes: Community Building, Cooperation
Badger is so fussy that his friends build their own home and enjoy it, leaving Badger out in the cold until he builds a sleigh for all of them.

How Are You Peeling?: Foods with Moods

Saxon Freymann and Joost Elffers

Illustrated by: Saxon Freymann and Joost Elffers
New York : Scholastic, 2004, ©1999
Grade Level: K-4
Themes: Recognizing Emotions
This book provides an entertaining format for building a feelings vocabulary and exploring the idea that the same situations can evoke a range of emotions for different individuals. The fruits and vegetables begin by asking the reader, "How are you peeling?" Emotions and illustrations are then linked to situations common in students' everyday lives, as well as their reactions to these situations.

How Jackrabbit Got His Very Long Ears

Heather Irbinskas

Illustrated by: Kenneth J. Spengler
Flagstaff, AZ: Northland, 2004, ©1994
Grade Level: K-3
Themes: Listening, Hurtful Words
After creating the desert creatures, the Great Spirit assigns Jackrabbit to acquaint the animals with their new homes. Because he doesn't listen carefully, Jackrabbit gives incorrect information to Tortoise, Bobcat, and Roadrunner. This harms their self-esteem. So the Great Spirit affirms the creatures and gives Jackrabbit ears that will help him in the future.

How Kind!

Mary Murphy
Illustrated by: Mary Murphy
Cambridge, MA: Candlewick Press, 2004,
 ©2002
Grade Level: P-1
Themes: Community Building
A chain reaction of barnyard kindness begins when Hen gives Pig an egg. (In *One Smile* by Cindy McKinley (Bellevue, WA: Illumination Arts Publishing, 2005, ©2002) a young girl's smile begins a sequence of good events which come full circle.)

How My Family Lives in America

Susan Kuklin
Photographs by: Susan Kuklin
New York: Aladdin, 1998, ©1992
Grade Level: P-2
Themes: Inclusion or Exclusion, Diversity of
 Cultures
Three children whose ancestors are from other countries (Sanu from Senegal, Eric from Puerto Rico, and April from Taiwan) tell how their families incorporate their cultures into life in the United States.

How to Behave and Why

Munro Leaf
Illustrated by: Munro Leaf
New York: Universe Publishing, 2002, ©1946
Grade Level: K-3
Themes: Social Skills, Honesty, Responsible
 Decision Making
This book gives upbeat reasons for behaving. If we want to be happy and get along, we will be honest, fair, strong, and wise. The letters of these four words structure the lessons. (*Manners Can be Fun* (2004, ©1936) also addresses social skills.)

How to Lose All Your Friends

Nancy Carlson
Illustrated by: Nancy Carlson
New York: Puffin Books, 1997, ©1994
Grade Level: K-3
Themes: Social Skills, Sharing
By humorously describing obnoxious behaviors not wanted in a friend, the author helps students infer the qualities it takes to be a good friend and member of a caring community.

Howie Helps Himself

Joan Fassler
Illustrated by: Joe Lasker
Chicago: Whitman, 1976, ©1975
Grade Level: K-3
Themes: Recognizing Emotions, Overcoming
 Obstacles, Respect for Elderly or Disabled
Howie, who has cerebral palsy, has many moods. However, he persists until he can move his wheelchair by himself.

100th Day Worries

Margery Cuyler
Illustrated by: Arthur Howard
New York: Aladdin Paperbacks, 2006, ©2000
Grade Level: K-2
Themes: Fear or Worry, Community in Action
Other: Audio, Video
When Jessica the worrier cannot find 100 items, her family helps her gather a collection that shows lots of love and some ingenuity.

Hunter's Best Friend at School

Laura Malone Elliott
Illustrated by: Lynn Munsinger
New York: HarperCollins, ©2002
Grade Level: K-2
Themes: Friendship, Peer Pressure
Other: Audio

Hunter is a little raccoon who enjoys Stripe's antics, even when they lead the two best friends into trouble at school. After Hunter destroys his own artwork in order to follow Stripe, Hunter becomes the leader and both friends are better off. (In *Hunter & Stripe and the Soccer Showdown* (©2005) the two friends deal with competition. In *Hunter's Big Sister* (2008, ©2007), Hunter loves his big sister Glenna and helps her when she is hurt, even though she is bossy.)

I Am I

Marie-Louise Fitzpatrick
Illustrated by: Marie-Louise Fitzpatrick
New Milford, CT: Roaring Book Press, 2008, ©2006
Grade Level: 2-5
Themes: Apologizing or Forgiving, Hurtful Words

Two young desert boys meet, compete with each other, and exchange hurtful words that destroy their lands. Their words of sorrow then bring healing and new life. This is a subtle and imaginative depiction of the power of words.

I Am René, the Boy = Soy René, el Nino

Laínez Colato
Illustrated by: Fabiola Graullera Ramírez
Houston, TX: Piñata, ©2005
Grade Level: 1-3
Themes: Accepting Limitations and Gifts, Diversity of Cultures

When René moves from El Salvador he is shocked to meet a girl named Renee. He goes on to win a writing contest, celebrating his name.

I Can't Stop! A Story about Tourette Syndrome

Holly L. Niner
Illustrated by: Meryl Treatner
Morton Grove, IL: Whitman, ©2005
Grade Level: K-4
Themes: Friendship, Coping, Respect for Elderly or Disabled

After discovering that he has Tourette Syndrome, Nathan finds ways to deal with his tics. His friend Josh helps him accept his disability. Background information is given.

I Could Do That!: Esther Morris Gets Women the Vote

Linda Arms White
Illustrated by: Nancy Carpenter
New York: Farrar, Straus and Giroux, ©2005
Grade Level: 2-4
Themes: Overcoming Obstacles, Discrimination, Gender Roles
Other: Audio, Video

Esther Morris confronted gender discrimination all her life. She helped achieve voting rights for Wyoming women and became a judge in 1869, the first woman in the country to hold public office.

I Did It, I'm Sorry

Caralyn Buehner
Illustrated by: Mark Buehner
New York: Puffin Books, 2000, ©1998
    Paw Prints, 2008, ©1998
Grade Level: K-3
Themes: Social Skills

This is a humorous multiple-choice quiz book with fourteen situations. The answers are hidden in the pictures. (*Yes, Please! No, Thank You!* by Valerie Wheeler (New York: Sterling Publishing Co., 2006, ©2005) has a sequence of questions that can be answered with "Yes, please!" or "No, thank you!")

I Hate English!

Ellen Levine
Illustrated by: Steve Björkman
New York: Scholastic, 1995, ©1989
Grade Level: 1-3
Themes: Diversity of Cultures
Other: Video
Mei Mei refuses to learn English, afraid she will lose her Chinese heritage, until her teacher helps her to want to communicate. (*My Name is Yoon* by Helen Recorvits (New York: Farrar, Straus and Giroux, 2003, ©2002) tells the story of Yoon who misses her country so much that she will not write her name, until she makes a friend.)

I Miss Franklin P. Shuckles

Ulana Snihura
Illustrated by: Leanne Franson
Toronto: Annick Press, 2001, ©1998
Grade Level: K-3
Themes: Diversity of Individuals, Peer Pressure, Apologizing or Forgiving
Molly Pepper enjoys Franklin P. Shuckles until they go to school and she realizes that her friends, who make fun of Franklin, might start making fun of her. After she shuns him, she misses his friendship and then they make up.

I Saw Your Face

Text by Kwame Dawes
Afterword by Jerry Pinkney
Illustrated by: Tom Feelings
New York: Dial, 2005, ©2004
Grade Level: 2-6
Themes: Diversity of Cultures
The text is a poem which addresses people of African descent. Each pair of pages shows lines from the poem and drawings of people who live in different parts of the world and have similar features.

I Wish I Were a Butterfly

James Howe
Illustrated by: Ed Young
New York: Scholastic, 1999, ©1987
Grade Level: P-3
Themes: Accepting Limitations and Gifts, Hurtful Words
After a frog tells him he is ugly, a little cricket wishes he were a butterfly. Finally an old spider helps the cricket find his own gifts, including fiddling, which leads to a nice surprise ending.

Ian's Walk

Laurie Lears
Illustrated by: Karen Ritz
Morton Grove, IL: Whitman, ©1998
Grade Level: 1-3
Themes: Empathy, Respect for Elderly or Disabled
Julie takes her brother Ian, who has autism and processes things differently, for a walk in the park. When he wanders off, Julie tries to understand his experience. (In *Waiting for Mr. Goose* (©1999), a young boy with ADHD learns the discipline to patiently wait for a goose that needs to have a metal trap and chain removed.)

Ice-Cold Birthday

Maryann Cocca-Leffler
Illustrated by: Maryann Cocca-Leffler
New York: Grosset & Dunlap, ©1992
Grade Level: K-3
Themes: Community in Action, Problem Solving
When a snow storm interferes with a seven-year-old girl's birthday party, her parents and sister improvise and provide a good time.

Ice Palace

Deborah Blumenthal

Illustrated by: Ted Rand

New York: Clarion Books, ©2003

Grade Level: K-4

Themes: Community in Action, Responsible
   Decision Making

A young girl from Saranac Lake, NY, tells of
the community effort (which includes her uncle
from a minimum-security correctional facility),
building an ice palace for the annual Winter
Carnival. An historical note is included.

If a Bus Could Talk: The Story of Rosa Parks

Faith Ringgold

Illustrated by: Faith Ringgold

New York: Scholastic, 2005, ©1999

Grade Level: K-3

Themes: Discrimination

A young girl narrates. She gets on a bus that tells
her the story of Rosa Parks's life; the passengers are
from Rosa's life. At the end, Rosa herself gets on
the bus and everyone has a birthday party for her.
The story emphasizes the significance of Rosa's
act and acknowledges the part of so many others
in working for civil rights. (*My Dream of Martin
Luther King* (New York: Dragonfly, 1999, ©1995)
also addresses the struggle for civil rights.)

If the World Were a Village: A Book about the World's People

David J. Smith

Illustrated by: Shelagh Armstrong

Tonawanda, NY: Kids Can Press, 2007, ©2002

Grade Level: 2-6

Themes: Community Building, Diversity of
   Cultures

Other: Video

The world is imagined as a village of 100
people. The village is then described in terms
of languages spoken, ages, religions, and
so on. Endnotes give teaching tips and add
background to the statistics given.

If You Could Wear My Sneakers

Sheree Fitch

Illustrated by: Darcia Labrosse

Buffalo, NY: Firefly Books, 1998, ©1997

Grade Level: K-3

Themes: Community Building, Peacemaking,
   Point of View, Respect in General

Children's human rights are addressed in 15
humorous poems featuring a variety of animals.
The rights are based on articles from the United
Nations Convention on the Rights of the Child.

I'm Gonna Like Me: Letting Off a Little Self-Esteem

Jamie Lee Curtis

Illustrated by: Laura Cornell

New York: Joanna Cotler Books, 2007, ©2002

Grade Level: P-2

Themes: Accepting Limitations and Gifts

Other: Audio

A little girl tells how she will like herself in all
kinds of situations.

I'm Not Going to Chase the Cat Today

Jessica Harper

Illustrated by: Lindsay Harper duPont

New York: Scholastic, ©2000

Grade Level: P-1

Themes: Peacemaking

The dog decides not to chase the cat, the cat
the mouse, and the mouse the lady. So, the lady
has a party for them all.

I'm Not Oscar's Friend Anymore

Marjorie Weinman Sharmat
Illustrated by: Tony DeLuna
New York: Dutton, ©1975
Grade Level: 1-3
Themes: Friendship, Conflict Nature
A young boy tells about all the misery Oscar must be in since their fight, and then decides they should make up.

I'm Tougher than Diabetes!

Alden R. Carter
Photographs by: Dan Young
Morton Grove, IL: Whitman, ©2001
Grade Level: K-3
Themes: Coping, Respect for Elderly or
    Disabled
Siri explains how she lives a normal life and takes care of her diabetes. The book contains many photos. (*I'm Tougher than Asthma* (Alden R. Carter and Siri M. Carter, 2001, ©1996) may also be of interest.)

In My Momma's Kitchen

Jerdine Nolen
Illustrated by: Colin Bootman
New York: Scholastic, 2001, ©1999
Grade Level: K-3
Themes: Community Building
Other: Audio
A variety of warm events take place in the kitchen. "… everything good that happens in my house happens in my momma's kitchen."

In the Small, Small Night

Jane Kurtz
Illustrated by: Rachel Isadora
New York: Greenwillow, ©2005
Grade Level: P-2
Themes: Fear or Worry, Diversity of Cultures
Abena's little brother Kofi is afraid they will forget their relatives in Ghana. She comforts him by telling him two stories: Tricky Anansi learns that a child has wisdom, and a turtle makes progress slowly. Kofi reciprocates by assuring Abena that she will know what to do if her classmates make fun of her way of talking.

Incredibly Lonely, That's Me

Ben Keckler
Illustrated by: Dick Davis
Creative Development by: Diana Barnard
Indianapolis, IN: Eagle Creek Publications,
    ©2007
Grade Level: 1-3
Themes: Coping, Feelings
In poetry-form, Melissa describes her feelings. She sorely misses her older sister Linda who was killed in a climbing accident when Melissa was nine. She listens to her loneliness and trusts it to help her feel connected to Linda. Endnotes give creative ideas, including journaling, for expressing feelings.

Ira Says Goodbye

Bernard Waber
Illustrated by: Bernard Waber
New York: Scholastic, 1990, ©1988
Grade Level: P-4
Pages: 40
Themes: Anger, Coping
Other: Audio, Video
Ira deals with his anger and disappointment over finding out that his best friend Reggie is moving away. (In *Ira Sleeps Over* (2008, ©1972) Ira is comforted when he learns that Reggie also has a teddy bear.)

Is There Really a Human Race?

Jamie Lee Curtis

Illustrated by: Laura Cornell
New York: Joanna Cotler Books, ©2006
Grade Level:K-3
Themes: Competition, Diversity of Individuals
Other: Audio

This play on words begins a series of clever questions about the strong role of competition in our society.

Isabel's House of Butterflies

Tony Johnston

Illustrated by: Susan Guevara
Salt Lake City, UT: Gibbs Smith, 2006, ©1997
Grade Level: K-3
Themes: Problem Solving

In Michoacán, Mexico, eight-year-old Isabel and her family have an oyamel tree where monarch butterflies come every winter. When times are hard, Isabel helps her mother raise money from tourists so that they don't have to sell the tree for wood. The book ends on a note of uncertainty mixed with hope.

Ish

Peter H. Reynolds

Illustrated by: Peter H. Reynolds
Cambridge, MA: Candlewick Press, ©2004
London: Walker Books, 2005, ©2004
Grade Level: K-3
Themes: Accepting Limitations and Gifts
Other: Audio, Video

Ramon's little sister uses his discards to teach him that he can draw vase-ish, boat-ish art, and he becomes free enough to be creative.

The Island of the Skog

Steven Kellogg

Illustrated by: Steven Kellogg
New York: Penguin Young Readers, 1993,
    ©1973
Grade Level: 2-4
Themes: Conflict Nature, Conflict Escalator,
    Win-Win Solutions
Other: Audio, Video

Jenny and her city-mouse friends set sail in search of a more peaceful place to live. They arrive on an island inhabited by a seemingly hostile Skog, with seemingly gigantic feet. But when the two parties finally meet face to face, they find they have a lot in common.

It Doesn't Have To Be This Way: A Barrio Story = No tiene que ser así: una historia del barrio

Luis J. Rodriguez

Illustrated by: Daniel Galvez
San Francisco: Children's Book Press, ©1999
Grade Level: 2-5
Themes: Peer Pressure, Responsible Decision
    Making

After Monchi decides to join a gang, his cousin Dreamer is shot in a gang-related activity. Monchi then reconsiders and decides not to join the gang.

It Is the Wind

Ferida Wolff

Illustrated by: James Ransome
New York: HarperCollins, 2005, ©2003
Grade Level: P-1
Themes: Fear or Worry, Listening

A young boy imagines many possible sources for the sound he hears in the night—the owl, the gate, the calf, and so on. Each of the possibilities is shown with a poetic passage describing the related sounds.

"It Was Me, Mom!"

Brigitte Weninger
Illustrated by: Stephanie Roehe
Translated by: Charise Myngheer
New York: Minedition, 2005, ©2004
Grade Level: P-K
Themes: Honesty, Apologizing or Forgiving
Miko, a little mouse, breaks his mother's vase and gets his toy mouse Mimiki to report the incident to Miko's mother. Then Miko tells the whole story and helps his mother glue the pieces into a candy dish, to be filled with candy from his grandma.

It Wasn't Me

Udo Weigelt
Illustrated by: Julia Gukova
Translated by: J. Alison James
New York: North-South, ©2001
Grade Level: P-3
Themes: Rumors or Suspicion, Apologizing or
    Forgiving
When Raven is falsely accused of stealing Ferret's raspberries, the animals all work to find out who took them, and have a party for all when the berries are found.

It's Mine!

Leo Lionni
Illustrated by: Leo Lionni
New York: Knopf, 1996, 1985
New York: Dragonfly Books, 1996, ©1985
Grade Level: K-3
Themes: Sharing
Other: Audio, Video
It's Mine! tells the story of three frogs, Lydia, Milton, and Robert, who inhabit the same pond and are unable to share their resources. It takes a severe thunderstorm and the help of a friend to help the three do some problem solving. They all enjoy the peacefulness that results when they end their bickering and stop competing.

It's Not My Fault!

Nancy Carlson
Illustrated by: Nancy Carlson
Minneapolis: Carolrhoda Books, ©2003
Grade Level: P-1
Themes: Responsible Decision Making
When George is called to the principal's office, he gets himself into trouble by making excuses for everything that has gone wrong.

Ivy's Icicle

Gary Bower
Illustrated by: Jan Bower
Wheaton, IL: Tyndale House Publishers, ©2002
Grade Level: K-4
Themes: Empathy, Apologizing or Forgiving
Ivy's heart feels as cold as an icicle toward her brother Dustin when he accidentally hits her new doll with his basketball and breaks it. Then Ivy drops and breaks her grandmother's glasses, giving her new insight into Dustin's situation. Her grandmother's quick forgiveness enables Ivy to forgive Dustin.

Jack's Talent

Maryann Cocca-Leffler
Illustrated by: Maryann Cocca-Leffler
New York: Farrar, Straus and Giroux, ©2007
Grade Level: P-2
Themes: Accepting Limitations and Gifts,
    Diversity of Individuals
On the first day of school, Miss Lucinda asks students to introduce themselves by telling their special talents. Jack, who is last, says he is good at nothing. As he goes on to name each student and the talent which he himself does not have, Miss Lucinda helps Jack recognize his special talent for remembering.

Jam & Jelly by Holly & Nellie

Gloria Whelan

Illustrated by: Gijsbert van Frankenhuyzen
Chelsea, MI: Sleeping Bear Press, ©2002
Grade Level: K-3
Themes: Cooperation
All through the summer Holly and her mother pick berries in northern Michigan. They sell the jam for 25¢ a jar so that Holly will have a winter coat and boots and not have to miss school.

Jamaica and the Substitute Teacher

Juanita Havill

Illustrated by: Anne Sibley O'Brien
Boston: Houghton Mifflin, ©1999
Grade Level: K-2
Themes: Accepting Limitations and Gifts, Honesty
Jamaica cheats on a spelling test in order to have a perfect paper. (*Jamaica's Find* (2004, ©1986) also deals with honesty.)

Jamaica's Blue Marker

Juanita Havill

Illustrated by: Anne Sibley O'Brien
Boston: Houghton Mifflin, 1997, ©1995
Grade Level: P-2
Themes: Sharing, Empathy
After acting mean, Russell uses Jamaica's blue marker to mess up her art. When Jamaica learns that Russell is moving, she is able to forgive him. (*Jamaica and Brianna* (2004, ©1993) and *Jamaica Tag-Along* (2004, ©1989) also address conflict resolution.)

Jingle Dancer

Cynthia Leitich Smith

Illustrated by: Cornelius Van Wright and Ying-Hwa Hu
New York: Morrow Junior Books, ©2000
Grade Level: K-3
Themes: Sharing, Diversity of Cultures
Jenna wants to jingle dance like Grandma Wolfe, but the pow-wow will come before the jingles can be ordered. So Jenna goes to four women in her life, borrows a row of jingles from each, and dances for them.

Jonkonnu: A Story from the Sketchbook of Winslow Homer

Amy Littlesugar

Illustrated by: Ian Schoenherr
New York: Philomel, ©1997
Grade Level: 3-6
Themes: Assertiveness, Racism, Diversity of Cultures
In 1876, Winslow Homer traveled south to paint daily life of African Americans and their freedom celebration. He is challenged by some racist townspeople and responds assertively. The story is told by the young daughter of the hotel-keeper where Homer stayed.

Julio's Magic

Arthur Dorros

Illustrated by: Ann Grifalconi
New York: HarperCollins, ©2005
Grade Level: K-4
Themes: Sharing, Respect for Elderly or Disabled
Julio puts aside his own desire to enter a wood-carving contest in order to help his teacher Iluminado (whose eyesight is failing) to win. Julio trusts that his turn will come next year.

Jungle Drums

Graeme Base
Illustrated by: Graeme Base
New York: Harry N. Abrams, ©2004
Grade Level: K-3
Themes: Accepting Limitations and Gifts,
    Jealousy, Diversity of Cultures
Ngiri, the smallest warthog in Africa is taunted by the bigger warthogs who are jealous of the other animals who hold their own parade for the most beautiful animals. The wise Wildebeest, Nnyumbu, gives Ngiri magic drums that cause the animals to go through several changes until they appreciate their diversity. A Swahili pronunciation guide is included.

Just the Way You Are

Marcus Pfister
Illustrated by: Marcus Pfister
Translated by: Marianne Martens
New York: North-South, ©2002
Grade Level: P-K
Themes: Accepting Limitations and Gifts
Through a series of misunderstandings, each animal thinks he needs a different feature to be accepted. In the end, each is affirmed.

A Kaleidoscope of Kids

Emma Damon
Illustrated by: Emma Damon
New York: Dial, ©1995
Grade Level: K-2
Themes: Alike and Different, Diversity of
    Cultures
A lift-the-flap book shows differences in kids.

Karate Hour

Carol Nevius
Illustrated by: Bill Thomson
Tarrytown, NY: Marshall Cavendish, 2006,
    ©2004
Grade Level: K-4
Themes: Respect in General
A description in poetry shows the respect and discipline found in a karate class. Notes on karate are included.

Keep Your Ear on the Ball

Genevieve Petrillo
Illustrated by: Lea Lyon
Gardiner, Maine: Tilbury House, ©2007
Grade Level: 1-3
Themes: Cooperation, Respect for Elderly or
    Disabled
Peter and his elementary school classmates realize from the beginning that the new student, Davey, who is blind, is very capable and prefers to do things by himself. On the kickball field, however, Davey is unwelcome on the teams until the students find a way to help Davey follow the ball and find the bases. By calling out the location of the ball and the bases, the students work with Davey so that they are all successful. (*Going with the Flow* by Claire H. Blatchford (Minneapolis: Carolrhoda Books, ©1998) features a 5th grader who is deaf and joins the basketball team.)

Kindness Is Cooler, Mrs. Ruler

Margery Cuyler

Illustrated by: Sachiko Yoshikawa
New York: Simon & Schuster Books for Young
    Readers, 2007, ©2006
Grade Level: K-2
Themes: Community Building, Social Skills
After they are mean to each other, Anaya, Tawana, Connor, Raquelita, and David are each assigned five acts of kindness for their families. When their kindergarten teacher Mrs. Ruler records the deeds at show-and-tell, other students join in and the class accumulates one hundred acts of family, school, and community kindness.

King of the Playground

Phyllis Reynolds Naylor

Illustrated by: Nola Langner Malone
New York: Aladdin Paperbacks, 1994, ©1991
Grade Level: K-3
Themes: Assertiveness, Bullying
Kevin goes to the playground every day, only to be ousted by Sammy's threats. Kevin's dad mildly points out that Sammy's fierce notions are impractical and unlikely, and helps Kevin realize that he's not helpless. Finally, Kevin gets up his courage and counters Sammy's threats with an imaginative—and logical—verbal exchange. Then, the two settle down to play in the sandbox together.

The Knight and the Dragon

Tomie De Paola

Illustrated by: Tomie De Paola
New York: Putnam, 1998, ©1980
Grade Level: K-4
Themes: Win-Win Solutions
The Kight and the Dragon arrange a fight, because that's what Knights and Dragons do. After learning that they are failures at fighting, they use their talents in an extremely clever enterprise.

Knockin' on Wood

Lynne Barasch

Illustrated by: Lynne Barasch
Markham, Ontario: Fitzhenry & Whiteside,
    2005, ©2004
Grade Level: 1-4
Themes: Overcoming Obstacles,
    Discrimination
This is based on the true story of Clayton "Peg Leg" Bates, who danced, even after losing one leg in a cottonseed mill accident. He endured discrimination and went on to open his own Country Club in the Catskill Mountains.

Knots on a Counting Rope

Bill Martin, Jr., and John Archambault

Illustrated by: Ted Rand (1987 on), Joseph A. Smith, 1966
Columbus, OH: SRA/McGraw Hill, 2003,
    ©1966
Grade Level: K-3
Themes: Fear or Worry, Diversity of Cultures
Other: Audio, Visual
A Native American grandfather tells his blind grandson the story of the grandson's birth and the source of his courage.

The Last Badge

George McClements

Illustrated by: George McClements
New York: Hyperion, ©2005
Grade Level: K-2
Themes: Honesty, Respect in General
Samuel Moss wants to earn a place in the family album with those who earned Grizzly Scout achievements. However, he can only see the album after he earns his badge for finding the Moon Frog which only appears every 30 years. After Samuel finds and photographs the Moon Frog, he realizes scientists will reveal its hiding place. So he tells his dad he cannot claim the badge and then learns that he has just joined his ancestors who made the same decision.

Last One In Is a Rotten Egg

Diane deGroat

Illustrated by: Diane deGroat
New York, NY: Scholastic, 2008, ©2007
Grade Level: P-2
Themes: Competition, Sharing
When their cousin Wally visits them, oppossums Gilbert and Lola discover how competitive Wally is. During the Easter egg hunt, when Wally snatches the prize egg after Lola had spotted it, Gilbert teaches his cousin a lesson. (In *Me First!* by Helen Lester (New York: Scholastic, 1996, ©1992) the main character learns that being first is not always the best.)

Least of All

Carol Purdy

Illustrated by: Tim Arnold
New York: Aladdin, 1993, ©1987
Grade Level: K-2
Themes: Gender Roles
It seems that Raven Hannah cannot do anything when compared with her five brothers. But the little Amish girl teaches herself to read while she churns the butter and ends up teaching the rest of her family.

The Lemonade Club

Patricia Polacco

Illustrated by: Patricia Polacco
New York: Philomel Books, ©2007
Grade Level: 2-4
Themes: Empathy, Overcoming Obstacles
Traci and Marilyn's 5th-grade teacher Miss Wichelman encourages her students to take the sour lemons of life and make lemonade. When Marilyn gets leukemia and needs chemo, her teacher and classmates shave their heads for her return to school. Then they discover that Miss Wichelman has breast cancer and is modeling the attitude which she has taught. This book, written by Traci's mother, is based on a true story. The end page contains pictures and an update on the three main characters.

Leonardo, the Terrible Monster

Mo Willems

Illustrated by: Mo Willems
New York: Hyperion, ©2005
Grade Level: P-1
Themes: Bullying
Leonardo is a failure as a monster. When he finally finds Sam, someone easy to scare, he finds out that Sam is crying because of other things that happened to him. So, Leonardo tries instead to be a friend, and succeeds.

Let's Talk about Race

Julius Lester

Illustrated by: Karen Barbour
New York: HarperCollins, ©2005
Grade Level: 1-5
Themes: Prejudice or Dislike, Respect in
   General
The reader is told that each of us is a story that includes our history, our likes and dislikes, our religion and nationality and race. Some of us get caught in comparisons based on race, economics, and so on. But, if each of us took off our skin and our hair, we would look alike. In the end, unless we get to know each other, we really know very little about each person's story.

Liar, Liar, Pants on Fire!

Miriam Cohen

Illustrated by: Ronald Himler, 2008; Lillian
   Hoban, 1985
New York: Star Bright Books, 2008, ©1985
Grade Level: 1-4
Themes: Inclusion or Exclusion, Honesty,
   Empathy
Other: Audio
Alex tells stories and is shunned by his classmates, until Jim feels sorry for him.

The Librarian of Basra: A True Story from Iraq

Jeanette Winter

Illustrated by: Jeanette Winter
Orlando, FL: Harcourt, 2005, ©2004
Grade Level: 2-4
Themes: Community Building, Problem
    Solving
When war came to Basra, Alia Muhammad Baker, the librarian, hid the precious books of the library with friends. There they will stay until peace comes and the library can be rebuilt.

Lilly's Purple Plastic Purse

Kevin Henkes

Illustrated by: Kevin Henkes
New York: Greenwillow, 2005, ©1996
Grade Level: P-2
Themes: Recognizing Emotions, Apologizing
    or Forgiving
Other: Audio
Lilly wants to show her musical purse at school and has a conflict with her teacher Mr. Slinger. Together they resolve their conflict.

Listen Buddy

Helen Lester

Illustrated by: Lynn Munsinger
New York: Scholastic, 1997, ©1990
Grade Level: P-K
Themes: Listening
Buddy Rabbit learns the hard way that for his own safety he needs to listen.

Listen to the Wind

Greg Mortenson and Susan L. Roth

Illustrated by: Susan L. Roth
New York: Dial Books for Young Readers,
    ©2009
Grade Level: 1-3
Themes: Community Building, Cooperation,
    Diversity of Cultures, Peacemaking
The children of Korphe, Pakistan, tell the story of Greg Mortenson who got lost in their mountains and went to their village to be nursed back to health. When Greg asked how he could repay them, his mentor, Haji Ali, told Greg to listen to the wind. Greg heard the voices of the children and knew he should build them a school. The children tell how the whole village helped build the school and then celebrated. Endpapers include a Korphe Scrapbook and Artist's Note. Artifacts from the Pakistani region of Baltistan contributed to the creation of the collages in the book. (The chapter book *Three Cups of Tea* (Mortenson and Relin, 2008, ©2006) tells the story in fuller detail.)

Little Bear and the Big Fight

Jutta Langreuter

Illustrated by: Vera Sobat
Brookfield, CT: Millbrook Press, ©1998
Grade Level: P-2
Themes: Anger, Conflict Escalator, Apologizing
    or Forgiving
When Little Bear's best friend Brandon won't share the pink clay, Little Bear gets so angry he bites Brandon's ear. After losing his best friend, Little Bear takes some time to decide to say, "Sorry."

Little Raccoon's Big Question

Miriam Schlein
Illustrated by: Ian Schoenherr
New York: Scholastic, 2005, ©2004
Grade Level: P-2
Themes: Accepting Limitations and Gifts
Other: Audio
Little Raccoon finds out that his mother loves him all the time, not just when he is performing well. (In *Why Do You Love Me?* by Laura Schlessinger and Martha Lambert (New York: HarperCollins, ©1999) a mother tells her little boy that she loves him unconditionally for himself.)

The Littlest Witch

Jeanne Massey
Illustrated by: Adrienne Adams
New York: Alfred A. Knopf, ©1959
Grade Level: K-3
Themes: Peacemaking, Diversity of Individuals
Littlest Witch wants to help, not scare, others on Halloween. So, she gives up the ways of the other witches, helps others, and gets her own rewards.

Lizzie and Harold [Also named The Best Friends Club: A Lizzie and Harold Story]

Elizabeth Winthrop
Illustrated by: Martha Weston
New York: Lothrop, Lee & Shepard, 1989, ©1986
Grade Level: P-2
Themes: Gender Roles
Lizzie decides that Harold can no longer be her best friend, because he is not a girl.

Lizzy's Ups and Downs: Not an Ordinary School Day

Jessica Harper
Illustrated by: Lindsay Harper duPont
New York: HarperCollins, ©2004
Grade Level: P-3
Themes: Recognizing Emotions
After a day in school, Lizzy finds satisfaction in listing for her mother all the feelings she has had during the day.

Long-Long's New Year: A Story about the Chinese Spring Festival

Catherine Gower
Illustrated by: He Zhihong
Boston: Tuttle Publishers, ©2005
Grade Level: K-2
Themes: Cooperation, Diversity of Cultures
Long-Long helps his grandfather repair his bicycle. Then he helps sell fresh cabbage so that they have enough money for Chinese Spring Festival supplies. An historical note is included.

Loretta Ace Pinky Scout

Keith Graves
Illustrated by: Keith Graves
New York: Scholastic, ©2002
Grade Level: K-3
Themes: Accepting Limitations and Gifts
Loretta, who comes from a line of perfectionists, meets failure in roasting marshmallows. Then she learns that her ancestors were also flawed.

Louanne Pig in Making the Team

Nancy Carlson

Illustrated by: Nancy Carlson
Minneapolis: Carolrhoda Books, 2005, ©1985
Grade Level: K-3
Themes: Gender Roles
Other: Audio
Louanne makes the football team and Arnie leads the cheerleaders.

Louanne Pig in Witch Lady

Nancy Carlson

Illustrated by: Nancy Carlson
Minneapolis: Carolrhoda Books, 2006, ©1985
Grade Level: P-3
Themes: Rumors or Suspicion
Other: Audio
Louanne Pig trips near the witch lady's house and learns that all the rumors are false.

Loudest Noise in the World

Benjamin Elkin

Illustrated by: James Daugherty
New York: Viking, 1966, ©1954
Grade Level: K-3
Pages: 64
Themes: Listening
For his birthday, Prince Hulla-Baloo wants to hear everyone shout at once. Instead he gets the gift of silence.

Loudmouth George and the New Neighbors

Nancy Carlson

Illustrated by: Nancy Carlson
Minneapolis: Carolrhoda Books, 2003, ©1983
Grade Level: K-3
Themes: Prejudice or Dislike
Other: Audio
George hesitates to meet the pigs who have moved into the neighborhood until he sees others enjoying them.

Love, Lizzie: Letters to a Military Mom

Lisa Tucker McElroy

Illustrated by: Diane Paterson
Morton Grove, IL: Whitman, ©2005
Grade Level: K-3
Themes: Coping
This is a collection of letters from Lizzie during the year her mother is out of the country on military duty. Tips for families are included.

Low-Down, Bad-Day Blues

Derrick D. Barnes

Illustrated by: Aaron Boyd
New York: Scholastic, ©2004
Grade Level: K-1
Themes: Recognizing Emotions, Coping
A boy tells all the rotten things that happened to him in one day. He goes on to say that he waited, and things got better. Discussion questions and activities are included.

Magid Fasts for Ramadan

Mary Matthews

Illustrated by: Earl B. Lewis
New York: Clarion Books, 2000, ©1996
Grade Level: 2-4
Pages: 48
Themes: Honesty, Diversity of Cultures, Win-
    Win Solutions
Magid, who is almost eight years old, tries to fast even though his parents have said he is too young. In the end, Magid and his family resolve the problem.

The Making of My Special Hand: Madison's Story

Jamee Riggio Heelan

Illustrated by: Nicola Simmonds Carter
Atlanta: Peachtree, 2002, ©1998
Grade Level: P-3
Themes: Respect for Elderly or Disabled
Madison, a very young child, was born without a left hand. The book is narrated from her point of view, telling how she was fitted for her "helper hand," how it was made, and how it works.

Making Plum Jam

John Warren Stewig

Illustrated by: Kevin O'Malley
New York: Hyperion, ©2002
Grade Level: 2-4
Themes: Sharing, Peacemaking
Jackie visits his country aunts. When they make their annual visit to a neighbor's plum tree, the new owner chases them away. Jackie makes peace by taking some plum jam to that farmer, and begins a round of sharing.

Making the World

Douglas Wood

Illustrated by: Yoshi and Hibiki Miyazaki
New York: Simon & Schuster, ©1998
Grade Level: K-2
Themes: Community Building
Here is a secret: the world is not yet finished. This book tells ways that all the creatures of nature, including humans, can help make the world.

Mama Loves Me from Away

Pat Brisson

Illustrated by: Laurie Caple
Honesdale, PA: Boyds Mills Press, ©2004
Grade Level: 1-3
Themes: Coping
Sugar, born on her mother's 19th birthday, loves to hear Mama's story of that night. Although Mama is in prison, she finds a way to share her stories with Sugar.

Mama Panya's Pancakes: A Village Tale from Kenya

Mary Chamberlin and Rich Chamberlin

Illustrated by: Julia Cairns
Cambridge, MA: Barefoot Books, 2006, ©2005
Grade Level: K-3
Themes: Community Building, Sharing
While Mama Panya is at market getting the makings for pancakes, her son Adika invites all of their friends. Mama gets home and worries they will not have enough—until the friends arrive with abundant gifts of food. Endnotes discuss the life and language of Kenya.

Mama Went to Jail for the Vote

Kathleen Karr

Ilustrated by: Malene Laugesen
New York: Hyperion, ©2005
Grade Level: K-3
Themes: Discrimination, Gender Roles
Susan Elizabeth, the daughter of a suffragist, tells the story of her mother picketing President Wilson's White House and being jailed for six months. Historical background is included.

Manuela's Gift

Kristyn Rehling Estes
Illustrated by: Claire B. Cotts
San Francisco: Chronicle Books, ©1999
Grade Level: K-3
Themes: Community Building, Coping
Instead of the yellow dress she wants for her birthday, Manuela gets her mother's blue dress altered to fit. She fills the piñata with good wishes for each of her family, and grows to love and appreciate her dress.

Martha Walks the Dog

Susan Meddaugh
Illustrated by: Susan Meddaugh
New York: Scholastic, 2000, ©1998
Boston: Houghton Mifflin, 2000
Grade Level: K-3
Themes: Hurtful Words
Martha the talking dog learns that mean words anger Bob, the new dog on the block whose owner tells him he is a bad dog. Then Melissa, a neighboring parrot, tells Bob he is good and Bob changes his attitude.

Masai and I

Virginia Kroll
Illustrated by: Nancy Carpenter
New York: Aladdin, 1997, ©1992
Grade Level: 2-4
Themes: Point of View, Diversity of Cultures
Linda learns about the Masai in East Africa and imagines what her life would be like if she were Masai. (*Joshua's Masai Mask* by Dakari Hru (New York: Lee & Low, 1996, ©1993) tells a story for younger students in which a young boy receives a Masai mask that allows him to be in other people's shoes.)

Matthew and Tilly

Rebecca C. Jones
Illustrated by: Beth Peck
New York: Puffin Books, 1995, ©1991
Grade Level: K-2
Themes: Conflict Escalator
Matthew and Tilly are close friends who live in the inner city. They play and work together every day. Problems begin when they argue over a broken crayon and go their separate ways. The children soon discover that many of their favorite games aren't as much fun to play alone. They make up and play together again.

Max's Starry Night

Ken Wilson-Max
Illustrated by: Ken Wilson-Max
New York: Hyperion, ©2001
St. Albans: David Bennett, 2003, ©2001
Grade Level: P-K
Themes: Empathy
When Little Pink the pig makes fun of Big Blue the elephant who is scared of the night, Max helps Little Pink feel sorry.

May I Pet Your Dog?

Stephanie Calmenson
Illustrated by: Jan Ormerod
New York: Clarion Books Books, 2007, ©2006
Grade Level: P-2
Themes: Respect in General
A dog named Harry teaches a young boy how to approach a variety of dogs, always beginning by asking the owner if he may pet the dog. The tips on meeting dogs could serve as an introduction to respect for others.

McGillycuddy Could!

Pamela Duncan Edwards
Illustrated by: Sue Porter
New York: HarperCollins, ©2005
Grade Level: P
Themes: Accepting Limitations and Gifts
McGillycuddy is a kangaroo who feels like a failure in the barnyard because he cannot give milk or eggs, grow wool, or crow in the morning. Then a wolf comes for a goose and McGillycuddy's jumping and kicking scares the wolf away.

Me Too!

Jamie Harper
Boston: Little, Brown, ©2005
Grade Level: K-2
Themes: Point of View
Grace is bothered by the way her little sister Lucy always copies her. Then Grace realizes that she herself copies Coach Finn, her swimming coach, out of admiration.

Mean Chickens and Wild Cucumbers

Nathan Zimelman
Illustrated by: David Small
New York: Macmillan, ©1983
Grade Level: K-3
Themes: Conflict Escalator, Mediation or Negotiation
A hole in the fence leads to conflict and higher fences. Resolution comes with a coop and a trellis—and sun through the hole.

The Meanest Thing to Say

Bill Cosby
Illustrated by: Varnette P. Honeywood
New York: Scholastic, 2004, ©1997
Grade Level: K-3
Themes: Assertiveness, Peer Pressure
Michael Reilly cannot get Little Bill to join him in saying mean things. Bill and his friends say, "So?" and later invite Michael to play with them.

Meet the Barkers: Morgan and Moffat Go to School

Tomie De Paola
Illustrated by: Tomie De Paola
New York: Puffin Books, 2003, ©2001
Grade Level: P-1
Themes: Diversity of Individuals
Other: Audio, Video
The Welsh terrier twins are introduced. Moffie gets gold stars and Morgie makes friends, and then they learn to diversify.

Megan's Birthday Tree: A Story about Open Adoption

Laurie Lears
Illustrated by: Bill Farnsworth
Morton Grove, IL: Whitman, ©2005
Grade Level: 1-4
Themes: Community Building, Coping
Megan stays in touch with her birth mother Kendra (who was too young to care for a baby when Megan was born). Kendra has a tree that she planted when Megan was born; each year she decorates it and sends a picture. When Megan learns that Kendra is getting married and will move away, Megan is concerned about the tree, so she digs up a tree from their yard to give Kendra—and then discovers that Kendra has already dug up Megan's tree so she can take it with her.

The Memory String

Eve Bunting
Illustrated by: Ted Rand
New York: Clarion Books, ©2000
Grade Level: K-3
Themes: Inclusion or Exclusion
Other: Video

The memory string was created by Laura's great-grandmother who began stringing special buttons. The treasure was passed down to Laura through her late mother. Then, the memory string breaks and one of the buttons cannot be found. Laura's stepmother Jane knows that no substitute button will do, just as she herself can never replace Laura's mother. When Laura learns of Jane's wise insight, their relationship reaches a new stage.

Mercedes and the Chocolate Pilot: A True Story of the Berlin Airlift and the Candy that Dropped from the Sky

Margot Theis Raven
Illustrated by: Gijsbert van Frankenhuyzen
Chelsea, MI: Sleeping Bear Press, ©2002
Grade Level: 3-5
Themes: Sharing, Basic Emotional Needs
Other: Audio

During the 1948–1949 Berlin Airlift, seven-year-old Mercedes Simon writes Col. Gail S. Halvorsen, the pilot who is dropping candy for the children. Years later the two meet. Historical notes are included.

Messy Lot

Larry Dane Brimner
Illustrated by: Christine Tripp
New York: Children's Press, ©2001
Grade Level: K-2
Themes: Cooperation

Alex bosses Three J and Gabby, and then they all work together to clean a corner lot. (*Trash Trouble* (New York: Scholastic, 2004, ©2003) and *Sidewalk Patrol* (New York: Children's Press, ©2002) also address cooperating to help the environment.)

Michael Rosen's Sad Book

Michael Rosen
Illustrated by: Quentin Blake
Cambridge, MA: Candlewick Press, 2005, ©2004
London: Walker, 2008, ©2004
Grade Level: 3-8
Themes: Recognizing Emotions, Coping

The author tells how he copes with the sadness in his life since his son Eddie's death.

Mighty Jackie: The Strike Out Queen

Marissa Moss
Illustrated by: C. F. Payne
New York: Simon & Schuster, 2004, ©2002
Grade Level: K-3
Themes: Discrimination, Gender Roles

This is the true story of Jackie Mitchell who, at age seventeen, was a pitcher for the Chattanooga Lookouts. In a single game on April 2, 1931, Jackie struck out both Babe Ruth and Lou Gehrig. After the game, Jackie's contract was voided because "baseball was 'too strenuous' for a woman." (*Girl Wonder: A Baseball Story in Nine Innings* by Deborah Hopkinson (New York: Aladdin, 2006, ©2003) tells the true story of another female baseball player, Alta Weiss, who pitched for an Ohio semipro team in 1907.)

Mike and Tony: Best Friends

Harriet Ziefert
Illustrated by: Catherine Siracusa
New York: Puffin Books, 1993, ©1987
Grade Level: K-1
Themes: Mediation or Negotiation

Mike and Tony, best friends, have a fight but settle it with words. (Negotiation is also found in *Mr. and Mrs. Muddle* by Mary Ann Hoberman (Boston: Joy Street, 1998, ©1988) when two donkeys find an agreeable solution.)

Mim, Gym, and June

Denis Roche
Illustrated by: Denis Roche
Boston, MA: Houghton Mifflin, ©2003
Grade Level: P-2
Themes: Competition, Conflict Escalator, Jealousy
Other: Video
Short Mim and tall June, two cats, are line leaders for the 2nd and 3rd grades. Their conflict begins when Mim gets to lead the entire group to gym, and ends when they find that they can win the obstacle course together.

The Mine-O-Saur

Sudipta Bardhan-Quallen
Illustrated by: David Clark
New York: G. P. Putnam's Sons, ©2007
Grade Level: P-K
Themes: Sharing
Because of his behavior, Mine-o-saur does not get to take part in many of the school activities with the other dinosaurs. After not letting the other dinosaurs play with any of the blocks, he finds that they are more interested in playing with each other than in admiring his tower. He returns their things and finds that they are more interested in playing with him than in just getting their things returned. Then he realizes that friends are what he really wants.

Miss Alaineus: A Vocabulary Disaster

Debra Frasier
Illustrated by: Debra Frasier
Orlando, FL: Voyager Books, 2007, ©2000
Grade Level: 3-5
Themes: Problem Solving
Sage misunderstands her spelling word. Later she cleverly deals with her mistake by using Miss Alaineus in the Vocabulary Parade.

Miss Rumphius

Barbara Cooney
Illustrated by: Barbara Cooney
Lexington, MA: Schoolhouse, 1999, ©1982
Grade Level: K-4
Themes: Peacemaking
Other: Audio, Video
Alice Rumphius wants to go to faraway places and then live by the sea. She learns from her grandfather that, in addition, she needs to make the world beautiful. At the end of her life she does that, when she plants lupines all over the countryside. [A statue of a "Cigar Store" Native American may require class discussion.]

Mississippi Morning

Ruth Vander Zee
Illustrated by: Floyd Cooper
Grand Rapids, MI: Eerdmans, ©2004
Grade Level: 3-5
Themes: Racism
Other: Audio
James Williams learns that his father, a store-owner whom he admires, is also a Klansman.

The Mixed-Up Chameleon

Eric Carle
Illustrated by: Eric Carle
Hong Kong: HarperFestival, 1998, ©1975
Grade Level: P-2
Themes: Accepting Limitations and Gifts
Other: Video
A chameleon tries to take on the characteristics of many zoo animals and finds it cannot function unless it is itself. (A similar situation is found in *The Perfect Tail: A Fred and LuLu Story* by Mie Araki (San Francisco: Chronicle Books, ©2004) where a rabbit accepts his own tail after trying to make it like those of the other animals.)

Molly in the Middle

Kim Morris
Photographs by: Dorothy Handelman
Brookfield, CT: Millbrook Press, ©1999
Grade Level: K-3
Themes: Accepting Limitations and Gifts
Molly tries to feel as special as Tina the oldest and Lucy the youngest. She tries cutest, loudest, funniest, meanest, and then her dad helps her see she is the luckiest.

Molly Rides the School Bus

Julie Brillhart
Illustrated by: Julie Brillhart
Morton Grove, IL: Whitman, ©2002
Grade Level: K-1
Themes: Assertiveness, Nonviolent Response
On Molly's first day in kindergarten, she drops her toy bear Willy as she boards the bus. The other students toss him around, but Ruby, a 4th grader, returns Willy to Molly and then sits with her, turning the ride into a good experience.

Morning Glory Monday

Arlene Aldo
Illustrated by: Maryann Kovalski
Toronto: Tundra Books, ©2003
Grade Level: P-3
Themes: Community Building, Recognizing
    Emotions
In an effort to cheer up her depressed mother, a little girl plants a morning glory seed that grows, helps her mother, and changes the whole neighborhood and city.

Moses Sees a Play

Isaac Millman
Illustrated by: Isaac Millman
New York: Farrar, Straus and Giroux, ©2004
Grade Level: K-3
Themes: Respect for Elderly or Disabled
Moses, who is deaf, attends a special school. When the Little Theatre of the Deaf comes to act out Cinderella, a class of hearing children spend the day with Moses's class. Moses makes a new friend, Manuel, who is just learning English. Sketches of sign language, ASL, are included throughout the book. (Millman has also written *Moses Goes to School* (©2000) and *Moses Goes to the Circus* (©2003).)

Moses: When Harriet Tubman Led Her People to Freedom

Carole Boston Weatherford
Illustrated by: Kadir Nelson
New York: Hyperion Books for Children,
    ©2006
Grade Level: 2-5
Themes: Community in Action, Overcoming
    Obstacles, Oppression
Other: Video
Full-page illustrations show Harriet Tubman in conversation with God as she begins her escape from slavery and makes her way to freedom. The story continues with Harriet's call to return for her family and many other slaves. An endnote explains how the events in Harriet's life prepared her for her role and states that, in nineteen trips, she helped three hundred others find freedom. (*Aunt Harriet's Underground Railroad in the Sky* by Faith Ringgold (New York: Crown Publishers, 1995, ©1992) is suitable for older children. Eight-year-old Cassie Lightfoot dreams that she and her baby brother Be Be are part of the Underground Railroad as Aunt Harriet tells them her story.)

Mouse, Mole, and the Falling Star

A. H. Benjamin
Illustrated by: John Bendall-Brunello
New York: Dutton, ©2002
London: Little Tiger, 2003, ©2002
Grade Level: P-K
Themes: Competition, Friendship
Mouse and Mole trust each other until both want to capture a star that has fallen and each thinks the other has it. In the end they realize the value of their friendship.

Mr. Lincoln's Way

Patricia Polacco
Illustrated by: Patricia Polacco
New York: Scholastic, 2003, ©2001
Grade Level: 1-4
Themes: Basic Emotional Needs, Prejudice or
    Dislike, Bullying
Principal Lincoln uses Eugene Esterhause's love for birds to help Eugene overcome his bullying and to teach him the value of diversity.

Mr. Peabody's Apples

Madonna (Ritchie)
Illustrated by: Loren Long
New York: Scholastic, 2004, ©2003
London: Puffin Books, 2006, ©2003
Grade Level: 3-6
Themes: Rumors or Suspicion
When Tommy spreads a rumor about him, Mr. Peabody, the baseball coach, tells Tommy the story of gossip being like the wind-blown feathers from a torn pillow.

Mrs. Biddlebox: Her Bad Day and What She Did About It

Older copies have only the title Mrs. Biddlebox.
Linda Smith
Illustrated by: Marla Frazee
San Diego, CA: Harcourt Children's, 2008,
    ©2002
Grade Level: 1-3
Themes: Recognizing Emotions, Coping
Mrs. Biddlebox wraps up a gloomy day, bakes it, and eats it.

Mrs. Watson Wants Your Teeth

Alison McGhee
Illustrated by: Harry Bliss
Orlando, FL: Harcourt, 2008, ©2004
Grade Level: K-2
Themes: Rumors or Suspicion
Other: Audio
A little girl with a loose tooth listens to the second grader who tells her the first-grade teacher wants the children's teeth. After keeping her mouth closed all day, the little girl gets some pleasant surprises.

Mud Pie for Mother

Scott Beck
Illustrated by: Scott Beck
New York: Dutton, ©2003
Grade Level: P-2
Themes: Sharing
After Little Pig respects the needs of the other animals, they each contribute to a birthday gift for Little Pig's mother.

Mufaro's Beautiful Daughters: An African Tale

John Steptoe
Illustrated by: John Steptoe
Boston: Houghton Mifflin, 2001, ©1987
Grade Level: K-3
Themes: Respect in General, Social Skills
Other: Audio, Video
In this folktale from Zimbabwe, Mufaro is the father of two beautiful daughters, Manyara and Nyasha. Manyara aspires to be queen and rule her sister. However, Nyasha is kind to everyone, including the king who comes in several disguises before selecting her to be queen.

Music for Alice

Allen Say
Illustrated by: Allen Say
Boston: Houghton Mifflin, 2004
Grade Level: 3-8
Themes: Basic Emotional Needs,
    Discrimination
Alice neglects her love of dance while she and her husband Mark move from internment in a World War II Japanese internment camp to bleak farming in Eastern Oregon. Years later, after Mark has died, Alice remembers the acres of gladiolas they had grown, and dances.

My Best Friend

Mary Ann Rodman
Illustrated by: Earl B. Lewis
New York: Puffin Books, 2007, ©2005
Grade Level: 1-3
Themes: Inclusion or Exclusion
At the pool, six-year-old Lily wants seven-year-old Tamika to be her best friend, but Tamika wants to be with seven-year-old Shanice. In the end, Lily appreciates six-year-old Keesha who has wanted all along to be her friend.

My Big Brother

Valorie Fisher
Illustrated by: Valorie Fisher
New York: Atheneum, ©2002
Grade Level: P-1
Themes: Point of View
The reader sees a boy from his baby brother's viewpoint. (*My Big Sister* (2004, ©2003) may also be of interest.)

My Diary from Here to There

Amanda Irma Perez
Illustrated by: Maya Christina Gonzalez
San Francisco: Children's Book Press, ©2002
Grade Level: 1-4
Themes: Coping, Diversity of Cultures
Young Amanda tells of her family's move from Juarez, Mexico, to Los Angeles. Her diary helps her cope with the loss of her friend Michi and the strangeness of a new land and language. This is a bilingual account, based on the author's own experience.

My Friend and I

Lisa Jahn-Clough
Illustrated by: Lisa Jahn-Clough
Boston: Houghton Mifflin, ©1999
Grade Level: P-K
Themes: Problem Solving
A girl and a boy play together until they fight over a toy bunny. After each is miserable, they get together, mending the toy and their friendship.

My Many Colored Days

Dr. Seuss
Illustrated by: Steve Johnson and Lou Fancher
New York: Knopf, 1998, ©1996
Grade Level: P-2
Themes: Recognizing Emotions
Other: Video
Using colors, a child describes his feelings on given days. In the end, he accepts the range of feelings he has. (*On Monday When It Rained* by Cherryl Kachenmeister (Boston: Houghton Mifflin, 1996, ©1989) features photographs of a young boy showing his feelings as he describes an event for each day of the week.)

My Name Is Bilal

Asma Mobin-Uddin
Illustrated by: Barbara Kiwak
Honesdale, PA: Boyds Mills Press, ©2005
Grade Level: 3-6
Themes: Prejudice or Dislike, Diversity of
   Cultures, Responsible Decision Making
Bilal stands by as his sister Ayesha is harassed by Scott because of her scarf. He decides to use the name Bill Al in class, but his Muslim teacher gives him a book about his namesake, an ancient Muslim prayer leader. Later Bilal invites Scott to join a basketball game and the two play together until an older student, who is Muslim, leaves to pray and Bilal joins him.

My Name Is Celia

Monica Brown
Illustrated by: Rafael López
Flagstaff, AZ: Luna Rising, ©2004
Grade Level: 2-4
Themes: Discrimination, Diversity of Cultures
With page-filling illustrations and brief bilingual accounts, Celia Cruz (1924–2003) tells her story. She describes the life in Cuba that she had to leave behind and the salsa music that she helped create.

My Name is Jorge: On Both Sides of the River

Jane Medina
Illustrated by: Fabricio Vandenbroeck
Honesdale, PA: Boyds Mills Press, ©1999
Grade Level: 2-5
Pages: 48
Themes: Discrimination
Through bilingual poems, 6th-grader Jorge, who has crossed the river to the U.S. and then returned to Mexico, tells of the hardships in the U.S.

My Name Was Hussein

Hristo Kyuchukov
Illustrated by: Allan Eitzen
Honesdale, PA: Boyds Mills Press, ©2004
Grade Level: P-3
Themes: Oppression
A young boy in Bulgaria tells how his Muslim family was captured and forced to take on Christian names. This story is based on the author's own experience.

My Rows and Piles of Coins

Tololwa M. Mollel
Illustrated by: Earl B. Lewis
Boston: Houghton Mifflin, 2000, ©1999
Grade Level: P-3
Themes: Community Building, Responsible
   Decision Making
Saruni, a young Tanzanian boy, saves for a bicycle so that he can help his mother take things to market.

My Secret Bully

Trudy Ludwig

Illustrated by: Abigail Marble
Berkeley, CA: Tricycle Press, 2005, ©2003
Grade Level: 1-4
Themes: Inclusion or Exclusion, Assertiveness,
    Bullying

Katie has been Monica's friend since kindergarten, and then she changes. When they are alone Katie is usually kind, but when others are around Katie makes fun of Monica or excludes her. After talking this over with her mother, Monica confronts Katie without being mean. In the end, Monica makes new friends and feels better about herself. Discussion questions and resources are included.

Myrtle

Tracey Campbell Pearson

Illustrated by: Tracey Campbell Pearson
New York: Farrar, Straus and Giroux, ©2004
Grade Level: K-2
Themes: Assertiveness

Her Aunt Tizzy teaches Myrtle, a mouse, how to cope with mean Frances. Myrtle can ignore Frances or she can tell her to stop being rude.

A New Coat for Anna

Harriet Ziefert

Illustrated by: Anita Lobel
New York: Scholastic, 1988, ©1986
Grade Level: P-2
Themes: Sharing, Community in Action
Other: Audio

By bartering with the sheep farmer, spinner, weaver, and tailor, Anna's mother secures a coat for Anna.

The New Hippos

Lena Landström

Illustrated by: Joan Sandin
New York: R & S Books, ©2003
Grade Level: P-2
Themes: Inclusion or Exclusion, Diversity of
    Individuals

Life in the hippo community is changed when new neighbors move in. The little hippo excels in diving, and his mother weaves a new kind of hut.

The New Kid

Larry Dane Brimner

Illustrated by: Christine Tripp
New York: Scholastic, 2004, ©2003
Grade Level: K-2
Themes: Inclusion or Exclusion, Empathy

Gabby does not want to welcome the new student, Lisa, until Three J and Alex remind her of how they had welcomed her.

New Kid

Susan Hood

Photographs by: Dorothy Handelman
Brookfield, CT: Millbrook Press, ©1998
Grade Level: P-1
Themes: Inclusion or Exclusion

Sid acts up until he feels accepted. The whole class is glad when Sid settles down.

Nice Wheels

Gwendolyn Hooks

Illustrated by: Renee Andríaní
New York: Scholastic, ©2005
Grade Level: K-2
Themes: Respect for Elderly or Disabled

A young boy reports that the new boy in his class, who is in a wheelchair, does most of the things that his classmates do.

Night Rabbits

Lee Posey

Illustrated by: Michael Montgomery
Atlanta: Peachtree, 2007, ©1999
Grade Level: P-K
Themes: Win-Win Solutions
Elizabeth loves the rabbits who run through their lawn at night, but her father thinks they will ruin the lawn. They work out a way to share the lawn with the rabbits.

Nine Animals and the Well

James Rumford

Illustrated by: James Rumford
Boston: Houghton Mifflin, ©2003
Grade Level: K-3
Themes: Friendship, Peer Pressure
This is a cumulative tale in which animals meet as they travel to the birthday party for the raja-king. Each time the group meets up with the next animal, that animal has enough gifts for each of them to take a better gift to the raja-king, and they discard their old gifts. At the end they lose everything and the raja-king assures them he just wants their company.

Nine Candles

Maria Testa

Illustrated by: Amanda Schaffer
Minneapolis: Carolrhoda Books, ©1996
Grade Level: 1-4
Themes: Coping
Raymond celebrates his seventh birthday but has a hard time waiting until he is nine and his mother is out of prison.

No One Can Ever Steal Your Rainbow

Barbara Meislin

Illustrated by: Helen Webber
Tiburon, CA: Purple Lady Productions, ©2005
Grade Level: K-5
Themes: Coping, Hope
Other: CD
The author learns a lesson of hope when she discovers that her mailbox has been stolen.

No Good in Art

Miriam Cohen

Illustrated by: Lillian Hoban
New York: Bantam Dell, 1996, ©1980
Grade Level: K-3
Themes: Accepting Limitations and Gifts
After his kindergarten teacher corrects his painting, Jim has the idea that he is no good in art. His 1st-grade teacher and his friends help him discover that he can create beautiful paintings.

No Red Monsters Allowed!

Liza Alexander

Illustrated by: David Prebenna
New York: Golden Books, 1997, ©1991
Grade Level: P-2
Themes: Prejudice or Dislike
Hazel refuses to let Elmo, a Red Monster, play in her tree house until her Blue Monster friends, Herry and Hannah, persuade her otherwise. They find out Elmo is different and also fun.

Nobody Likes Me!

Raoul Krischanitz
Illustrated by: Rosemary Lanning
New York: North-South, 2001, ©1991
Grade Level: K-3
Themes: Social Skills
Buddy, a new dog in the neighborhood, assumes nobody likes him. When he checks out his assumptions, he discovers the other animals are afraid of him.

Nora's Ark

Natalie Kinsey-Warnock
Illustrated by: Emily Arnold McCully
New York: HarperCollins, ©2005
Grade Level: K-4
Themes: Sharing, Community in Action
Wren's grandparents, Nora and Horace, have nearly finished building their new house when the 1927 Vermont flood comes. The neighbors and their animals arrive with provisions and the community waits out the flood in the house, built on high ground.

Nothing but Trouble: The Story of Althea Gibson

Sue Stauffacher
Illustrated by: Greg Couch
New York: Alfred A. Knopf, ©2007
Grade Level: 2-5
Themes: Discrimination, Social Skills
As a young girl in Harlem, Althea Gibson had the reputation of often being in trouble. Then, Buddy Walker, a local musician, saw Althea's potential and arranged tennis lessons at the Cosmopolitan Tennis Club for her. With the help of Buddy and several others, Althea eventually learned social skills as well, and went on to become the first African American to compete in the Wimbledon Cup, winning in 1957 and 1958. Althea always acknowledged those who had helped her. Historical notes are included.

Now One Foot, Now the Other

Tomie De Paola
Illustrated by: Tomie De Paola
New York: Puffin Books, 2005, ©1981
Grade Level: 2-5
Themes: Cooperation, Respect for Elderly or Disabled
Other: Audio, Video
Grandpa Bob teaches Bobbie to walk and, after Bob has a stroke, Bobbie helps Bob walk.

Nowhere to Run, Nowhere to Hide

Kathleen Duey and Ron Berry
Illustrated by: Bartholomew
San Diego, CA: Smart Kids Publishing, ©1997
Grade Level: P-2
Themes: Fear or Worry
Jenny is sure a monster is coming into her room at night. She finds out that it's only her baby sister making the noises. Tips for discussion are given. (In *Boogeyman in the Basement!* (©1997) tree branches against the basement window make scary noises.)

Numero Uno

Alex Dorros and Arthur Dorros
Illustrated by: Susan Guevara
New York: Henry N. Abrams, 2007, ©2006
Grade Level: K-3
Themes: Competition
Strong Hercules and smart Socrates argue incessantly about which man's gift is more important to the village. So, a young boy challenges them to leave the village for three days so that the village can decide which man they miss more. In the end, the village decides that they miss both men, but not their arguing.

Odd Velvet

Mary Whitcomb

Illustrated by: Tara Calahan King
San Francisco: Chronicle Books, ©1998
Grade Level: K-2
Themes: Diversity of Individuals

Velvet's classmates learn to appreciate the special gifts that she has, even though she is different.

Oh, Bother! No One's Listening

Nikki Grimes

Illustrated by: Sue DiCicco and John Kurtz
New York: Golden Books, ©1997
Grade Level: P-2
Themes: Listening

No one listens to Rabbit's directions for planning a picnic. They show up with the wrong things, but work out a solution. (*Oh, Bother! Someone's Fighting!* (1997, ©1991) may also be of interest.)

Oh, Bother! Someone's Jealous!

Betty Birney

Illustrated by: Nancy Stevenson
Racine, WI: Golden Books, 1997, ©1994
Grade Level: P-2
Themes: Jealousy

Tigger is jealous because Roo can bounce up the hill in fewer bounces. (Birney also wrote *Oh, Bother! Somebody's Grumpy!* (1994, ©1992) and *Oh, Bother! Someone Won't Share!* (1995, 1993).)

The Old Tree

Ruth Brown

Illustrated by: Ruth Brown
Cambridge, MA: Candlewick Press, ©2007
Grade Level: P-2
Themes: Cooperation, Problem Solving

At first, the animals are oblivious of the "X" which marks their old tree. However, Crow has seen what happens to such trees and alerts the others. So Captain Crow and the crew set to work, cleverly hiding the "X" and saving their home.

Old Turtle and the Broken Truth

Douglas Wood

Illustrated by: Jon J. Muth
New York: Scholastic, ©2003
Grade Level: 3-8
Pages: 56
Themes: Inclusion or Exclusion, Conflict
    Nature
Other: Audio

In this sequel to *Old Turtle* (2007, ©1992), human beings find a treasure in the partial truth, "You are loved." When they accept that as The Truth, they consider others as enemies. A young girl learns the rest of the truth from Old Turtle: "… and so are they."

Oliver Button Is a Sissy

Tomie De Paola

Illustrated by: Tomie De Paola
San Diego: Harcourt Brace: 1995, ©1979
Grade Level: K-3
Themes: Gender Roles
Other: Audio, Video

Oliver becomes a target of teasing because he prefers dancing to football. He rises above the taunts by doing what he does best and being recognized for his talent.

On Meadowview Street

Henry Cole

Illustrated by: Henry Cole
New York: Greenwillow, ©2007
Grade Level: K-2
Themes: Community, Peacemaking

It all begins with a single flower in a yard. Caroline wants to protect it from her father's mower and he agrees. Gradually, as more flowers appear, the protected area grows and the whole yard becomes a meadow. The neighbors join the movement, and their street lives up to its name.

On Sand Island

Jacqueline Briggs Martin

Illustrated by: David A. Johnson
Boston: Houghton Mifflin, ©2003
Grade Level: 1-3
Themes: Cooperation
Other: Audio

In the early 1900s, young Carl Dahl who lived on Lake Superior built a boat. At each stage, one of his neighbors helped and then they all celebrated.

Once Upon a Time

Niki Daly

Illustrated by: Niki Daly
New York: Farrar, Straus and Giroux, ©2003
Grade Level: K-3
Themes: Hurtful Words, Peer Pressure

Charmaine and Carmen laugh at Sarie, of the South African Karoo, when she reads in front of the class, but not Emile. After being able to read with her Auntie Anna, Sarie gets the confidence she needs.

One for Me, One for You

C. C. Cameron

Illustrated by: Grace Lin
Brookfield, CT: Roaring Brook Press, ©2003
Grade Level: P-K
Themes: Sharing

A hippo and an alligator find it easy to share four cookies. They have trouble figuring out how to distribute three toy trucks, and then find a nice solution.

One Green Apple

Eve Bunting

Illustrated by: Ted Lewin
New York: Clarion Books Books, ©2006
Grade Level: 1-4
Themes: Diversity of Cultures, Point of View
Other: Audio

On her second day in the new school, Farah and her classmates visit an apple orchard. She narrates the story, conveying her hesitation in speaking aloud. Her classmates encourage her enough that she is able to use her "first outside-myself word." The class makes apple cider with Farah's apple being the only green one, symbolizing a positive aspect to diversity. (*Sumi's First Day of School Ever* by Soyung Pak (New York: Viking, ©2003) features a young girl who speaks no English and finds school less frightening because of a new friend.)

One Million Men and Me

Kelly Starling Lyons

Illustrated by: Peter Ambush
East Orange, NJ: Just Us Books, ©2007
Grade Level: K-2
Themes: Community Building, Responsible
    Decision Making

Nia and her dad join a bus trip to Washington, D.C., for the October 16, 1996, Million Man March. Nia watches her dad and the other men pledge to improve themselves and their communities. The author's endnote comments on the original march and some of its effects.

Only One Neighborhood

Marc Harshman and Barbara Garrison

Illustrated by: Barbara Garrison
New York: Dutton Children's Books, ©2007
Grade Level: K-2
Themes: Community Building, Diversity of
    Cultures

Pictures are shown of several one-of-a-kind stores, each with a variety of goods, and then one school with many children. Finally many neighborhoods in a city and many countries in one world are mentioned with "only one wish: PEACE."

On That Day: A Book of Hope for Children

Andrea Patel

Illustrated by: Andrea Patel
Berkeley: Tricycle Press, 2004, ©2001
Grade Level: P-2
Themes: Fear or Worry, Peacemaking

The scary things that happened on September 11, 2001, are acknowledged. Then there are suggestions of helpful things everyone can do.

The Other Side

Jacqueline Woodson

Illustrated by: Earl B. Lewis
New York: Putnam, ©2001
Grade Level: 1-4
Themes: Prejudice or Dislike, Win-Win
    Solutions
Other: Audio

This book tells the story of two young girls, Clover who is black and Annie who is white, who live next door to each other and are separated by a fence. The girls notice their similarities, but are encouraged not to acknowledge each other by their friends and family. When one finally climbs the fence to sit beside the other, the fences of prejudice begin to crumble.

The Other Way to Listen

Byrd Baylor

Illustrated by: Peter Parnall
New York: Aladdin Paperbacks, 1997, ©1978
Fitzgerald Books, 2007, ©1978
Grade Level: 1-4
Themes: Listening, Respect in General
Other: Audio, Video

A wise old man teaches a young boy how to respect and listen to nature.

Over the Deep Blue Sea

Daisaku Ikeda

Illustrated by: Brian Wildsmith
Translated by: Geraldine McCaughrean
New York: Knopf, 1993, ©1992
Grade Level: 1-3
Themes: Conflict Nature

Pablo welcomes Akiko and Hiroshi to his island, but will no longer be a friend after he hears how Akiko and Hiroshi's ancestors were enemies to his people. After Hiroshi almost drowns and Pablo tries to save him, the children get a powerful lesson that all are one family.

Owen

Kevin Henkes

Illustrated by:
New York: Scholastic, 2004, ©1993
Findaway World LLC, 2007, ©1993
Grade Level: P-2
Themes: Win-Win Solutions
Other: Audio

Owen, a little mouse, has a yellow blanket that he takes with him wherever he goes. "Fuzzy goes where I go," says Owen, but his neighbor, Mrs. Tweezers, disagrees. Owen's parents are worried because he is going to kindergarten and they wonder if Mrs. Tweezers is right. After trying various ways to separate Owen from his blanket, Owen's mother comes up with a solution that leaves everyone pleased.

The Owl and the Woodpecker

Brian Wildsmith
Illustrated by: Brian Wildsmith
New York: Star Bright Books, 2007, ©1971
Grade Level: K-3
Themes: Conflict Nature, Problem Solving
Both Owl and Woodpecker want the same tree. After a long conflict, Woodpecker saves Owl's life and, although they both lose the tree, they find a workable solution.

Owl Moon

Jane Yolen
Illustrated by: John Schoenherr
New York: Philomel Books, 2007, ©1987
Grade Level: P-3
Themes: Listening
Other: Audio, Video
A little girl tells the story of a magical full-moon night when she and her dad search for an owl. Although she feels cold and wants to talk, she listens and watches until the owl appears.

The Pain and the Great One

Judy Blume
Illustrated by: Judy Blume
New York: Atheneum, 2002, ©1974
Grade Level: 1-4
Themes: Point of View
Other: Audio
This is a book about sibling rivalry, in which a brother (the Pain) and a sister (The Great One) view life in the same household from two very different points of view. In the first portion of the book, the sister is telling her story about her younger brother. She feels that he is treated much better than she, and describes a multitude of examples, such as how dad carries him in the kitchen in the morning, and helps him so he's not late for the school bus. Mom takes glory in his schoolwork, and he gets dessert when he doesn't eat all of his dinner. The second part of the story, The Great One, is told from the little brother's perspective. He describes things differently. He thinks his sister thinks she's so great because she can play the piano, work the can opener, baby-sit for their aunt, and remember phone numbers.

Papa Jethro

Deborah Bodin Cohen
Illustrated by: Jane Dippold
Minneapolis: Kar Ben Publishing of Lerner
    Publishing Group, ©2007
Grade Level: K-3
Themes: Diversity of Cultures
When Rachel asks her grandfather Nick why she goes to a synagogue and he goes to a church, Grandpa Nick says they have different religions. He tells the story of Moses's Jewish son Gersham whose grandfather Jethro was a Midianite. Although it was sometimes hard to be different, they liked to share what made them different. Grandpa Nick assures Rachel that he loves her just as she is.

Papa's Mark

Gwendolyn Battle-Lavert
Illustrated by: Colin Bootman
New York: Holiday House, 2003, ©2001
Grade Level: 2-5
Themes: Discrimination
Simms helps his father Samuel T. Blow to write his own name when he votes in the first election (1870) where black men are allowed to vote.

The Patched Heart: A Gift of Friendship and Caring

H. E. Stewart
Illustrated by: H. E. Stewart
Victoria, BC: Tudor House Press, ©2007
Grade Level: K-2
Themes: Community, Coping, Friendship
When Big Puppy needs heart surgery, he feels afraid and does not begin to heal until his young friend Mossy stays with him in the hospital. During Big Puppy's long time in the hospital, he acquires the name Patch. His second surgery goes much better because the animal staff in the hospital is more acquainted with his needs and Patch knows what to expect. In the end, Patch and Mossy become regular hospital visitors.

The Patchwork Quilt

Valerie Flournoy
Illustrated by: Jerry Pinkney
New York: Scholastic, 1996, ©1985
Grade Level: K-3
Themes: Community Building, Respect for
    Elderly or Disabled
Other: Audio, Video
Making a quilt becomes a family project and a storytelling legacy from Tanya's grandmother and mother.

Patrol: An American Soldier in Vietnam

Walter Dean Myers
Illustrated by: Ann Grifalconi
New York City: HarperTrophy, 2005, ©2001
Grade Level: 4+
Themes: Peacemaking
A young G.I. describes the world of Vietnam as he sees it during one day of combat. As he searches for his enemy, he endures the hardships of the landscape and the fear of being killed. When he does see the "enemy," he sees the harmless people of a village and a young man very much like himself. He ends the day, exhausted from the war.

The Peace Book

Todd Parr
Illustrated by: Todd Parr
Boston: Little, Brown, 2006, ©2004
Grade Level: K-2
Themes: Peacemaking
Peace is illustrated in many situations, ending with: "Peace is being different, feeling good about yourself, and helping others." (*Peace Begins with You* by Katherine Scholes (Boston: Little, Brown, 1994, ©1989) uses drawings and text to teach students in grades 2-4 various aspects of peace.)

Peace One Day: The Making of World Peace Day

Jeremy Gilley
Illustrated by: Karen Blessen
New York: Putnam, ©2005
Grade Level: 3-6
Themes: Community in Action, Peacemaking,
    Responsible Decision Making
Jeremy Gilley tells how he began to establish Peace One Day by meeting with world leaders in 1999. In September 2001, the UN declared that September 21, 2002 "would be the first UN International Day of Peace—a day of cease-fire and nonviolence." Jeremy's story shows how one person can make a difference, and how much help he had from friends, family, and organizations.

Peaceful Piggy Meditation

Kerry Lee MacLean
Illustrated by: Kerry Lee MacLean
Morton Grove, IL: Whitman, ©2004
Grade Level: P-3
Themes: Anger, Coping, Peacemaking
Other: Video
A group of pigs shows how to calm down in the midst of anxiety, stress, or anger. Tips for parents are included. (*The Happiest Tree: A Yoga Story* by Uma Krishnaswami (New York: Lee & Low, 2008, ©2005) tells how a young girl, who feels clumsy, learns to use Yoga breathing.)

Peach Heaven

Yangsook Choi
Illustrated by: Yangsook Choi
New York: Farrar, Straus and Giroux, 2005,
    ©2004
Grade Level: K-2
Themes: Cooperation, Peacemaking
A little girl in Puchon, Korea, loves the peaches that are washed down from the mountain farms in an extremely heavy rainfall. Then she organizes a group of children to take some of the peaches back to the farmers who lost them.

Peanut's Emergency

Cristina Salat
Illustrated by: Tammie Lyon
Watertown, MA: Charlesbridge, ©2002
Grade Level: K-2
Themes: Recognizing Emotions, Fear or Worry,
    Responsible Decision Making
Peanut Nwanda reports her feelings when her mother does not pick her up after school and she tries to remember the Safety Rules. She eventually contacts her family and they all celebrate her return.

Pearl Moscowitz's Last Stand

Arthur Levine
Illustrated by: Robert Roth
Boston: Houghton Mifflin, 2001, ©1993
Grade Level: K-4
Themes: Assertiveness, Problem Solving
When the electric company threatens to take down the last gingko tree in her block, Pearl tries to talk with the company representative and then chains herself to the tree.

Pearl's New Skates

Holly Keller
Illustrated by: Holly Keller
New York: Greenwillow, ©2005
Grade Level: K-2
Themes: Cooperation
Pearl needs to overcome her initial discouragement from falling, and her Uncle Jack gives her the help she needs so she can learn to skate.

Peer Pressure: Deal With It Without Losing Your Cool

Elaine Slavens
Illustrated by: Ben Shannon
Toronto: James Lorimer, ©2004
    Paw Prints, 2008, ©2004
Grade Level: 4-6
Themes: Assertiveness, Peer Pressure,
    Responsible Decision Making
This is a discussion about peer pressure and ways to respond, with cartoon-like illustrations. Advice and a quiz are given on the basics of peer pressure, for the Insider, the Outsider, and the Witness. (*Bullying: Deal With It Before Push Comes to Shove* (©2003) and *Fighting: Deal With It Without Coming to Blows* (2007, ©2004) may also be helpful.)

The Perfect Clubhouse

Daniel J. Mahoney
Illustrated by: Daniel J. Mahoney
New York: Clarion Books, ©2004
Grade Level: K-3
Themes: Cooperation, Win-Win Solutions
Four animal friends (Stanley, Heston, Floyd, and Julius) all have different ideas about the ideal clubhouse. When they try to build it, they find ways to satisfy all the needs. (In *The Mighty Pigeon Club* by David San Souci (©2007), friends find a win-win solution when taking care of a neighbor's pigeons.)

The Perfect Thanksgiving

Eileen Spinelli
Illustrated by: JoAnn Adinolfi
New York: Square Fish, 2007, ©2003
Grade Level: P-3
Themes: Alike and Different
The narrator contrasts the perfect Thanksgiving Day of Abigail Archer's family with the chaotic day at her own house. She concludes that both families are alike in how loving their families are.

A Picnic in October

Eve Bunting
Illustrated by: Nancy Carpenter
Orlando, FL: Voyager, 2004, ©1999
Grade Level: 1-3
Themes: Inclusion or Exclusion, Diversity of
    Cultures
Other: Video
Tony begrudgingly takes part in his family's annual birthday party for Lady Liberty. His grandma recalls arriving at Ellis Island from Italy. When Tony sees a Middle East family looking at Lady Liberty, he has a new appreciation of the significance of their celebration.

A Pig Is Moving In!

Claudia Fries
Illustrated by: Claudia Fries
New York: Orchard Books, 2000, ©1999
Grade Level: K-2
Themes: Prejudice or Dislike, Stereotypes
The neighbors cannot believe that the new neighbor can be neat and skilled.

Piggie Pie!

Margie Palatini
Illustrated by: Howard Fine
New York: Scholastic, 1997, ©1995
Sandpiper, 2008, ©1995
Grade Level: K-3
Themes: Cooperation
Other: Audio
When a witch goes to the farm to buy pigs, the pigs disguise themselves as other animals.

Pipaluk and the Whales

John Himmelman
Illustrated by: John Himmelman
Washington, DC: National Geographic Society,
    2002, ©2001
Grade Level: P-2
Themes: Cooperation, Community in Action
Pipaluk and her father discover thousands of beluga whales trapped in an ice opening. The villagers chop at the ice and feed the whales while they wait many weeks for a ship to cut a canal. Then, when the whales will not follow the ship, Pipaluk sings from the ship and lures them to the open waters. This is based on an event from December 1984, until February 1985, off the coast of Russa where the scientists onboard used classical music to attract the whales.

Pirate's Eye

Robert Priest
Illustrated by: Robert Priest
Boston: Houghton Mifflin, ©2005
Grade Level: 2-4
Themes: Point of View
Captain Black loses his glass eye and Sandpiper, an artistic pauper, finds it. When Sandpiper sees images in the eye, he writes a book about Black's life and then returns the eye to the captain. Black reforms his life when he sees in the eye the kindness of Sandpiper's life.

Pitching In for Eubie

Jerdine Nolen
Illustrated by: Earl B. Lewis
New York: Amistad of Harper Collins, ©2007
Grade Level: K-3
Themes: Community, Cooperation
Young Lily Shorter's sister Eubie is offered a college scholarship, on the condition that her family raise $3,000. Lily's parents, Eubie, and their brother Jacob all take on extra jobs to make Lily's dream come true, After all of Eubie's efforts fail, she is offered $5 an hour for helping the mother of Mrs. Tollinger, one of Mrs. Shorter's sewing customers, and Eubie becomes part of the family endeavor.

A Place to Grow

Soyung Pak

Illustrated by: Marcelino Truong
New York: Arthur A. Levine Books, ©2002
Grade Level: K-4
Themes: Basic Emotional Needs, Diversity of
    Cultures

An Asian girl's father explains that people are like seeds needing favorable conditions to grow. So some of them immigrate to other countries.

A Place Where Sunflowers Grow

Amy Lee-Tai

Illustrated by: Felicia Hoshino
San Francisco: Children's Book Press, ©2006
Grade Level: 1-4
Themes: Coping, Discrimination,

Young Mari and her family are interned in Topaz, Utah, during World War II. In the community Art School, Mari is only able to draw when she can draw on the happy memories of her former back yard. Meanwhile, her sunflower seeds finally sprout and give hope in the desert where they are staying.

Planting the Trees of Kenya:
The Story of Wangari Maathai

Claire A. Nivola

Illustrated by: Claire A. Nivola
New York: Farrar, Straus and Giroux, ©2008
Grade Level: 1-3
Themes: Community Building, Responsible
    Decision Making

Wangari Maathai, born in 1940, grew up in the fertile land of Kenya. After five years at Benedictine College in Atchison, KS, Wangari returned to a land where the land was barren because harvesting of trees removed topsoil. Wangari taught the women of Kenya how to plant and nurture new trees. Endnotes give additional background.

A Play's the Thing

Aliki

Illustrated by: Aliki
New York: Harper Collins, ©2005
Grade Level: 1-3
Themes: Cooperation

A class creates a play of "Mary had a little lamb" and everyone, including Jose who had bullied, cooperates. (*Communication* (New York: Mulberry, 1999, ©1993) and *Feelings* (New York: Scholastic, 1991, ©1984) are also by Aliki.)

Players in Pigtails

Shana Corey

Illustrated by: Rebecca Gibbon
New York: Scholastic, 2006, ©2003
Grade Level: K-4
Themes: Gender Roles
Other: Audio, Video

This is the story of Katie Casey who played for Kenosha Comets in the All-American Girls Professional Baseball League (1943–1954).

Please Is a Good Word to Say

Barbara Joosse

Illustrated by: Jennifer Plecas
New York, NY: Philomel Books, ©2007
Grade Level: K-3
Themes: Social Skills

An upbeat little girl demonstrates a variety of situations where she can good words, including Please, Thank You, I'm Sorry, Excuse Me, and May I Help You? (*Time to Say Please!* by Mo Willems (New York: Hyperion, ©2005) is a humorous look at the uses of "Please," "Thank you," and "Excuse me.")

Please, Louise!

Frieda Wishinsky

Illustrated by: Frieda Wishinsky
Berkeley, CA: House of Anansi Press, 2008,
    ©2007
Grade Level: P-1
Themes: Conflict Nature

Jake's little sister Louise is constantly pestering him, and Jake only wants to be left alone. After wishing Louise were a little dog who would let him be, a little dog happens by and gives him a scare. Then Louise appears with their new neighbor boy, and to Jake's relief, they want to play by themselves—after Jake and Louise say they will see each other later.

A Pocket Full of Kisses

Audrey Penn

Illustrated by: Barbara Leonard Gibson
Terre Haute, IN: Tanglewood, 2006, ©2004
Grade Level: P-1
Themes: Sharing, Jealousy
Other: Audio

When Chester the raccoon sees his mother give his little brother Ronnie a kissing hand, Chester is jealous. Their mother assures Chester that she will not run out of kisses. This is a sequel to *The Kissing Hand* (New York: Scholastic, 1998, 1993) in which the mother kisses Chester's hand, giving him a reminder throughout the day of her love.

Pop's Bridge

Eve Bunting

Illustrated by: C. F. Payne
Orlando: Harcourt, ©2006
Grade Level: 1-4
Themes: Cooperation, Diversity of Individuals

Robert's and Charlie's fathers are building the Golden Gate Bridge. Robert, the narrator, thinks his dad who does iron work on the high sections is more essential to the project than Charlie's father who paints. An accident involving a variety of workers convinces Robert that all the workers are important. The assembly and clever placement of the last piece of a jigsaw puzzle symbolize the lesson on cooperation.

The Pot That Juan Built

Nancy Andrews-Goebel

Illustrated by: David Diaz
Translated by: Eunice Cortés
New York: Lee & Low, ©2002
London: Turnaround, 2003, ©2002
Grade Level: K-5
Themes: Community Building, Diversity of
    Cultures
Other: Audio, Video

A cumulative rhyme tells how Juan Quezada of Mata Ortiz, a village in Mexico, creates pottery that uses local resources and contributes to the village's economy.

Presidents' Day

Anne Rockwell

Illustrated by: Lizzy Rockwell
New York: HarperCollinsPublishers, 2008,
    ©2007
Grade Level: K-2
Themes: Cooperation, Diversity of Individuals,
    Gender Roles

The narrator tells of her class creating a play about the four Mount Rushmore presidents. Each student is matched with his or her role. After the narrator, who shares his birthday, plays George Washington and then is elected class president, she gets the idea that she might be the first woman president of the United States.

Princess Pooh

Kathleen M. Muldoon

Illustrated by: Linda Shute
Niles, IL: Whitman, ©1989
Grade Level: K-3
Themes: Empathy, Respect for Elderly or
    Disabled

Patty Jean tells about her sister who is treated like a princess because she uses a wheelchair. After Patty Jean tries to depend on a wheelchair, she appreciates what her sister deals with.

The Printer

Myron Uhlberg

Illustrated by: Henri Sørensen
Atlanta: Peachtree, ©2003
Grade Level: 2-4
Themes: Inclusion or Exclusion, Respect for
    Elderly or Disabled

This story of the author's father, who was deaf, is set in the 1940s. A fire begins in the newspaper plant where narrator's father works. It is the deaf printers who alert the others of danger and save their lives. After the plant is rebuilt, the hearing printers, who had previously not communicated with the narrator's father, use sign language to express their thanks.

Psssst! It's Me ... the Bogeyman

Barbara Park

Illustrated by: Stephen Kroninger
New York: Aladdin, 2001, ©1988
Grade Level: 1-4
Themes: Fear or Worry, Point of View,
    Stereotypes

A clever monologue by the Bogeyman refutes the headline, "Evil Bogeyman Bellows Boo."

The Quarreling Book

Charlotte Zolotow

Illustrated by: Arnold Lobel
Topeka, KS: Econo-Clad Books, 1999, ©1963
Grade Level: K-3
Themes: Anger, Conflict Nature
Other: Audio, Video

A chain reaction of anger ends with the dog who reverses the reaction by just playing.

Queen of the Class

Mary Engelbreit

Illustrated by: Mary Engelbreit
New York: HarperCollins, 2007, ©2004
Grade Level: K-2
Themes: Cooperation

Although Ann Estelle has what it takes to be queen in the class play, she is a star as the stage manager.

Queen of the World

Thomas F. Yezerski

Illustrated by: Thomas F. Yezerski
New York: Farrar, Straus and Giroux, ©2000
Grade Level: P-3
Themes: Competition

The narrator and her two sisters Amanda and Natalie have a hard time getting along. They have a contest to make their mother's favorite birthday gift. The winner would be crowned Queen of the World and wear the crown they made. Their conflicts over the gifts causes their mother to cry, and the girls feel terrible. In the morning, they work together to make breakfast for their mother and crown her the Queen of the World.

A Quiet Place

Douglas Wood

Illustrated by: Dan Andreasen
New York: Aladdin, 2005, ©2002
Grade Level: K-3
Themes: Listening

The book suggests many ways and places, including books and his own solitude, where a child can find quiet.

The Quiltmaker's Gift

Jeff Brumbeau
Illustrated by: Gail De Marcken
New York: Scholastic, 2002, ©2000
Grade Level: 1-4
Themes: Sharing, Peacemaking
The quiltmaker teaches the selfish king to find happiness in giving.

Raccoon's Last Race: A Traditional Abenaki Story

Joseph Bruchac and James Bruchac
Illustrated by: Jose Aruego & Ariane Dewey
New York: Dial, ©2004
Grade Level: K-4
Themes: Competition
Azban the Raccoon with his long legs is so proud of his racing abilities that he taunts other animals. When he challenges a rock and gives it a push, he is flattened. When ants try to pull him back into shape, he brushes them off before they have finished the job, and so he has to live with his short legs.

Rachel Parker, Kindergarten Show-Off

Ann Martin
Illustrated by: Nancy Poydar
New York: Scholastic, 1993, ©1992
Grade Level: K-3
Themes: Cooperation, Competition, Jealousy
Other: Audio
Olivia is the only one in kindergarten who can read, until Rachel Parker moves next door. Olivia becomes so competitive with Rachel that she almost misses out on having a friend. Then their teacher Mrs. Bee arranges for the two girls to cooperate as they read to the class.

The Rag Coat

Lauren Mills
Illustrated by: Lauren Mills
New York: Trumpet Club, 1995, ©1991
Boston: Little, Brown, 1991
Grade Level: 1-4
Themes: Community in Action, Apologizing or
    Forgiving
Minna's coal-mining father dies when she is eight. The Quilting Mothers make her a coat from cloths that each have a story. After her schoolmates make fun of the coat, she tells the stories and they apologize.

Rain Romp: Stomping Away a Grouchy Day

Jane Kurtz
Illustrated by: Dyanna Wolcott
New York: Greenwillow, ©2002
Grade Level: P-1
Themes: Recognizing Emotions
A little girl, helped by her parents, loses her grouchiness on a gray day that becomes brighter.

The Rainbow Fish and the Big Blue Whale

Marcus Pfister
Translated by: J. Alison James
New York: North-South, 2003, ©1998
Grade Level: P-1
Themes: Rumors or Suspicion, Mediation or
    Negotiation
Other: Audio
Rainbow Fish and the others are suspicious and afraid of the Big Blue Whale, who then retaliates. After Rainbow Fish talks to the whale, they become friends and work together. (*The Rainbow Fish* (2007, ©1992) shows that sharing can overcome loneliness. Several themes are addressed by the Rainbow Fish books.)

Rainbow Joe and Me

Maria Diaz Strom
Illustrated by: Maria Diaz Strom
New York: Lee & Low, 2002, ©1999
Grade Level: P
Themes: Respect for Elderly or Disabled
Eloise tries to explain colors to her blind friend Joe, and he expresses them in music.

Raising Yoder's Barn

Jane Yolen
Illustrated by: Bernie Fuchs
Boston: Little, Brown, ©1998
Grade Level: K-3
Themes: Cooperation, Community in Action
After fire destroys a barn, an eight-year-old boy helps the neighbors build a new one. (In *Barn Raising* by Craig McFarland Brown (New York: Greenwillow, 2002) Amish neighbors help raise a barn.)

Raymond and Nelda

Barbara Bottner
Illustrated by: Nancy Hayashi
Atlanta: Peachtree Publishers, ©2007
Grade Level: 1-3
Themes: Anger, Conflict Escalator, Friendship
Raymond and Nelda are two animals who are comfortable friends, until Nelda falls and Raymond laughs at her. Their conflict continues for several days, with both feeling miserable and needing the help of another friend to help them reconcile with each other.

Reach High: The Delany Sisters

Amy Hill Hearth
Illustrated by: Tim Ladwig
Nashville, TN: Abingdon Press, ©2002
Grade Level: 1-3
Themes: Overcoming Obstacles, Discrimination
Although Sarah (1889–1999) and Bessie (1891–1995) Delany were daughters of a man who had been a slave, their entire family including their parents were college-educated. Events are related from Sarah's and Bessie's early years, including the beginning of the Jim Crow laws. A biographical note is included.

The Real Winner

Charise Neugebauer
Illustrated by: Barbara Nascimbent
New York: North-South, ©2000
Grade Level: K-2
Themes: Competition
Humphrey the hippo teaches his friend Rocky the raccoon that not everything needs to be a contest. Rocky wants to catch a fish so that his mother will be proud of him. After watching Humphrey's care of little animals, however, Rocky catches a fish and lets it go when he sees it struggling to live. Then his mother really is proud of him.

A Really Good Snowman

Daniel J. Mahoney
Illustrated by: Daniel J. Mahoney
New York: Clarion Books, ©2005
Grade Level: K-3
Themes: Competition, Empathy
Jack, a dog, can make a snowman with his little sister Nancy or with his friends Angie, a rabbit, and Melden, a mouse. Although his friends win a trophy, Jack is happy about his decision, because he chooses to work with Nancy who needs him.

The Recess Queen

Alexis O'Neill

Illustrated by: Laura Huliska-Beith
New York: Scholastic, 2006 ©2002
Grade Level: K-4
Themes: Assertiveness, Bullying
Other: Audio, Video

Mean Jean is the reigning Recess Queen, and no one dares touch a ball, swing a bat, or use a slide until she says so. One day Katie Sue a puny new girl shows up and catches Mean Jean completely offguard by making her an offer she finds hard to refuse—an invitation to play. Soon they are best friends, and the playground is safe for all. [The problem might be too easily resolved.]

Recycle Every Day!

Nancy Elizabeth Wallace

Illustrated by: Nancy Elizabeth Wallace
Tarrytown, NY: Marshall Cavendish, 2006, ©2003
Grade Level: K-2
Themes: Community in Action, Respect in General

When Minerva rabbit enters a Recycling Poster Contest, her family gives her an idea for each day of the week. A recycling game and an activity are included.

The Reluctant Dragon

Kenneth Grahame

Abridged and Illustrated by: Inga Moore
Cambridge, MA: Candlewick Press, 2004, ©1898
London: Walker, 2005, ©1898
London: Egmont, 2008, ©1898
Grade Level: 1-5
Pages: 54
Themes: Peacemaking, Rumors or Suspicion, Win-Win Solutions
Other: Audio, Video

Young Jack helps St. George and the dragon stage a duel, letting St. George look like a hero and securing a home near the village for the dragon. (*The Reluctant Dragon* retold by Robert D. San Souci (New York: Orchard Books, ©2004) is a shorter book for older students.)

Ring! Yo?

Chris Raschka

Illustrated by: Chris Raschka
New York: DK Publishing, ©2000
Grade Level: 1-4
Themes: Conflict Nature

A one-sided phone conversation, that could lead to a conflict, is later filled in by supplying the other party's words.

Romina's Rangoli

Malathi Michellev Iyengar

Illustrated by: Jennifer Wanardi
Fremont, CA: Shen's Books, ©2007
Grade Level: 1-3
Themes: Diversity of Culture, Problem Solving

Romina's mother is from India where people paint designs on floors in an art form called rangoli. Her father is from Mexico where papel picado is practiced; designs are cut in paper. When Miss McMahon assigns each student to create something which represents where his or her ancestors came from, Romina is torn between the two forms of art. Then she uses cut paper to create a floor design.

Room for a Little One: A Christmas Tale

Martin Waddell

Illustrated by: Jason Cockcroft
New York: Margaret K. McElderry, 2006, ©2004
London: Orchard, 2008, ©2004
Grade Level: P-1
Themes: Inclusion or Exclusion
Other: Audio

Kind Ox, Old Dog, Stray Cat, Small Mouse, and Tired Donkey each make room for the next animal. Then they welcome Jesus into the stable.

Rooster Can't Cock-a-Doodle-Doo

Karen Rostoker-Gruber

Illustrated by: Paul Rátz de Tagyos
New York: Penguin Young Readers, 2006,
    ©2004
Grade Level: P-2
Themes: Cooperation
When everyone on the farm oversleeps because of Rooster's sore throat, the other animals help Farmer Ted finish the chores before dark.

Rosa

Nikki Giovanni

Illustrated by: Bryan Collier
New York: Scholastic, 2006, ©2005
New York: Square Fish, 2008, ©2005
Grade Level: 3-5
Themes: Discrimination
Other: Audio, Video
This story describes the day, December 1, 1955, when Rosa Parks (1913–2005) decided to say no to being treated as a second class citizen and was arrested for not leaving her bus seat. The reader also sees the beginning and the growth of the bus boycott which ended with the Supreme Court declaring bus segregation illegal on November 13, 1956. (*The Bus Ride That Changed History: The Story of Rosa Parks* by Pamela Duncan Edwards (Boston: Houghton Mifflin, ©2005) tells the story in a cumulative poem.)

Rosie & the Yellow Ribbon

Paula De Paolo

Illustrated by: Janet Wolf
Boston: Little, Brown, ©1992
Grade Level: K-2
Themes: Rumors or Suspicion, Apologizing or
    Forgiving
When Rosie's favorite yellow ribbon is missing, she blames her best friend Lucille. Their friendship is in jeopardy until they work together to rescue a bird nest.

Rotten Island

William Steig

Illustrated by: William Steig
Jeffrey, NH: David R. Godino, 2007, ©1969
London: National Maritime Museum, 2008,
    ©1969
Grade Level: 2-4
Themes: Peacemaking
Other: Video
A flower blooms on an island that only has mean creatures, and everything gets changed.

Ruby the Copycat

Peggy Rathmann

Illustrated by: Peggy Rathmann
New York: Scholastic, 2007, ©1991
Grade Level: K-2
Themes: Accepting Limitations and Gifts
Other: Audio, Video
Ruby, a new student, thinks she must copy Angela, another student, to be accepted. When Ruby discovers a unique talent that impresses her classmates, she realizes that her uniqueness makes her a valued member of the community.

The Rumor: A Jataka Tale from India

Jan Thornhill

Illustrated by: Jan Thornhill
New York: Firefly Books, 2002
Toronto: Maple Tree Press, 2005, ©2002
Grade Level: K-2
Themes: Fear or Worry, Rumors or Suspicion
After wondering what would happen if the world broke apart, a hare hears a mango fall and then alarms every animal in the country that the world is breaking apart. A wise lion helps her find the truth.

Ruthie and the (Not So) Teeny Tiny Lie

Laura Rankin

Illustrated by: Laura Rankin
New York: Bloomsbury Children's Books,
   ©2007
Grade Level: P-2
Themes: Honesty

A little fox named Ruthie finds Martin's camera on the playground. When Martin claims the camera, Ruthie tells both Martin and their teacher Mrs. Olsen that the camera is her own. Her lie bothers her until that night when she tells her parents and decides she has to tell the truth. The next day, after telling Mrs. Olsen and returning the camera to Martin, Ruthie realizes she does not miss the camera at all. (*That's Mine, Horace* by Holly Keller (New York: Greenwillow, 2001, ©2000) tells a similar story where one little boy finds another's truck.)

Samantha the Snob

Kathryn Cristaldi

Illustrated by: Denise Brunkus
New York: Random House, 2003, ©1994
Grade Level: 1-3
Pages: 48
Themes: Stereotypes
Other: Audio

Before she gets to know Samantha S. Van Dorf, the narrator decides that Samantha is a snob. Only after being Samantha's partner in some relay races does the narrator realize that she has a new friend.

Sami and the Time of the Troubles

Florence Parry Heide and Judith Heide Gilliland

Illustrated by: Ted Lewin
New York: Clarion Books, ©1992
Grade Level: K-3
Themes: Fear or Worry, Peacemaking
Other: Audio

Ten-year-old Sami and his family live in Beirut and often must seek cover from war. His grandfather tells of the time when children demonstrated for peace.

Sammy Wakes His Dad

Chip Emmons

Illustrated by: Shirley Venit Anger
New York: Star Bright Books, ©2002
Grade Level: P-2
Themes: Respect for Elderly or Disabled

After his dad has an accident and is confined to a wheelchair, Sammy goes fishing alone each morning and returns to describe his experience to his dad. Finally, Sammy encourages his dad to join him in fishing.

The Saturday Escape

Daniel J. Mahoney

Illustrated by: Daniel J. Mahoney
New York: Clarion Books, ©2002
Grade Level: K-2
Themes: Honesty, Responsible Decision
   Making

Jack, a dog, and his friends Angie, a rabbit, and Melden, a mouse, each sneak away from Saturday chores to go to Story Hour. Each regrets the decision; so the three leave early, help each other finish their chores, and then have their own story hour.

Saving Strawberry Farm

Deborah Hopkinson

Illustrated by: Rachel Isadora
New York: Greenwillow, 2005, ©2004
Grade Level: P-2
Themes: Cooperation, Overcoming Obstacles,
   Community in Action

During the Depression, Davey and Rosey's parents are struggling to keep their farm. When Elsie Elkins's strawberry farm is going to be auctioned, Davey helps spread the word that everyone should plan a Penny Auction. The community keeps the bids low enough that Elsie can buy back her farm for $9.75.

Say Something

Peggy Moss

Illustrated by: Lea Lyon
Gardiner, ME: Tilbury House, 2008, ©2004
Grade Level: K-5
Themes: Empathy, Bullying, Nonviolent
    Response

A middle-school girl tells about a boy who always gets picked on, another who gets called names, and a girl who always sits by herself on the bus. When the narrator sits alone in the cafeteria because her friends are gone, she is taunted until she cries. Although the students at another table seem to feel sorry for her, no one says anything, and the narrator realizes what she needs to do. Later, she sits by the girl on the bus and finds herself enjoying the girl's company. (In *Nobody Knew What to Do: A Story about Bullying* by Becky Ray McCain (Morton Grove, IL: Whitman, ©2001) a student tells his teacher and gets help for a boy who is being bullied.)

Saying Goodbye to Lulu

Corinne Demas

Illustrated by: Ard Hoyt
Boston: Little, Brown, ©2004
Grade Level: P-2
Themes: Recognizing Emotions, Coping

A young girl tells about her dog LuLu dying. The girl is angry and sad and refuses to think of a new dog. Then time passes and a new dog is on his way.

The School Is Not White!:
A True Story of the Civil Rights Movement

Doreen Rappaport

Illustrated by: Curtis James
New York: Hyperion, ©2005
Grade Level: 2-5
Themes: Overcoming Obstacles, Community
    in Action, Racism

Set in 1965, this is the story of the Mae Bertha and Matthew Carter family of Drew, MS. Their seven oldest children, ages six to 16, were the first African Americans to attend a school which had previously been all white. When Matthew lost his plantation job and the family was turned out of their home, social and church groups helped. Although the children were harassed at school, they persevered, some going on for graduate degrees. An historical note is included.

A Season for Mangoes

Regina Hanson

Illustrated by: Eric Velasquez
New York: Clarion Books, ©2005
Grade Level: K-4
Themes: Cooperation, Diversity of Cultures

Sareen tells of the sit-up for her Nana. This is a wake on the ninth night which includes a ritual of storytelling. Sareen needs the encouragement of her brother Desmond to tell how hard she and Desmond had tried to get a sweet mango for their Nana, finally succeeding near the time of Nana's death. In the telling, Sareen realizes that her Nana would have been happy whether or not she had the mangoes. An endnote describes the sit-up ritual in Jamaica.

Sebastian's Roller Skates

Joan de Déu Prats

Illustrated by: Francesc Rovira
La Jolla, CA: Kane/Miller Book Publishers,
    2005, ©2003
Grade Level: K-3
Themes: Overcoming Obstacles

Though he has many things to say, Sebastian is very shy. After he finds an old pair of roller skates in the park and learns to skate, his new skill enables him to begin sharing his thoughts. (*Ready, Set, Skip!* by Jane O'Connor (New York: Viking, ©2007), a story for younger children, tells about a little girl who learns to skip when her mother teaches her that skipping is a variation of hopping.)

The Secret Birthday

Rosemary Wells

Jacket Art by: Rosemary Wells;
Interior Illustrations by: John Nez
New York: Hyperion, ©2002
Grade Level: K-3
Themes: Inclusion or Exclusion, Problem
    Solving

Nora is miserable, knowing that she can only invite five children to her party. However, she finds a way to include all her friends as well as the children in the hospital.

Secret of the Peaceful Warrior

Dan Millman

Illustrated by: T. Taylor Bruce
Tiburon, CA: H J Kramer, ©1991
Grade Level: 3-5
Themes: Fear or Worry, Bullying

Danny learns from an old man, Socrates, that courage is needed to deal with someone who is bullying him.

The Secret Seder

Doreen Rappaport

Illustrated by: Emily Arnold McCully
New York: Hyperion, 2005, ©2003
Grade Level: 2-6
Themes: Coping, Community in Action,
    Oppression

Jacques, a French Jewish boy, and his family pretend to be Catholic as they hide from the Nazis. On Passover, Jacques and his father attend a Seder meal at a small shack in the mountains. The men support each other and relate their present struggle to that of the Jews in Egypt.

Selavi: A Haitian Story of Hope

Youme (Landowne)

Illustrated by:
El Paso, TX: Cinco Puntos, 2005, ©2004
Grade Level: 1-4
Pages: 40
Themes: Cooperation, Overcoming Obstacles,
    Community in Action

A group of homeless children in Haiti help each other. When they are dispersed, one boy, Selavi, goes to a church group for help; they build an orphanage which is destroyed and then replaced by another. A children's radio station is also established. This story is based on the orphanage begun by Jean-Bertrand Aristide in 1986 and includes historical notes and photos.

Selfish Sophie

Damian Kelleher

Illustrated by: Georgie Birkett
Minneapolis: Picture Window Books, 2005,
    ©2000
Grade Level: P-2
Themes: Sharing

Sophie won't share anything and has no friends, until a classmate shares his umbrella.

Seven Blind Mice

Ed Young

Illustrated by: Ed Young
New York: Puffin Books, 2002, ©1992
Grade Level: K-3
Themes: Point of View
Other: Audio, Video
The story of the blind men and the elephant is retold, in seven colors and seven days of the week, with a seventh mouse who has the overview.

Seven Brave Women

Betsy Hearne

Illustrated by: Bethanne Andersen
New York: Greenwillow Books, 1998, ©1997
Grade Level: K-4
Themes: Gender Roles, Peacemaking
The young narrator tells how seven women in her ancestry acted bravely, even though they were women who did not fight in the wars of their times. Their accomplishments include: surviving a cross-Atlantic boat trip with young children, traveling in a covered wagon, riding a horse all day to art lessons, entering medical school during World War I, becoming an architect, raising a family, and passing on family stories. The women are based on the author's own ancestors.

Shanghai Messenger

Andrea Cheng

Illustrated by: Ed Young
New York: Lee & Low, 2006, ©2005
Grade Level: 3-6
Themes: Diversity of Cultures
Eleven-year-old Xiao Mai (May) Johanson from Ohio is invited to visit her relatives in China. May's Grandma Nai Nai asks May to remember everything. Although apprehensive at first, May loves her visit and shares it when she returns home. The text is written in free verse.

She Did It!

Jennifer A. Ericsson

Illustrated by: Nadine Bernard Westcott
New York: Farrar, Straus and Giroux, ©2002
Grade Level: K-3
Themes: Cooperation
Four sisters blame each other for the messes they make during a day. When they decide to clean up, they can say, "We did it!"

A Shelter in Our Car

Monica Gunning

Illustrated by: Elaine Pedlar
San Francisco: Children's Book Press, ©2004
Grade Level: K-3
Themes: Sharing, Coping, Hurtful Words
Zettie's dad has died, and she and her mother have moved from Jamaica. Now, they are living in their car while Mama studies at the Community College and finds a job. Ettie suffers from their poverty, as well as from the teasing at school.

Shop Talk

Juwanda G. Ford

Illustrated by: Jim Hoston
New York: Scholastic, ©2004
Fitzgerald Books, 2007, ©2004
Grade Level: K-3
Themes: Respect in General
Young Solomon describes a visit to the All-Star Barbershop where he is treated well. His barber Alton and the customers are friendly with each other, and when a woman comes in they speak to her with respect.

Show Way

Jacqueline Woodson

Illustrated by: Hudson Talbott
New York: Putnam, ©2005
Grade Level: K-5
Pages: 42
Themes: Coping, Community in Action,
    Oppression, Problem Solving
Other: Video

Quiltmaking has been part of eight generations in Jacqueline's family. Her story begins with her great-grandma Soonie's great-grandma who, at age seven, was sold from a Virginia plantation to one in South Carolina. The child had only a piece of cloth given her by her mother. Through the generations, the women made "Show Way" quilts, giving directions to freedom. The lineage ends with Jacqueline's daughter Toshi Georgiana. (In *The Patchwork Path: A Quilt Map to Freedom* by Bettye Stroud (Cambridge, MA: Candlewick Press, 2007, ©2005) a young girl's mother gives her the Patchwork Code, quilt symbols which held the instructions for running from slavery in Georgia to freedom.)

Simon and Molly plus Hester

Lisa Jahn-Clough

Illustrated by: Lisa Jahn-Clough
Boston: Houghton Mifflin, ©2001
Grade Level: P-2
Themes: Inclusion or Exclusion

Simon is jealous when Hester joins him and his best friend Molly. But they grow to enjoy and learn from each other.

The Sissy Duckling

Harvey Fierstein

Illustrated by: Henry Cole
New York: Aladdin, 2005, ©2002
Grade Level: K-3
Themes: Gender Roles, Hurtful Words

Elmer duckling doesn't enjoy any of the things the other boys do. Even his father calls him a sissy until, by caring for his wounded father, Elmer proves his strength. Throughout, Elmer remains true to himself.

Sitti's Secrets

Naomi Shihab Nye

Illustrated by: Nancy Carpenter
New York: Aladdin, 1997, ©1994
Grade Level: K-3
Themes: Diversity of Cultures, Peacemaking
Other: Audio

After visiting her Sitti (the Arabic word for "Grandma"), young Mona is able to imagine Sitti's activities throughout the day and feels connected with her, even though Sitti lives in Palestine, "on the other side of the earth." Mona writes the U.S. president, saying that she and Sittie both "vote for peace" and assures him that he would like Sitti if he could meet her.

Six Crows

Leo Lionni

Illustrated by: Leo Lionni
New York: Scholastic, 1995, ©1988
Grade Level: P-3
Themes: Conflict Escalator, Mediation or
    Negotiation
Other: Audio

Six crows and a farmer with his scarecrow spend so much time trying to scare each other that the wheat field is neglected. A wise owl gets them to talk to each other.

Skin Again

bell hooks

Illustrated by: Chris Raschka
New York: Hyperion, 2005, ©2004
Grade Level: K-4
Themes: Alike and Different, Prejudice or
    Dislike

Each person has a story that is more than skin deep. "The skin I'm in will always be just a covering. It cannot tell my story." (*The Skin You Live In* by Michael Tyler (Chicago: Chicago Children's Museum, ©2005) is a poem with whimsical illustrations that celebrates our skin in its usefulness and diversity.)

Snail Started It!

Katja Reider

Illustrated by: Angela von Roehl
Translated by: Rosemary Lanning
New York: North-South, 1999, ©1997
Grade Level: K-3
Themes: Hurtful Words, Apologizing or
    Forgiving

Snail's unkind words to pig set off a chain
reaction that continues until unkind words reach
snail. Snail's apology then sets off a healing
chain reaction.

Snail's Birthday Wish

Fiona Rempt

Illustrated by: Noëlle Smith
New York: Sterling Publishing, 2007, ©2006
Grade Level: P-1
Themes: Cooperation, Diversity of Individuals

Snail has a hard time keeping up with his friends
when they play. So, at his birthday party Snail's
friends give him the parts for a car and then they
assemble it for him.

Snarlyhissopus

Alan MacDonald

Illustrated by: Louise Voce
Wilton, CT: Tiger Tales, 2003, ©2002
Grade Level: P-2
Themes: Fear or Worry, Rumors or Suspicion

Pelican tries to describe the hippopotamus.
Rumors, fears, and misunderstandings grow,
until the animals themselves actually meet the
hippo.

"The Sneetches" in The Sneetches & Other Stories

Dr. Seuss

Illustrated by: Dr. Seuss
New York: Random House, 1989, ©1961
London: Harper Collins Children's, 2006,
    ©1961
Grade Level: 2-4
Themes: Inclusion or Exclusion, Peer Pressure
Other: Audio, Video

Star-Belly Sneetches and Plain-Belly Sneetches
think one group is better than the other. (This
story is also included in *A Hatful of Seuss* by
Dr. Seuss (©1996), and *Your Favorite Seuss: 13
Stories Written and Illustrated By Dr. Seuss With
13 Introductory Essays* (©2004).)

Snow in Jerusalem

Deborah da Costa

Illustrated by: Cornelius Van Wright & Ying-
    Hwa Hu
Morton Grove, IL: Whitman, 2008, ©2001
Grade Level: K-3
Themes: Prejudice or Dislike

Avi who lives in the Jewish Quarter of Old
Jerusalem and Hamudi who lives in the Muslim
Quarter are both tending the same stray cat. In
the end they discover each other and together
experience new life as snow covers their city.

So Happy / So Sad

Julie Paschkis

Illustrated by: Julie Paschkis
New York: Henry Holt, ©1995
Grade Level: P-1
Themes: Recognizing Emotions

This is a reversible book, with happy animals in
one half and sad ones in the other.

So What?

Miriam Cohen
Illustrated by: Lillian Hoban
New York: Bantam, 1998, ©1982
Grade Level: K-3
Themes: Competition
Other: Audio
Elinor Woodman from Chicago teaches Jim that ranking does not matter.

Some Things Are Scary

Florence Parry Heide
Illustrated by: Jules Feiffer
Cambridge, MA: Candlewick Press, 2003, ©1969
Grade Level: P-2
Themes: Fear or Worry
This is a humorous list of scary things.

Somebody Loves You, Mr. Hatch

Eileen Spinelli
Illustrated by: Paul Yalowitz
New York: Aladdin, 2006, ©1991
Grade Level: K-4
Themes: Community Building, Sharing
Mr. Hatch is a lonely man who keeps to himself until he receives a large heart-shaped box of chocolates on Valentine's Day from an anonymous person. The attached note reads, "Somebody Loves You." Mr. Hatch suddenly views the world differently because he feels that someone cares about him. His behavior changes as he wonders who his secret admirer could be. As he becomes more extroverted, he is more aware of the needs of others, and shares his time and talents as an active member of his community. The community responds in kind when Mr. Hatch needs them most.

Something Might Happen

Helen Lester
Illustrated by: Lynn Munsinger
Boston: Houghton Mifflin, ©2003
Grade Level: P-2
Themes: Fear or Worry
Twitchly Fidget, a lemur, won't try anything because of what might happen. Then his Aunt Bridget Fidget visits him and helps him to change.

Sometimes Bad Things Happen

Ellen Jackson
Photographs: by Shelley Rotner
Brookfield, CT: The Millford Press, ©2002
Grade Level: P-2
Themes: Coping
After acknowledging some of the things that can go wrong, focus is shifted to the ways people help each other and cope with disappointment and pain.

Sometimes I'm Bombaloo

Rachel Vail
Illustrated by: Yumi Heo
New York: Scholastic, 2005, ©2002
    Paw Prints, 2008, ©2002
Grade Level: P-1
Themes: Anger
Other: Audio, Video
Katie Honors tells how she usually behaves, how she acts when she lets her anger get away, and how she then gets back to normal.

Sometimes My Mommy Gets Angry

Bebe Moore Campbell

Illustrated by: Earl B. Lewis
New York: Puffin Books, 2005, ©2003
Grade Level: 1-3
Themes: Anger, Coping

Annie, whose mother has bipolar disorder, tells of how she copes with her mother's extreme moods from one school day to the next. She has the support of her grandmother, friends, and neighbors.

Somewhere Today: A Book of Peace

Shelley Moore Thomas

Photographs by: Eric Futran
Morton Grove, IL: Albert Whitman, ©1998
Grade Level: P-2
Themes: Peacemaking

Ten scenarios of peacemakers in everyday life are given.

Sorry!

Trudy Ludwig

Illustrated by: Maurie J. Manning
Berkeley: Tricycle Press, ©2006
Grade Level: 2-5
Themes: Apology

Jack is skeptical when his friend Charlie makes insincere apologies. When the two boys accidentally break Leena's science project, Jack learns that a sincere apology can actually strengthen a relationship. Endnotes provide further explanation and questions for discussion.

Spaghetti Park

DyAnne DiSalvo-Ryan

Illustrated by: DyAnne DiSalvo-Ryan
New York: Holiday House, 2003, ©2002
Grade Level: 1-4
Themes: Conflict Nature, Responsible Decision Making

Angelo's grandfather teaches him the Italian bowling game of bocce. When Richie, grandson of a top bocce player, and his friends disrupt the park (recently cared for by the neighbors) with noise and graffiti, the neighbors meet and discuss improving park conditions. When they return to work on the park, Richie and his friends have already started the cleaning process. Notes on bocce are included.

Speak to Me (And I Will Listen Between the Lines)

Karen English

Illustrated by: Amy June Bates
New York: Farrar, Straus and Giroux, ©2004
Grade Level: 3-5
Themes: Recognizing Emotions, Point of View

The book showcases poems by six young students (Malcolm, Brianna, Lamont, Rica, Tyrell, and Neecy) that reveal what is going on in their lives.

The St. Patrick's Day Shillelagh

Janet Nolan

Illustrated by: Ben F. Stahl
Morton Grove, IL: Whitman, ©2002
Grade Level: K-3
Themes: Coping, Diversity of Cultures

When Fergus and his parents flee the Irish Potato Famine, Fergus makes a shillelagh from his favorite blackthorn tree and takes a piece of Ireland with him. Through the generations, the shillelagh and its story are passed on.

Stars in the Darkness

Barbara M. Joosse
Illustrated by: R. Gregory Christie
San Francisco: Chronicle Books, ©2002
Grade Level: 1-5
Themes: Community Building, Peacemaking,
    Responsible Decision Making
When his older brother Richard joins a gang, the narrator and his mother organize Peace Walks to help the neighborhood cope and resist. The narrator and his mother acknowledge the mixture of "good and bad in everybody." This story is based on a "real Richard" and includes a note on him.

Stella and the Berry Thief

Jane B. Mason
Illustrated by: Loek Koopmans
Tarrytown, NY: Marshall Cavendish, ©2004
Grade Level: P-3
Themes: Sharing
A bear, whom Stella names Bernie, steals Stella's raspberries, but leads her to prize-winning berries. Then, for the first time, Stella shares with others.

Still My Grandma

Veronique Van den Abeele
Illustrated by: Claude K. Dubois
Grand Rapids, MI: Eerdmans Publishing Co.,
    2007, ©2006
Grade Level: K-4
Themes: Respect for Elderly or Disabled
Camille, the young narrator, tells all the things she and her Grandma did together before her grandmother got Alzheimer's disease. Although much has changed, now that her grandmother is in a care center, Camille has found ways to continue some of the things they enjoyed earlier. (*Memory Box* by Mary Bahr Fritts (Morton Grove, IL: Whitman, ©1992) tells the story of a young boy who makes a Memory Box with his grandparents when his grandfather has early Alzheimer's.)

Stolen Smile

Thierry Robberecht
Illustrated by: Philippe Goossens
New York, NY: Doubleday, ©2002
Grade Level: P-2
Themes: Social Skills, Hurtful Words
Sophie tells how Willard stole her smile when he said the boys didn't play with girls, and how she got it back when she learned that he teased her because he liked her.

Stormy Ride on Noah's Ark

Patricia Hooper
Illustrated by: Lynn Munsinger
New York: Putnam, ©2001
Grade Level: P-3
Themes: Peacemaking
The animals on Noah's Ark manage to get along.

Story of a Dolphin

Katherine Orr
Illustrated by: Katherine Orr
Minneapolis: Carolrhoda Books, 1995, ©1993
Grade Level: 2-4
Themes: Respect in General
This is the true story of a dolphin named JoJo, who befriended Laura's father and the tourists. Both the dolphin and the tourists had to learn how to treat each other.

The Story of Ferdinand

Munro Leaf
Illustrated by: Munro Leaf
New York: Viking, 2007, ©1936
Grade Level: K-3
Themes: Gender Roles, Diversity of Individuals
Other: Audio, Video
Ferdinand is a bull, who would rather smell the flowers than fight.

The Sunday Blues: A Book for Schoolchildren, Schoolteachers, and Anybody Else Who Dreads Monday Mornings

Neal Layton
Illustrated by: Neal Layton
Cambridge, MA: Candlewick Press, 2002, ©2001
Grade Level: K-1
Themes: Fear or Worry
Steve so dreads returning to school on Monday, that this ruins Sunday. When he gets to the friendly playground, he decides Monday morning is not so bad after all. [The playground might be unrealistically upbeat.]

The Summer My Father Was Ten

Pat Brisson
Illustrated by: Andrea Shine
Honesdale, PA: Boyds Mills Press, 1999, ©1998
Grade Level: K-4
Themes: Responsible Decision Making, Apologizing or Forgiving
A father tells his young daughter the story of Mr. Bellavista, an Italian immigrant who lived in the father's neighborhood when he was young. Although Mr. Bellavista kept to himself, the neighborhood boys often taunted him because of his accent. Each year, Mr. Bellavista cleared debris from a vacant lot and planted a garden, spending hours caring for the garden. One day, a group of neighborhood boys vandalized the garden, pulled up the vegetables, and threw them at surrounding buildings. The father admits to his daughter that he was one of the boys who destroyed the garden, and although he was sorry for his actions, he could not bring himself to apologize to Mr. Bellavista. It was not until the following year, when Mr. Bellavista refused to plant his garden, that the father apologized. When he offered to help Mr. Bellavista replant the garden, the two began a friendship that lasted for years.

Sunshine Home

Eve Bunting
Illustrated by: Diane de Groat
New York: Clarion Books, 2005, ©1994
Grade Level: 1-4
Themes: Recognizing Emotions
When 7-year-old Tim and his parents visit his grandmother in a nursing home, Tim is uneasy because neither his mother nor his grandmother talk about their feelings. At the end, Tim helps them share their feelings of sadness and all feel better for having talked about what was happening.

Super-Completely and Totally the Messiest

Judith Viorst
Illustrated by: Robin Preiss-Glasser
New York: Aladdin, 2004, ©2000
Grade Level: P-2
Themes: Diversity of Individuals
Olivia, who is perfectly neat, tells about her messy but lovable sister Sophie.

Sweet Clara and the Freedom Quilt

Deborah Hopkinson
Illustrated by: James Ransome
New York: Knopf, 2003, ©1993
Grade Level: 1-4
Themes: Community in Action, Oppression
Other: Audio, Video
As a slave on Home Plantation, Clara is a seamstress in the Big House. She listens to those passing through and uses scraps of material to make a quilt which can guide herself and others along the Underground Railroad to freedom.

Sweet Strawberries

Phyllis Reynolds Naylor

Illustrated by: Rosalind Charney Kaye
New York: Atheneum, ©1999
Grade Level: K-3
Themes: Social Skills, Hurtful Words

As a man and his wife go to market, he puts down everyone they see. After he refuses to let his wife buy strawberries, she tells him off. He assumes the people along the way had upset his wife. So, the next week the man treats everyone with kindness, and they reciprocate.

Swimmy

Leo Lionni

Illustrated by: Leo Lionni
Orlando, FL: Harcourt Brace, 1999, ©1963
    Paw Prints, 2008, ©1963
Grade Level: K-2
Themes: Cooperation
Other: Audio, Video

Swimmy is the only fish in his family born black instead of red. When he outswims a big fish that devours the rest of this family, he is left all alone. When he least expects it, Swimmy stumbles across another group of small red fish, and his quick thinking helps them to band together to fight the big fish in the sea.

T-Rex Is Missing!

Tomie De Paola

Illustrated by: Tomie De Paola
New York: Grosset & Dunlap, 2003, ©2002
Grade Level: 1-2
Themes: Rumors or Suspicion, Apologizing or
    Forgiving

Morgie accuses his friend Billy of taking his stuffed T-Rex and then finds that his little brother Marcos had taken it.

The Table Where Rich People Sit

Byrd Baylor

Illustrated by: Peter Parnall
New York: Aladdin, 1998, ©1978
Fitzgerald Books, 2007, ©1978
Grade Level: 3-5
Themes: Community Building, Accepting
    Limitations and Gifts

In an ingenious way of calculating assets, Mountain Girl learns the wealth of her family.

TACKY the Penguin

Helen Lester

Illustrated by: Lynn Munsinger
New York: Houghton Mifflin, 2008, ©1988
Grade Level: K-2
Themes: Diversity of Individuals
Other: Audio

Tacky, with his loud ways, is not accepted by the other penguins, until he saves them by being himself.

Talk Peace

Sam Williams

Illustrated by: Mique Moriuchi
New York: Holiday House, ©2005
London: Hodder Children's, 2006, ©2005
Grade Level: P-1
Themes: Peacemaking

This primary book has a poetic message, that we can talk peace anywhere, anytime.

Tawny, Scrawny Lion

Kathryn Jackson
Illustrated by: Gustaf Tenggren
New York: Golden Books, 2004, ©1952
Grade Level: K-3
Themes: Mediation or Negotiation
Other: Audio, Video

A lion, thin from chasing them, tells the animals to slow down so he can gain some weight and not need to eat so much. The animals appoint a small rabbit to talk to the lion. Instead, he and his nine siblings feed the lion vegetable stew and entertain him, so satisfying the lion that he has no need to chase the other animals.

Teammates

Peter Golenbock
Illustrated by: Paul Bacon
San Diego: Harcourt Brace, 2002, ©1990
Grade Level: 1-6
Themes: Friendship, Discrimination,
   Nonviolent Response

This picture book, with both color illustrations and black and white photos, is the story of how Jackie Robinson became the first black player on a major league baseball team, and how PeeWee Reese took a stand and declared Jackie his teammate.

Tear Soup

Pat Schwiebart and Chuck Deklyen
Illustrated by: Taylor Bills
Portland, OR: Grief Watch, 2007, ©1999
Grade Level: 3-8
Themes: Coping, Feelings

When Grandy and her husband Pops suffer a loss, each makes tear soup. Grandy makes a big pot, the process taking a long time. Various people help her make it, and she determines when to eat it. Several pages of "cooking tips" and resources are included.

Ten Tall Soldiers

Nancy Robison
Illustrated by: Hilary Knight
New York: Aladdin Paperbacks, 2001, ©1991
Grade Level: P-1
Themes: Fear or Worry

A king is frightened by several monsters who all turn out to be his own shadow.

The Tenth Good Thing about Barney

Judith Viorst
Illustrated by: Erik Blegvad
New York: Atheneum, 1995, ©1971
Grade Level: K-4
Themes: Recognizing Emotions, Coping
Other: Audio, Video

A child deals with the death of his pet cat Barney.

The Terrible Thing that Happened at Our House

Marge Blaine
Illustrated by: Marge Blaine
Parsippany, NJ: Silver Burdett Ginn, 1998,
   ©1975
Grade Level: 1-3
Themes: Listening, Win-Win Solutions

When the mother of a family returns to teaching, things are miserable at home. The daughter finally gets heard, and the family finds a solution.

Thank You, Mr. Falker

Patricia Polacco
Illustrated by: Patricia Polacco
New York: Philomel, 2001, ©1998
Grade Level: 2-5
Pages: 40
Themes: Overcoming Obstacles
Other: Audio, Video

Trisha cannot read until 5th grade when her teacher gives her special help. This is the author's own story.

The Thanksgiving Door

Debby Atwell

Illustrated by: Debby Atwell
Boston: Houghton Mifflin, 2006, ©2003
Grade Level: K-3
Themes: Inclusion or Exclusion, Diversity of
　　Cultures

Ed and Ann, an elderly couple, decide to eat Thanksgiving dinner at the New World Café because Ann has burned their dinner. Meanwhile, the owners, preparing to spend their first Thanksgiving in this country at their own café, are surprised to see Ann and Ed. All have a wonderful feast.

There's Only One of Me!

Pat Hutchins

Illustrated by: Pat Hutchins
New York: HarperCollins, 2006, ©2003
Grade Level: P-2
Themes: Community Building, Diversity of
　　Individuals
Other: Audio

A birthday girl identifies all the relationships she has to the members of her family. (In *My Family: Love and Care, Give and Share* by Lisa Bullard (Minneapolis: Picture Window Books, ©2003) a young boy draws a picture of his extended family, including stepfamily members.)

That's What Friends Are For

Valeri Gorbachev

Illustrated by: Valeri Gorbachev
New York: Philomel, ©2005
Grade Level: P-2
Themes: Fear or Worry, Rumors or Suspicion

When Goat sees Pig crying, he imagines all the disasters that could have happened. Goat calls on Pig, ready to help, and finds that Pig was cutting onions.

Through Grandpa's Eyes

Patricia MacLachlan

Illustrated by: Deborah Kogan Ray
New York: HarperCollins, 1995, ©1980
Grade Level: K-3
Themes: Point of View, Respect for Elderly or
　　Disabled
Other: Video

During John's visits to Grandpa's house, he learns about the special ways his blind grandfather sees and moves in the world.

That's What Friends Are For

Florence Parry Heide and Sylvia Van Clief

Illustrated by: Holly Meade
Cambridge, MA: Candlewick Press, 2007,
　　©1968
Grade Level: P-1
Themes: Listening
Other: Audio

Theodora the elephant has hurt his leg and cannot visit his cousin. The other animals give him useless advice, and then the opossum suggests they bring Theodora's cousin to him.

Thunder Cake

Patricia Polacco

Illustrated by: Patricia Polacco
New York: Philomel, 1999, ©1990
Grade Level: P-3
Themes: Fear or Worry
Other: Audio, Video

Her Grandma helps Patricia overcome her fear of thunder by making Thunder Cake. When the thunder starts, they hurry to assemble the ingredients from around the farm and try to make the cake before the storm comes. Then they enjoy cake and tea during the storm.

Tico and the Golden Wings

Leo Lionni

Illustrated by: Leo Lionni
New York: Knopf, 2007, ©1964
Grade Level: P-3
Themes: Accepting Limitations and Gifts,
    Diversity of Individuals, Peacemaking
Other: Audio, Video
After Tico loses his golden feathers to good deeds, he looks like his fellow birds but knows he will always be different because of his memories.

Tiggers Hate to Lose

Isabel Gaines

Illustrated by: Francese Rigol
New York: Disney Press, 2002, ©1999
Grade Level: P-2
Themes: Competition
Tigger keeps losing at the game of Pooh sticks until Eeyore shows him the way to win.

Timid Timmy

Andreas Dierssen

Illustrated by: Felix Scheinberger
Translated by: Marianne Martens
New York: North-South, ©2003
Grade Level: K-2
Themes: Honesty
Timmy wants to be a brave hare like his bold friend Rocket. When Timmy confesses to eating all the carrots, his mother observes that he really is brave.

Timothy Goes to School

Rosemary Wells

Illustrated by: Rosemary Wells
New York: Scholastic, 2004, ©1981
Grade Level: P-2
Themes: Peer Pressure
Other: Audio, Video
Timothy cannot seem to wear the right clothes at school, but Claude seems perfect. Then he discovers that Violet is having the same experience with Grace.

Tiny's Hat

Ann Grifalconi

Illustrated by: Ann Grifalconi
New York: HarperCollins, ©1999
Grade Level: K-3
Themes: Recognizing Emotions
Other: Audio, Video
Tiny wears her father's hat and sings the blues in order to cope with her sadness after her father left.

Today I Feel Silly & Other Moods That Make My Day

Jamie Lee Curtis

Illustrated by: Laura Cornell
New York: HarperCollinsPublishers, 2007,
    ©1998
Grade Level: P-2
Themes: Recognizing Emotions
Other: Audio
"A child's emotions range from silliness to anger to excitement, coloring and changing each day." (*Some Days, Other Days* by P. J. Petersen (New York: Scribner, ©1994) tells of a young boy who is not sure he wants to get up because some days things go well and other days they do not.)

Tomas and the Library Lady

Pat Mora

Illustrated by: Raúl Colón
New York: Dragonfly, 2000, ©1997
    Paw Prints, 2008, ©1997
Grade Level: 2-4
Themes: Overcoming Obstacles
Other: Audio
A librarian encourages a young migrant worker to read, and he later becomes a university chancellor. This is based on a true story.

Too Close Friends

Shen Roddie
Illustrated by: Sally Anne Lambert
New York: Dial, 1998, ©1997
Grade Level: P-2
Themes: Social Skills, Friendship
Pig and Hippo get along better when they go to visit each other, and their hedge is high enough for privacy.

Too Many Babas

Carolyn Croll
Illustrated by: Carolyn Croll
Boston: Houghton Mifflin, 1999, ©1979
Grade Level: K-3
Pages: 63
Themes: Cooperation
Four women learn that independently seasoning the soup does not work; they try again and find success.

The Tree

Dana Lyons
Illustrated by: David Lane Danioth
New York: Scholastic, 2003, ©2002
Grade Level: K-4
Themes: Community Building, Respect in General
Other: Audio
An 800-year-old Douglas Fir in the Olympic River Forest describes its life and its fear of bulldozers. Forewords are given by Julia Butterfly Hill and Pete Seeger.

Tree of Cranes

Allen Say
Illustrated by: Allen Say
New York: Scholastic, 1992, ©1991
Grade Level: P-3
Themes: Diversity of Cultures
A boy in Japan is given a Christmas tree by his mother who had lived in California.

Trouble in the Barkers' Class

Tomie De Paola
Illustrated by: Tomie De Paola
New York: Putnam, 2006, ©2003
Grade Level: P-2
Themes: Social Skills, Basic Emotional Needs, Empathy
Other: Audio, Video
Carole Anne, the new student, is unpleasant and mean. Then Morgie learns that she is just afraid no one will like her and really wants friends.

The True Story of the 3 Little Pigs

Jon Scieszka
Illustrated by: Lane Smith
New York: Viking, 1999, ©1989
Grade Level: K-4
Themes: Point of View
Other: Audio, Video
Jon Scieszka writes the story of the three little pigs from the wolf's perspective. A. Wolf claims that it's not his fault that wolves are carnivores. He tries to gain sympathy by stating that he did not threaten any of the pigs; he had to sneeze each time he was waiting at the door for someone to answer. When the houses of the first two pigs fall down due to his terrible sneeze, he had two wonderful dinners, since it would be silly just to leave a ham dinner lying there. The pig in the third house was supposedly so rude to A. Wolf that it put him into a rage, which is what the police saw when they arrived at the scene. (*The Three Little Wolves and the Big Bad Pig* by Eugene Trivizas also varies the point of view (New York: Aladdin, 1997, ©1993).)

Two Mrs. Gibsons

Toyomi Igus
Illustrated by: Daryl Wells
San Francisco: Children's Book Press, ©1996
Grade Level: K-3
Themes: Diversity of Cultures
A young girl describes her African American grandmother and her Japanese mother.

Two Bad Ants

Chris Van Allsburg

Illustrated by: Chris Van Allsburg
New York: Scholastic, 1997, ©1988
Grade Level: 1-5
Themes: Point of View
The reader sees the world as the ants see it.

Two Eyes, a Nose, and a Mouth

Roberta Grobel Intrater

Illustrated by: Roberta Grobel Intrater
New York: Scholastic, 1995, ©2000
Grade Level: P-2
Themes: Alike and Different
Poetry and photos celebrate a diversity of faces.

Two Old Potatoes and Me

John Coy

Illustrated by: Carolyn Fisher
Oak Park, CA: Dragonfly, 2009, ©2003
Grade Level: K-2
Themes: Cooperation
Other: Video
A girl tells how she and her dad planted and tended two old potatoes until they had over fifty, and then they made mashed potatoes.

The Ugly Vegetables

Grace Lin

Illustrated by: Grace Lin
Watertown, MA: Tale Winds, 2007, ©1999
Grade Level: K-3
Themes: Community Building, Diversity of
    Cultures
A little girl thinks her mother's Chinese vegetables are ugly, until the neighbors exchange their flowers for bowls of the soup her mother makes.

Uncle Jed's Barbershop

Margaree King Mitchell

Illustrated by: James Ransome
New York: Aladdin, 1998, ©1993
Grade Level: K-3
Themes: Sharing, Overcoming Obstacles
Other: Audio, Video
Sarah Jean tells about her great uncle, the only black barber in the county. All his life, Uncle Jed saved to build a barbershop. As a young man, he funded the narrator's surgery, and then he lost his savings in the Depression. Finally, on his 79th birthday, he opened the shop.

Upstairs Mouse, Downstairs Mole

Wong Herbert Yee

Illustrated by:
Boston: Houghton Mifflin, ©2005
Grade Level: K-3
Pages: 48
Themes: Cooperation, Mediation or
    Negotiation
Mouse and Mole cooperate and solve several of their difficulties.

The Valentine Express

Nancy Elizabeth Wallace

Illustrated by:
New York: Scholastic, ©2004
Grade Level: P-2
Themes: Overcoming Obstacles, Respect for
    Elderly or Disabled
Other: Audio
Two young rabbits, Minna and Pip, exchange valentines at school. When they get home they make valentines for their elderly neighbors, matching the type of gift with the person getting it. When mishaps occur, they change their designs.

Video Shop Sparrow

Joy Cowley
Illustrated by: Gavin Bishop
Honesdale, PA: Boyds Mills Press, ©1999
Grade Level: K-3
Themes: Responsible Decision Making
George and Harry discover a sparrow trapped in a video store while the owner is on vacation. The boys seek help, even involving the mayor, and manage to rescue the sparrow.

The View

Harry Yoaker and Simon Henwood
Illustrated by: Simon Henwood
New York: Dial, 1992, ©1991
Grade Level: 2-4
Themes: Point of View, Conflict Nature
In a little group of houses, each has a beautiful view. Then, one by one, the neighbors build additions that cut off others' lookouts. Finally, no one has a good view. [Although no solution is given, this might start a thoughtful discussion.]

The Village that Vanished

Ann Grifalconi
Illustrated by: Kadir Nelson
New York: Puffin Books, 2004, ©2002
Grade Level: 2-6
Pages: 40
Themes: Cooperation, Oppression,
    Community in Action, Problem Solving
When slavers threaten their Yao village, Njemile and her daughter Abikanile take action. After dismantling the village, so that Njemile's mother Chimwala appears to be a hermit, they lead the people safely across the river.

The Viper

Lisa Thiesing
Illustrated by: Lisa Thiesing
New York: Puffin Books, 2003, ©2002
Grade Level: K-2
Themes: Rumors or Suspicion
When Peggy the Pig gets a call, "I am zee Viper. I will come in one year," she goes on with her life. As the time draws closer and calls get more frequent, Peggy gets more scared, until a dog appears and says, "I have come to vipe your windows!"

Visiting Day

Jacqueline Woodson
Illustrated by: James E. Ransome
New York: Scholastic, ©2002
Grade Level: P-2
Themes: Coping
Other: Video
A young girl describes the monthly visiting day when Grandma and she take a long bus ride to the prison and spend loving time with her dad.

Waiting for Papá = Esperando a Papá

Laínez Colato
Illustrated by: Anthony Accardo
Houston, TX: Piñata Books, ©2004
Grade Level: 1-3
Themes: Community in Action, Diversity of
    Cultures
Other: Audio
Beta and his mother move to the United States, but Papá needs to stay in El Salvador and wait for a visa. He gets the visa after an immigration lawyer hears Beta's letter (written for a class assignment) telling why his father is special. Then Beta's class helps him get funds to buy a special gift for his father's arrival.

Walter Was Worried

Laura Vaccaro Seeger
Illustrated by: Laura Vaccaro Seeger
New Milford, CT: Roaring Brook Press, 2006,
    ©2005
Grade Level: P-2
Themes: Recognizing Emotions
A sequence of faces shows different feelings.
Each face is drawn with the letters in the feeling
word.

The War Between the Vowels and the Consonants

Priscilla Turner
Illustrated by: Whitney Turner
New York: Farrar, Straus and Giroux, 1999,
    ©1996
Grade Level: 2-4
Themes: Conflict Escalator, Win-Win Solutions
War escalates until the two groups of letters unite
against the common enemy, a senseless scrawl.
They go on to create all forms of literature.

Watch Out for These Weirdos!

Rufus Kline
Illustrated by: Nancy Carlson
New York: Puffin Books, 1992, ©1990
Grade Level: 1-4
Themes: Diversity of Individuals
The narrator describes a group of characters
in the neighborhood, who happen to be his
friends.

Way to Go, Alex!

Robin Pulver
Illustrated by: Elizabeth Wolf
Morton Grove, IL: Whitman, ©1999
Grade Level: K-2
Themes: Respect for Elderly or Disabled
Carly wishes her developmentally disabled
brother Alex were able to do more things.
However, as she watches him participate in
Special Olympics, she realizes how much he has
learned about coping.

We All Sing with the Same Voice

J. Philip Miller and Sheppard M. Greene
Illustrated by: Paul Meisel
New York: HarperCollins, 2001, ©1982
Grade Level: P-2
Themes: Diversity of Cultures, Diversity of
    Individuals
Other: Audio
A song from Sesame Street celebrates personal
and cultural diversity.

We Belong Together: A Book About Adoption and Families

Todd Parr
Illustrated by: Todd Parr
Boston: Little, Brown and Company, 2008,
    ©2007
Grade Level: P-2
Themes: Basic Needs, Building Community
Parents tell their adopted child all the reasons
they belong together, filling each other's needs
and adding to their happiness. (In *The Family
Book* (2006, ©2003) various kinds of families
are described, ways they are alike and different
in their activities and customs. *It's Okay to Be
Different* (2004, ©2001) assures the reader that
there are many ways of being different, but all
are okay.

We Can Work It Out: Conflict Resolution for Children

Barbara K. Polland
Photographs by: Craig DeRoy
Berkeley, CA: Tricycle Press, ©2000
Grade Level: 1-3
Themes: Problem Solving, Mediation or Negotiation
Positive strategies for 14 areas of conflict are offered. Discussion questions and a three-step approach are included for parents and teachers. *We Can Get Along: A Child's Book of Choices* by Lauren Murphy Payne (Minneapolis: Free Spirit Publishing, ©1997) addresses a younger audience.

We Go in a Circle

Peggy Parry Anderson
Illustrated by: Peggy Parry Anderson
Boston: Houghton Mifflin, ©2004
Grade Level: P-2
Themes: Respect for Elderly or Disabled, Win-Win Solutions
After an injury, a race horse goes to a ranch where children with physical disabilities can ride horses for therapy. Both the horse and the children feel special.

The Wednesday Surprise

Eve Bunting
Illustrated by: Donald Carrick
New York: Houghton Mifflin, 1991, ©1989
Grade Level: K-3
Themes: Cooperation, Overcoming Obstacles
Other: Audio, Video
As a birthday surprise for her father, Anna teaches her grandmother to read.

Wemberly Worried

Kevin Henkes
Illustrated by: Kevin Henkes
New York: Scholastic, 2001, ©2000
Grade Level: P-1
Themes: Fear or Worry
Other: Audio
Wemberly worried about everything, including the first day of school—where she had so much fun that she forgot to worry.

What Are You So Grumpy About?

Tom Lichteneld
Illustrated by: Tom Lichteneld
Boston: Little, Brown, 2006, ©2003
Grade Level: 1-4
Themes: Recognizing Emotions
This is a humorous list of reasons why someone might feel grumpy. The final one is that you might forget what you were grumpy about. [If read aloud, some items might need to be edited for appropriateness.]

What Aunts Do Best; What Uncles Do Best

Laura Joffe Numeroff
Illustrated by: Lynn Munsinger
New York: Scholastic, 2006, ©2004
Grade Level: P-2
Themes: Gender Roles
Two books in one show that aunts and uncles do many of the same things, the most important one being love.

What Do You Do with a Grumpy Kangaroo?

Jane Belk Moncure

Illustrated by: Linda Hohag and Lori Jacobson
Mankato, MN: The Child's World, 2001, ©1987
Grade Level: P-2
Themes: Recognizing Emotions
A kangaroo experiences a variety of feelings throughout the day. The feelings are summarized in sketches at the end.

What Does PEACE Feel Like?

V. Radunsky and children just like you from around the world

Illustrated by: V. Radunsky
New York: Atheneum, ©2004
Grade Level: K-2
Themes: Peacemaking
Ideas contributed by children tell what peace smells, looks, sounds, tastes, and feels like.

What If?

A. H. Benjamin

Illustrated by: Jane Chapman
New York: Scholastic, 1997, ©1996
London: Little Tiger, 2003, ©1996
Grade Level: P-2
Themes: Rumors or Suspicion
Other: Audio
The barnyard animals speculate that the kangaroo will come and take over their places.

What If It Never Stops Raining?

Nancy Carlson

Illustrated by: Nancy Carlson
New York: Puffin Books, 1994, ©1992
Grade Level: P-3
Themes: Fear or Worry
Tim worries throughout the day and finds out that he can survive the worst that can happen.

What If the Zebras Lost Their Stripes?

John Reitano

Illustrated by: William Haines
New York: Scholastic, 2000, ©1998
Grade Level: P+
Themes: Prejudice
Colorful drawings show animals in the wild, watching as some zebras lose their black stripes and others lose their white stripes. Then the question is considered: would the black and white zebras still remember their commonalities, or would they separate themselves from each other? In the end, the story concludes that the zebras "would be much too smart to let their colors tear them apart!"

What Is Goodbye?

Nikki Grimes

Illustrated by: Raúl Colón
New York: Hyperion, ©2004
Grade Level: 3-8
Pages: 64
Themes: Recognizing Emotions, Coping, Point of View
For over a year after their older brother Jaron suddenly dies, Jerilyn and her younger brother Jesse speak in poems about their experiences of grief. Each pair of poems addresses a common aspect: "The Funeral," "Mad," etc.

What Is My Song?

Dennis Linn, Sheila Fabricant Linn, and
Matthew Linn
Illustrated by: Francisco Miranda
New York: Paulist Press, ©2005
Grade Level: K-4
Themes: Accepting Limitations and Gifts,
    Community in Action
In Africa a young child is given a song, and is
reminded of that song at every stage of life.
Even if he or she does something harmful to the
community, the song is used to reconnect with
him or her.

What Lies On the Other Side?

Udo Weigelt
Illustrated by: Maja Dusíková
Translated by: J. Alison James
New York: North-South, ©2002
Grade Level: K-4
Themes: Point of View, Prejudice or Dislike,
    Peacemaking, Rumors or Suspicion
Little Fox is afraid of the witches and dragons
on Raccoon's side of the river, and Raccoon is
afraid of the giants and robbers on Fox's side.
When they show each other around and explain
the origins of the rumors, the animals on both
sides of the river become friends.

What's That Sound?

Mary Lawrence
Illustrated by: Lynn Adams
New York: The Kane Press, ©2002
Fitzgerald, 2007, ©2002
Grade Level: 1-3
Themes: Fear or Worry
When the narrator's family stays in the country,
her brother Tim is scared of the sounds until he
can identify their source.

What's Wrong with Timmy?

Maria Shriver
Illustrated by: Sandra Speidel
New York: Warner, 2002, ©2001
Grade Level: 3-5
Themes: Respect for Elderly or Disabled
When Kate first meets Timmy, who is mentally
challenged, she is afraid of him. However, her
mother helps her discover the ways they are
alike, and the two become friends. (In *What's
Happening to Grandpa?* (New York: Little,
Brown, and Company, 2004) Kate learns how
to cope when her grandfather has Alzheimer's
disease. Both books list resources.)

When Mommy Was Mad

Lynne Jonell
Illustrated by: Petra Mathers
New York: Putnam, ©2002
Grade Level: P-2
Themes: Anger
Although Christopher and Robbie's mom is
mad at their dad, she acts mad around them,
too. Robbie helps her calm down and then the
mother helps their dad.

When Sophie Gets Angry— Really, Really Angry ...

Molly Bang
Illustrated by: Molly Bang
New York: Scholastic, 2007, ©1999
Grade Level: K-2
Themes: Anger
Other: Audio, Video
Sophie is so angry that she is ready to explode.
When her sister grabs a toy that Sophie must
share with her, Sophie falls over a toy truck.
Sophie handles her anger by running and crying,
and then retreating into nature until she is calm
enough to go home. Sophie is welcomed back
when she returns home.

When They Fight

Kathryn White

Illustrated by: Cliff Wright
Delray Beach, FL: Winslow Press, ©2000
Grade Level: K-3
Themes: Conflict Nature
A small badger tells how he feels when his parents, shown in giant shadows on the wall, fight. Then he tells how great he feels when they are friends.

Where's Jamela?

Niki Daly

Illustrated by: Niki Daly
New York: Farrar, Straus and Giroux, ©2004
Grade Level: P-2
Themes: Coping
Although Jamela does not want to move to a hew house, she finds ways to cope, and she discovers some good aspects to her new home. (*Goodbye to Griffith Street* by Marilynn Reynolds (Custer, WA: Orca, ©2004) shows how a boy copes with moving away.)

The White Swan Express: A Story about Adoption

Jean Davies Okimoto and Elaine M. Aoki

Illustrated by: Meilo So
New York: Clarion Books, ©2002
Grade Level: K-3
Themes: Community Building, Diversity of
    Cultures, Diversity of Individuals
Four Chinese girls are adopted by parents from Miami; Seattle; Minnetonka, MN; and Toronto. Single and lesbian parents are included.

Whitewash

Ntozake Shange

Illustrated by: Michael Sporn
New York: Walker, ©1997
Grade Level: K-3
Themes: Fear or Worry, Racism
Other: Video
A young African American girl and her brother are spray-painted by a gang.

Who Moved My Cheese? for Kids: An A-Mazing Way to Change and Win!

Spencer Johnson

Illustrated by: Steve Pileggi
New York: Putnam, 2003, ©1998
Grade Level: 2-5
Pages: 61
Themes: Fear or Worry, Responsible Decision
    Making
Other: Audio, Video
Four mice, Sniff and Scurry, Hem and Haw, learn life lessons on their daily search for cheese in a maze.

Who Stole the Gold?

Udo Weigelt

Illustrated by: Julia Gukova
Translated by: J. Alison James
New York: North-South, ©2000
Grade Level: P-2
Themes: Problem Solving, Apologizing or
    Forgiving
When Raven takes his gold, Hamster figures out a way to resolve the problem.

Who's in Rabbit's House?

Verna Aardema

Illustrated by: Leo Dillon and Diane Dillon
New York: Dial Press, 1979, ©1977
Findaway World LLC, 2008, ©1977
Grade Level: K-4
Themes: Fear or Worry, Problem Solving
Other: Audio, Video
All the animals are afraid of "The Long One" who is hiding in Rabbit's house and who turns out to be a caterpillar.

Whoa Jealousy!

Woodleigh Marx Hubbard

Illustrated by: Madeleine Houston
New York: Putnam, ©2002
Grade Level: K-3
Themes: Jealousy
Jealousy is depicted as a mean chicken. When you let it in the door, it brings its friends, Envy the snake, Greed the rude rat, and Rivalry the angry red hornet.

Whoever You Are

Mem Fox

Illustrated by: Leslie Staub
San Diego: Harcourt Children, 2008, ©1997
Grade Level: K-3
Themes: Alike and Different, Diversity of
    Cultures
Several drawings of children around the world show their differences. A second set of drawings shows that the children are the same in their feelings and needs. (*We are a Rainbow = Somos un Arco Iris* by Nancy Maria Grande Tabor (Watertown, MA: Charlesbridge, 1999, ©1997) and (*We are All Alike, We are All Different* by Laura Dwight & The Cheltenham Elementary School Kindergartners (New York: Scholastic, 2002, ©1991) also feature the similarities and differences of children.)

Whose Garden Is It?

Mary Ann Hoberman

Illustrated by: Jane Dyer
Orlando, FL: Gulliver Books, ©2004
Grade Level: P-1
Themes: Community Building
Other: Video
Mrs. McGee thinks the garden is hers. However, the gardener, the animals, insects, and plants all tell her that it is their garden.

Why?

Nikolai Popov

Illustrated by: Nikolai Popov
New York: North-South, 1998, ©1996
Grade Level: 1-4
Themes: Conflict Nature, Conflict Escalator
A book without pictures shows frogs and mice in a conflict that escalates into a war. (*The Upstairs Cat* by Karla Kuskin (Boston: Houghton Mifflin, 1998, ©1997) two cats who never become friends and repeatedly fight.)

Why a Disguise?

Laura Joffe Numeroff

Illustrated by: David McPhail
New York: Aladdin, 1999, ©1996
Grade Level: P-2
Themes: Accepting Limitations and Gifts
There are times when you would like to hide behind a mask, but at the end of day, it's best to be yourself.

Why Are You Fighting, Davy?

Brigitte Weninger
Illustrated by: Eve Tharlet
Translated by: Rosemary Lanning
New York: North-South, 2002, ©1999
Grade Level: P-2
Themes: Anger, Conflict Escalator
Eddie builds a dam and Davy builds a boat and they have a fight and then resolve it.

Why is the Sky Blue?

Sally Grindley
Illustrated by: Susan Varley
Simon & Schuster, 1997, ©1996
London: Andersen Press, 2006, ©1996
London: Hodder Children's, 1998, ©1996
Grade Level: P-K
Themes: Listening
When Rabbit can settle down long enough to listen, he learns from Donkey, who also learns from Rabbit.

Why Mosquitoes Buzz in People's Ears

Verna Aardema
Illustrated by: Leo Dillon and Diane Dillon
New York: Puffin Books, 2007, ©1975
Grade Level: K-3
Themes: Listening, Rumors or Suspicion
Other: Audio, Video
The iguana puts sticks in his ears so he can no longer hear mosquito's stories. This begins a chain reaction of misunderstandings.

Why War Is Never a Good Idea

Alice Walker
Illustrated by: Stefano Vitale
New York: HarperCollins Publishers, ©2007
Grade Level: 3+
Themes: Nature of Conflict, Peacemaking
War is personified, and its pervasive destruction is made real through scenarios of unsuspecting victims living in areas that are later ruined by war. The art work and attention to specific people and animals add to the poignancy of this story.

Wild & Woolly

Mary Jessie Parker
Illustrated by: Shannon McNeill
New York: Dutton, 2005, ©2004
Grade Level: K-3
Themes: Alike and Different
Wild, a bighorn sheep who lives in the hills, and Woolly, a ranch sheep from a field below, are each surprised to learn that the other is a sheep. When they visit each other's homes, they each know they prefer their own.

The Wild Wombat

Udo Weigelt
Illustrated by: Anne-Katrin Piepenbrink
Translated by: Kathryn Grell
New York: North-South, ©2002
Grade Level: P-1
Themes: Rumors or Suspicion
A zookeeper says that the wild wombat should be treated with care. The parrot, having overheard, spreads the word that the newcomer is to be feared. The rumor spreads until all the animals are hiding in fear of the little endangered creature.

Will I Have a Friend?

Miriam Cohen
Illustrated by: Lillian Hoban
Long Island City, NY: Star Bright Books, 2007,
    ©1967
Grade Level: K-3
Themes: Social Skills
Other: Audio, Video
On Jim's first day of school he tries to find a friend, and by the end of the day he has found one.

William's Doll

Charlotte Zolotow
Illustrated by: William Pène Du Bois
New York: HarperTrophy, 2000, ©1972
Grade Level: P-3
Themes: Gender Roles
Other: Video
William wants a doll even though others tell him he would be a sissy. His grandmother tells William's father that William needs a doll so he can learn how to be a father.

Winners Never Quit!

Mia Hamm
Illustrated by: Carol Thompson
New York: Scholastic, 2006, ©2004
Grade Level: P-2
Themes: Competition
Other: Video
After young Mia quits because she is losing a soccer game, her teammates refuse to let her on their team. The next day Mia is chosen first for the team and, even though she might not win, she chooses to play rather than quit because playing is more important to her than winning. The book includes historical notes about the author, who is a soccer champion.

Winston of Churchill: One Bear's Battle against Global Warming

Jean Davies Okimoto
Illustrated by: Jeremiah Trammell
Seattle, WA: Sasquatch Books, ©2007
Grade Level: 1-3
Themes: Community in Action
Winston, an elder white polar bear of Churchill, Manitoba, realizes that the ice near their home is melting. He calls a meeting and enlists the other bears to join him in a march, alerting the tourists that their cars and smoke stacks are causing the climate change. His wife refuses to support Winston until he does his part and stops smoking his cigar. The result is a group of polar bears holding signs that say, "We must all do our part, no matter how small." They are led by a bear with a twig in his mouth.

Wolf's Coming

Joe Kukla
Illustrated by: Joe Kukla
Minneapolis: Carolrhoda Books, ©2007
Grade Level: P-1
Themes: Rumors or Suspicion
Everyone in the forest is running for cover, because the word is out that Wolf's coming. In the end, they are all tucked into a dark house when Wolf opens the door, enters, and is greeted at his surprise birthday party.

Worst Kid Who Ever Lived on Eighth Avenue

Laurie Lawlor
Illustrated by: Cynthia Fisher
New York: Scholastic, 2001, ©1998
Grade Level: 1-3
Themes: Rumors or Suspicion
Rumors abound about Leroy, the grownup who was the "worst kid." The truth is quite different.

A Wreath for Emmett Till

Marilyn Nelson
Illustrated by: Philippe Lardy
Boston: Houghton Mifflin, ©2005
Grade Level: 8-12
Pages: 40
Themes: Oppression
Other: Audio
This is a depiction of the crime of Emmett Till's (1941–1955) lynching, the mourning, and the seeds of change. The artwork enhances the form which is a heroic crown of sonnets (14 sonnets with the last line of each one similar to the first line of the next, followed by the 15th, which is composed of the first lines of the 14 sonnets.) Each verse is annotated.

Yanni Rubbish

Shulamith Levey Oppenheim
Illustrated by: Doug Chayka
Honesdale, PA: Boyd Mills Press, 2005, ©1999
Grade Level: K-3
Themes: Hurtful Words, Nonviolent Response
Yanni takes his cart and donkey Lamia to collect garbage. After being called "Yanni Rubbish," he finds a way to earn the respect of the other boys.

Yes We Can!

Sam MacBratney
Illustrated by: Charles Fuge
HarperCollinsPublishers, 2007, ©2006
Grade Level: P-K
Themes: Accepting Limitations and Gifts,
　　Competition
Roo challenges Duck to jump, and Mouse laughs at Duck who cannot jump as well as Roo. Then Roo laughs at Mouse who can't float, and so on. Finally, the three friends, each having failed and been laughed at, are depressed. Roo's mother asks each to show what he or she is good at, and they again feel confident.

Yesterday I Had the Blues

Jeron Ashford Frame
Illustrated by: R. Gregory Christie
Berkeley, CA: Tricycle Press, 2008, ©2003
Grade Level: 1-4
Themes: Recognizing Emotions
Using an array of colors and down-to-earth descriptions, a young African American boy tells about the feelings he and his family have.

Yo! Yes?

Chris Raschka
Illustrated by: Chris Raschka
New York: Orchard Books, 2001, ©1993
Grade Level: K-4
Themes: Friendship, Listening
Other: Audio, Video
In a two-sided conversation, someone admits he has no friends and the other person becomes a friend.

Yoko

Rosemary Wells
Illustrated by: Rosemary Wells
New York: Scholastic, 1999, ©1998
Grade Level: P-2
Themes: Diversity of Cultures
Other: Audio
At school lunch, the other animals make fun of the kitten Yoko's sushi. However, when international foods are shared, Timothy learns to like sushi.

You and Me Together: Moms, Dads, and Kids Around the World

Barbara Kerley

Photographs by: Barbara Kerley
Washington, DC: National Geographic, ©2005
Grade Level: P-2
Themes: Alike and Different, Diversity of
  Cultures

Photographs from around the world show parents and their children in a wide variety of activities. A message by Marian Wright Edelman is included. Endnotes identify the geographic location of each photo.

You'll Grow Soon, Alex

Andrea Shavick

Illustrated by: Russell Ayto
New York: Orchard, 2001, ©2000
Grade Level: P-1
Themes: Accepting Limitations and Gifts

Alex tries everything and cannot stop being the smallest boy in his grade. Then his uncle advises him to take care of himself and others, and he becomes the happiest boy.

Your Dad Was Just Like You

Dolores Johnson

Illustrated by: Dolores Johnson
New York: Macmillan, ©1993
Grade Level: 3-5
Themes: Empathy

Peter learns that his dad was a runner who had a disappointment.

You're All My Favorites

Sam McBratney

Illustrated by: Anita Jeram
Cambridge, MA: Candlewick Press, 2008,
  ©2004
Grade Level: P-K
Themes: Competition, Accepting Limitations
  and Gifts

When three little bears start to compare themselves with each other, their parents assure them of their special love of each.

You're Not My Best Friend Anymore

Charlotte Pomerantz

Illustrated by: David Soman
New York: Dial, 1998, ©1997
Grade Level: K-2
Themes: Conflict Escalator

Molly and Ben are best friends until they fight about which kind of tent to buy. After several miserable days, they reconcile.

You've Got Dragons

Kathryn Cave

Illustrated by: Nick Maland
Atlanta: Peachtree, 2003, ©2002
Grade Level: P-2
Themes: Fear or Worry

Ben learns that having dragons, being afraid, is normal, and there are ways to cope.

Yum! Yuck!: A Foldout Book of People Sounds

Linda Sue Park and Julia Durango

Illustrated by: Sue Ramá
Watertown, MA: Charlesbridge, ©2005
Grade Level: P-3
Themes: Recognizing Emotions
Eight different situations and related English expressions are presented in two-page spreads. Before each two-page spread is opened, the reader views four children of different nationalities saying the corresponding sound and conveying the appropriate body language.

"The Zax" in The Sneetches & Other Stories

Dr. Seuss

Illustrated by: Dr. Seuss
New York: Random House, 1989, ©1961
London: Harper Collins Children's, 2006, ©1961
Grade Level: 2-4
Themes: Conflict Escalator
Other: Audio, Video
Stubborn characters get nowhere because they will not give in to each other.

Ziggy's Blue-Ribbon Day

Claudia Mills

Illustrated by: R. W. Alley
New York: Farrar, Straus and Giroux, ©2005
Grade Level: K-2
Themes: Competition, Accepting Limitations and Gifts
Ziggy knows he will get silver ribbons for last place when the second graders have their Track and Field Day. Then he decorates his classmates' envelopes, and they give him blue ribbons.

Chapter Books

Alt Ed

Catherine Atkins

New York: Speak, 2004, ©2003
Grade Level: 8-12
Pages: 198
Themes: Empathy, Diversity of Individuals,
    Hurtful Words
Other: Audio

Sophomore Susan Callaway lives with her widowed father and her older brother Tom who lacks self esteem and feels ashamed of Susan because she is overweight. No one talks about her mother's death of cancer. Kale Krasner and others harass Susan because of her weight and her friend Brendan Slater because of his homosexuality. When Brendan vandalizes Kale's truck and Susan is considered an accomplice, they are given a second chance by Mr. Duffy, a counselor. In weekly counseling sessions, six diverse students learn to respect and even appreciate each other.

Amanda Pig and the Awful, Scary Monster

Jean Van Leeuwen

Illustrated by: Ann Schweninger
New York: Puffin Books, 2004, ©2003
Grade Level: K-2
Pages: 48
Themes: Fear or Worry

Amanda gradually overcomes her fear of monsters at bedtime.

Anna Is Still Here

Ida Vos

Translated by: Terese Edelstein and Inez Smidt
New York: Scholastic, 1995, ©1993
Grade Level: 4-7
Pages: 139
Themes: Anger, Coping, Oppression

After hiding for three years during Nazi occupation of Holland, Anna is now back with her parents and all three are trying to adjust. Anna befriends Mrs. Neumann, a neighbor who is still waiting for her daughter Fannie who looks like Anna. Although she continues to feel angry with those associated with Nazis and is taunted at school because of wearing a yellow star, Anna gradually finds healing and finally discovers Fannie who had survived.

Any Small Goodness: A Novel of the Barrio

Tony Johnston

Illustrated by: Raul Colón
New York: Scholastic, 2002, ©2001
Grade Level: 4-7
Pages: 128
Themes: Community in Action, Diversity
    of Cultures, Nonviolent Response,
    Peacemaking

Although life in the East Los Angeles barrio is dangerous, Arturo Rodriguiz and his family find many examples of kindness. Arturo then forms his own Green Needle Gang that gives Christmas gifts anonymously. Many Spanish words are explained in the text, and a Selected Glossary is included.

Absolutely Normal Chaos

Sharon Creech

New York: Scholastic, 2004, ©1990
Grade Level: 6-9
Pages: 230
Themes: Accepting Limitations and Gifts,
    Empathy, Respect in General
Other: Audio

Thirteen-year-old Mary Lou Finney's journal shows insights acquired during the summer. It also includes reflections on events in Homer's *Odyssey*, which is on her reading list and parallels some of her own experiences. Mary Lou's first impressions of her 17-year-old cousin Carl Ray from West Virginia and of her classmate Alex Cheevey, with whom she falls in love, both change after she gets to know them better.

Adam's War

Sonia Levitin

Illustrated by: Vincent Nasta
New York: Dial, ©1994
Grade Level: 5-8
Pages: 87
Themes: Fear or Worry, Conflict Escalator,
    Peer Pressure

Adam, head of the Angels, claims an abandoned shack in the park for their clubhouse. When the Terrestrials take it over, the two clubs are at war. The situation becomes more serious when a beloved dog is killed, the companion of an older man who is a veteran and frequents the park.

Agony of Alice

Phyllis Reynolds Naylor

New York: Simon & Schuster Children's
    Publishing, 2007, ©1985
Grade Level: 5-7
Pages: 131
Themes: Accepting Limitations and Gifts,
    Prejudice or Dislike
Other: Audio

Because her own mother has died, Alice McKinley needs a mother's guidance. Alice discovers the inner beauty of her 6th-grade teacher Mrs. Plotkin, recognizes her own talent for writing, and learns that everyone makes mistakes as they grow up.

Aldo Applesauce

Johanna Hurwitz

Illustrated by: John Wallner
New York: Puffin Books, 1989, ©1979
Grade Level: 3-6
Pages: 127
Themes: Hurtful Words

Aldo Sossi, 4th grader, moves to a new school and has to cope with a nickname that he dislikes.

All Alone in the Universe

Lynne Rae Perkins

New York: HarperTrophy, 2007, ©1999
Grade Level: 5-8
Pages: 140
Themes: Friendship, Inclusion or Exclusion
Other: Audio

Maureen Berck, Debbie Pelbry's best friend since 3rd grade, and Glenna Flaiber begin to leave Debbie out of their activities. After a summer of loneliness, Debbie begins to enjoy friendships which are reciprocal. Debbie's English teacher, Miss Epler, encourages Debbie and Alice Dahlpke, who have much in common, to become friends. Then, a chance encounter with a police officer leads Debbie to a lasting friendship with his daughter, Patty Tsimmicz. Debbie and Patty are also featured in *Criss Cross*, 2005. The uncertainties of growing up are given a sense of hope, and are seen in the context of the randomness of some encounters.

The Bad News Bully

Marcia Leonard

Illustrated by: Julie Durrell
New York: Pocket Books, 1996
Grade Level: 2-5
Pages: 76
Themes: Bullying, Nonviolent Response
Third grader Natalie and her friend James work with classmates and adults to stop Hank from bullying everyone on their bus.

Bat 6

Virginia Euwer Wolff

Austin, TX: Holt, Rinehart and Winston, 2002, ©1998
Grade Level: 5-7
Pages: 230
Themes: Apologizing or Forgiving, Point of View, Prejudice or Dislike
Other: Audio
The 6th-grade girls' softball teams of two Oregon towns tell the story of the Fiftieth Anniversary BAT 6 Game in 1949. Bear Creek Ridge player Aki has returned from over three years in a desert internment camp. Barlow player Shirley "Shazam" fears and resents the Japanese people because of her father's death at Pearl Harbor. During the game, when Shazam is out at Aki's base, Shazam causes a head injury to Aki that leaves her in a brace for several weeks. Both team and community members blame themselves for not speaking up about warning signs. Shazam does community service for Japanese families, eventually coming to some understanding of the hurt she has caused Aki.

The Beast in Ms. Rooney's Room

Patricia Reilly Giff

Illustrated by: Blanche Sims
New York: Scholastic, 2006, ©1984
Grade Level: 2-4
Pages: 76
Themes: Overcoming Obstacles, Hurtful Words
Other: Audio
Richard "Beast" Best is repeating 2nd grade. He endures the teasing of his former classmates, makes new friends, and learns to read.

Because of Anya

Margaret Peterson Haddix

New York: Aladdin, 2004, ©2002
Grade Level: 3-6
Pages: 114
Themes: Friendship, Peer Pressure
When Anya Seaver loses her hair because of alopecia areata, Keely Michaels cares enough to break away from Stef Englewood and the rest of the group in order to give Anya the support she needs. Information on alopecia areata is included.

Because of Winn-Dixie

Kate DiCamillo

New York: Scholastic, 2005, ©2000
Grade Level: 4-6
Pages: 182
Themes: Community Building, Accepting Limitations and Gifts, Diversity of Individuals
Other: Audio, Video
India Opal Buloni adopts a stray dog, Winn-Dixie, who helps her to make many friends in her new town. Opal also learns more about the mother who left her and her preacher father when Opal was three.

Because She's My Friend

Harriet Sirof

New York: Atheneum, 1993, ©1983
    Lincoln, NE: Universe.com, 2000, ©1983
Grade Level: 5-9
Pages: 184
Themes: Friendship, Anger, Point of View
Teri D'Angelo befriends Valerie Ross who has paralyzed her leg in an accident. In alternating chapters the two girls tell the story of their rocky friendship.

Becoming Naomi León

Pam Munoz Ryan

New York: Scholastic, 2007, ©2004
Grade Level: 5-8
Pages: 246
Themes: Community Building, Accepting
    Limitations and Gifts, Diversity of Cultures,
    Respect for Elderly or Disabled
Other: Audio
Fifth-grader Naomi Soledad León Outlaw and her 2th-grade brother Owen, born with his head to one side, have lived in Southern California with Mary "Gram" Outlaw since their parents' divorce. When their mother, Terri Lynn, returns after many years and demands custody, neighbors Bernardo and Fabiola Morales help Gram and the children go to Oaxaca City. Naomi continues a León tradition by carving radishes for the Christmas festival and meets her father Santiago León, who helps Gram obtain legal custody of the two children. As the story unfolds, Naomi's self-confidence grows.

Beethoven in Paradise

Barbara O'Connor

New York: Farrar, Straus and Giroux, 1999,
    ©1997
Grade Level: 5-8
Pages: 153
Themes: Overcoming Obstacles
Other: Audio
Martin Pittman's dad tries to keep Martin from following his love of music. Sybil and the recluse Wylene, Martin's friends, help him to realize his dream.

Being Bee

Catherine Bateson

New York: Holiday House, 2007, ©2006
Grade Level: 4-6
Pages: 126
Themes: Anger, Inclusion or Exclusion, Point of
    View, Respect for Elderly or Disabled
Beatrice "Bee" who was young when her mother died, reacts angrily when her dad's girlfriend Jasmine "Jazzi" moves in. Although not all goes smoothly, Bee benefits by some of the household changes, appreciates Jazzi's brother Harley who lives in a group home, and grows an understanding of Jazzi as a person. The story is set in Australia.

The Beloved Dearly

Doug Cooney

New York: Aladdin, 2003, ©2002
Grade Level: 4-7
Pages: 183
Themes: Cooperation, Friendship,
    Recognizing Emotions
Other: Audio
Ernie Castellano begins a funeral business for pets. Along the way he and his "staff" learn about friendship, cooperation, and grief.

Benjamin Dove

Fririk Erlings

New York: North-South Books, 2007, ©2006
Grade Level: 5-8
Pages: 206
Themes: Anger, Bullying, Community in
     Action, Competition, Conflict Escalator,
     Inclusion or Exclusion, Stereotypes

Benjamin Dove and Jeff, each 12, and Emmanuel "Manny", 9, are best friends threatened by the bullying of Howard and Eddie and protected by Adele "Grandma Dell." Then Roland McIntosh from Scotland moves in and forms the Order of the Red Dragon with Benjamin and his friends. After a series of events, including a serious disagreement, Jeff leaves his friends and forms the Order of the Black Feather with Eddie and others. While Red Dragon does much that is admirable, their exclusion of Jeff leads to tragedy when Black Feather kidnaps Manny and inadvertently causes his death. The poignant story, narrated by Benjamin, shatters stereotypes and shows the complexity of everyday life.

The Best School Year Ever

Barbara Robinson

New York: HarperTrophy, 2005, ©1994
Grade Level: 3-6
Pages: 117
Themes: Empathy, Diversity of Individuals
Other: Audio

When Beth Bradley is assigned to think of compliments for Imogene Herdman, she thinks it will be impossible, until she recognizes some of Imogene's strengths. This is the sequel to *The Best Christmas Pageant Ever* (2005, ©1972).

The Best Worst Day

Bonnie Graves

Illustrated by: Nelle Davis
New York: Hyperion, ©1996
Grade Level: 2-5
Pages: 64
Themes: Competition, Accepting Limitations
     and Gifts

Lucy tries to get Maya to be her best friend and to get a paper on the BEST board. She also tries to stay away from Zach. Things work out when her art paper is not best but is "lively, unique, and colorful."

Big Talk: Poems for Four Voices

Paul Fleischman

Illustrated by: Beppe Giacobbe
Cambridge, MA: Candlewick Press, 2008,
     ©2000
Grade Level: 4-7
Pages: 44
Themes: Cooperation

Three poems of varying difficulty and content are to be read by four voices. (*I am Phoenix: Poems for Two Voices* (HarperTrophy, 1989, ©1985) and *Joyful Noise: Poems for Two Voices* (HarperTrophy, 2005, ©1988) contain poems about birds and insects, respectively.)

Biggest Klutz in Fifth Grade

Bill Wallace

New York: Aladdin, 2002, ©1992
Grade Level: 5-8
Pages: 148
Themes: Empathy, Hurtful Words, Diversity of
     Individuals

After Neal Moffett constantly taunts overweight Pat Berry who takes dancing lessons, Neal makes a bet that he will need to kiss Kristine Blimpton if Pat gets stitches or broken bones by the end of summer. By the end of summer, this is not a penalty.

Bird Shadow: An Ike and Mem Story

Patrick Jennings

Illustrated by: Anna Alter
New York: Holiday House, ©2001
Grade Level: 2-4
Pages: 55
Themes: Honesty, Responsible Decision
    Making, Apologizing or Forgiving

Second-grader Ike Nunn and his preschool sister Mem follow Dave Hove to the old Hawkins place. After they see pigeons in a shed and Dave breaks a window to let them out, Culver T. Hawkins appears and everyone runs. After telling their parents what happened, Ike and Mem apologize to Mr. Hawkins and make a friend; Dave pays restitution. (*The Weeping Willow* (2002) also deals with conflict resolution.)

Bird Springs

Caroline Marsden

New York: Viking, ©2007
Grade Level: 3-6
Pages: 124
Themes: Coping, Diversity of Cultures,
    Friendship

After a drought at the Bird Springs Navaho Reservation, 10-year-old Gregory's father left. While Gregory, his mother, and his baby sister Jeanine stay at a shelter, Gregory's coping skills evolve. Gregory accepts his Native American heritage, replaces his imaginary friend with his classmate Matt, and learns that talking about problems is an effective way to cope.

Birdie for Now

Jean Little

Custer, WA: Orca, ©2002
Grade Level: 2-5
Pages: 154
Themes: Friendship, Coping

Dickon Fielding's father has left them; he and his mother are in a new town where Dickon, who has ADHD, helps train Birdie, a Papillon; makes new friends; and becomes more focused. Because of his mother's phobia of dogs, Dickon needs to convince her to let him keep Birdie.

Blizzard's Wake

Phyllis Naylor

New York: Simon Pulse, 2004, ©2002
Grade Level: 5-8
Pages: 231
Themes: Anger, Apologizing or Forgiving
Other: Audio

A 1941 blizzard forces Zeke Dexter into the lives of 15-year-old Kate Sterling, her father, and her young brother Jesse. Zeke has just been released from prison for driving drunk and killing Mrs. Sterling four years earlier. This is a story of painful forgiveness.

Blubber

Judy Blume

New York: Dell Yearling, 2004, ©1974
Grade Level: 4-6
Pages: 153
Themes: Empathy, Bullying, Hurtful Words

Jill Brenner joins Wendy in naming and harassing Linda. The 5th-grade bullying shifts after Jill gets to know Linda and Jill herself becomes the victim of bullying.

Bone by Bone by Bone

Tony Johnston

New Milford, CT: Roaring Book Press, ©2007
Grade Level: 6+
Pages: 184
Themes: Friendship, Racism
This story, set in the South during the 1950s, tells of young David Church's deep friendship with Malcolm Deeter, in spite of the warning of David's father Franklin that he would shoot if Malcolm, an African American, ever came into their house. David feels both love and hatred toward his father, whose moods quickly shift. Although Franklin, a doctor, wants David to follow in his footsteps, his racism turns David away from him. [The author uses the "raw language" that was part of her racist environment when she was growing up.]

The BossQueen, Little BigBark, and the Sentinel Pup

Sarah Clark Jordan

Berkeley: Tricycle Press, 2006, ©2004
Grade Level: 3-6
Pages: 133
Themes: Point of View, Mediation or
    Negotiation
This story is told from the viewpoints of Chris (BossQueen, an Australian Shepherd), Layla (Little BigBark, a Rottweiler), and Mina (Sentinel Pup, a black dog), whose female owner (OurShe) marries a man with two children and Thomas (The Cat). While Chris and Layla try to evict The Cat, Mina negotiates with him and eventually appreciates his friendship. When Chris dies, it is The Cat who convinces Mina that she needs to take the lead.

Bravo, Grace!

Mary Hoffman

Illustrated by: June Allan
London: Frances Lincoln Children's Books,
    2007, ©2004
Grade Level: 3-5
Pages: 112
Themes: Hurtful Words, Nonviolent Response
Grace adjusts to her mother's marriage to Vince, a new baby brother Benjamin, and moving to a new house. Grace also takes action to stop the verbal bullying of her classmate Russell. (*Encore, Grace!* (New York: Dial, 2003) addresses jealousy and other friendship issues.)

The Breadwinner

Deborah Ellis

New York: Scholastic, 2002, ©2000
Grade Level: 5-8
Pages: 170
Themes: Anger, Gender Roles, Oppression
Other: Audio
After the Taliban imprisons her father, young Parvana, clad in her late brother Hossain's clothes, works in the market to earn food for her mother, older sister Nooria, and younger siblings Maryam and Ali. When her mother and siblings go to Mazar, Parvana stays behind to wait for her father. Parvana's father is finally released, and then word comes that many have fled Mazar. The story ends as Parvana and her father set out to find the rest of their family. (In *Parvana's Journey* (2002), after her father's death, Parvana sets out to find her family. Along the way she meets other young refugees and they make their way to the camp where her family is staying. *Mud City* (2003) completes the trilogy with the story of Shauzia, Parvana's friend from her working days.

Bridge to Terabithia

Katherine Paterson

Illustrated by: Donna Diamond
New York: HarperEntertainment, 2007, ©1972
Grade Level: 4-7
Pages: 191
Themes: Friendship, Fear or Worry
Other: Audio, Video
Jess Aarons learns confidence and values from his friend Leslie Burke. This poignant story of friendship ends with Leslie's accidental death.

The Broken Bike Boy and the Queen of 33rd Street

Sharon G. Flake

Illustrated by: Colin Bootman
New York: Hyperion, ©2007
Grade Level: 5-7
Pages: 132
Themes: Friendship, Respect in General
Other: Audio
Queen Marie Rosseau takes her name seriously, looking upon her 5th-grade classmates as her subjects. Leroy, who claims he came from Africa, challenges Queen to look beyond appearances. Leroy's elderly friend Cornelius teaches Queen some important lessons about friendship and respect.

The Bully of Barkham Street

Mary Stolz

Illustrated by: Leonard Shortall
New York: Harper & Row, 2006, ©1963
Grade Level: 4-7
Pages: 194
Themes: Point of View, Bullying, Responsible
    Decision Making
Sixth-grader Martin Hastings, who had been bullying Edward Frost, tells his story. This is the sequel to *The Dog on Barkham Street* (New York: HarperCollins Publishers, 1993, ©1960), in which 5th-grader Edward Frost tells the same story from his viewpoint.

Busybody Nora

Johanna Hurwitz

Illustrated by: Debbie Tilley
New York: Scholastic, 2002, ©1976
Grade Level: 2-5
Pages: 96
Themes: Community Building
Other: Audio
Nora helps create community in her New York apartment complex. One chapter is like *Stone Soup*.

Call Me Hope: A Novel

Gretchen Olsen

New York: Little, Brown and Company, ©2008
Grade Level: 4-7
Pages: 272
Themes: Coping, Hurtful Words
Other: Background Notes
Sixth-grader Hope Elliott's mother is a single parent who belittles and verbally abuses her. Although she tries to cope by following the example of Anne Frank, Hope suffers from headaches and teeth grinding. Then she finds help from friends and adults, including her school counselor Mrs. Nelson who teaches students and their parents to name verbal abuse and deal with it. The Hands & Words Are Not For Hurting Project (www.handsproject.org) is part of the story.

The Canning Season

Margaret Carlson

Illustrated by: Kimanne Smith
Minneapolis: Carolrhoda Books, ©1999
Grade Level: 2-6
Pages: 40
Themes: Community in Action, Prejudice or
    Dislike
The author tells the true story of a time when her best friend is no longer permitted to sleep over because of racial fear. The author, Peggy, finds refuge in her family community.

Center Court Sting

Matt Christopher

Boston: Little, Brown, ©1998
Grade Level: 4-8
Pages: 140
Themes: Cooperation, Empathy, Responsible
　　Decision Making
Other: Audio

Daren McCall thinks everyone has it in for him. Eventually his whole basketball team is falling apart because they won't support each other. He learns why Lou is not playing well and also realizes he was too hard on eight-year-old Gary who idolizes him.

The Chalk Box Kid

Clyde Robert Bulla

Illustrated by: Thomas B. Allen
New York: Scholastic, 2000, ©1987
Grade Level: 3-5
Pages: 59
Themes: Coping
Other: Audio

Nine-year-old Gregory knows how to cope with the setbacks in his life. When his Uncle Max comes to share his room, Gregory finds space in an old building that was once a chalk factory. Although there is no place to plant seeds, Gregory uses his gift of art to draw a garden on the walls in "his" building. This leads to a friendship with his classmate Ivy.

Charlie Is a Chicken

Jane Denitz Smith

New York: HarperTrophy, 2000, ©1998
Grade Level: 4-7
Pages: 168
Themes: Hurtful Words, Peer Pressure,
　　Apologizing or Forgiving

In order to be Jessica's friend, Maddie writes mean notes to her longtime friend Charlie. Both 5th-graders are miserable until they resolve their conflict and mend their friendship.

Charlie's Raven

Jean Craighead George

New York: Puffin Books, 2006, ©1974
Grade Level: 6-9
Pages: 190
Themes: Community Building, Respect in
　　General
Other: Audio

After Singing Bird, Charlie Carlisle's Teton Sioux friend, says ravens can cure people, Charlie steals a baby raven for his naturalist grandfather. For a year 13-year-old Charlie (and Grandad, Grandma Sally and Singing Bird) study Blue Sky and his sister Pinecone. They find that ravens are neither bad nor good, but mysterious, and that both the people and the ravens have changed each other.

The Cheat

Amy Goldman Koss

New York: Scholastic, 2004, ©2003
Grade Level: 6-8
Pages: 176
Themes: Honesty, Point of View

Six 8th graders are involved in cheating on a geography midterm.

Chess Rumble 5-8

G. Neri

Illustrated by: Jesse Joshua Watson
New York: Lee & Low Books, 2008, ©2007
Grade Level: 5-8
Pages: 64
Themes: Anger, Nonviolent Response,
　　Responsible Decision Making

After Marcus's sister died of a heart attack and his grieving father left, 11-year-old Marcus, his 8-year-old twin brothers, and their mother found life more difficult. After fighting with his former friend Latrell Jones, who had taunted him about his weight, Marcus gets sent to the library where he meets CM, a chess master. CM teaches Marcus the chess strategy of thinking ahead three moves. When Marcus applies this to life, he helps Latrell also learn to channel his energy and make wise decisions. (This book is written in free verse.)

Children Just Like Me: A Unique Celebration of Children Around the World

Barnabas Kindersley and Anabel Kindersley

Compiled and written by: Sue Copsey
New York: DK Publishing, 1999, ©1997
Grade Level: 3-6
Pages: 79
Themes: Diversity of Cultures

Photographs of children from over 30 countries are shown, and many details about their lives are given. This was produced in association with UNICEF.

Children of the River

Linda Crew

New York: Bantam, 1991, ©1989
Grade Level: 7-12
Pages: 213
Themes: Prejudice or Dislike, Diversity of Cultures
Other: Audio

In 1975 13-year-old Sundara Sovann and her Aunt Soka's family left Cambodia. This story takes place four years later when Sundara is trying to be true to her Cambodian heritage but struggles with her aunt's orders to stay away from Jonathan McKinnon whom she loves. Eventually Sundara and her aunt accept the changes that come in the river of life.

Cliques, Phonies, & Other Baloney

Trevor Romain

Minneapolis: Free Spirit, 2001, ©1998
Grade Level: 3-8
Pages: 129
Themes: Inclusion or Exclusion
Other: Video

With humor, the author offers advice on being one's self and avoiding the negative effects of cliques.

Close Encounters of a Third-World Kind

Jennifer J. Stewart

New York: Holiday House, 2008, ©2004
Grade Level: 4-7
Pages: 148
Themes: Diversity of Cultures, Responsible Decision Making

Twelve-year-old Annie Ferris and her five-year-old sister Chelsea spend two months in Nepal where their parents are on a medical mission. Ten-year-old Nirmala, the youngest of seven daughters, helps the Ferris family and returns with the family in order to be educated in the United States. Annie does without daily comforts, gives medical assistance, and learns that: "You will not change Nepal. Nepal will change you."

Cockroach Cooties

Laurence Yep

New York: Hyperion, 2001, ©2000
Grade Level: 3-4
Pages: 135
Themes: Bullying

Teddy and his little brother Bobby use some bugs to stand up to Arnie, who has been bullying them.

Colder than Ice

David Patneaude

Chicago: Albert Whitman & Co., ©2003
Grade Level: 4-6
Pages: 168
Themes: Friendship, Respect for Elderly or
    Disabled, Bullying, Nonviolent Response

Josh Showalter, an overweight 6th grader, who has just moved from Seattle to Rathborn, Idaho, has seen 7th-grader Corey Kitchen bullying Mark who has Asperger Syndrome and Skye. Still, Josh wants to believe that Corey's invitations to play soccer are based on friendship rather than the fact that Josh's father coaches high school sports. The moment of truth comes when Corey's bullying sends Josh's classmate Alex onto thin ice. Josh, Skye, and Mark risk their lives to rescue Alex after he falls through the ice. Then Mark gets the courage to report Corey and stop the bullying.

The Color of My Words

Lynn Joseph

New York: HarperTrophy, 2002, ©2000
Grade Level: 4-7
Pages: 138
Themes: Accepting Limitations and Gifts,
    Oppression, Community in Action,
    Responsible Decision Making, Apologizing
    or Forgiving
Other: Audio

Twelve-year-old Ana Rosa is a passionate writer who lives in the Dominican Republic. Undaunted by being labeled different by the villagers, as well as by the dangers of living in a country where words are suppressed, she writes about her experiences, her loving family, and the interconnectedness of a caring community. The culture and spirit of life in the Dominican Republic come alive through Ana Rosa's words.

A Corner of the Universe

Ann M. Martin

New York: Scholastic, 2004, ©2002
Grade Level: 5-8
Pages: 189
Themes: Respect for Elderly or Disabled
Other: Audio

Hattie Owen tells about her tenth summer when her Uncle Adam moves home because the mental institution where he had spent many years has closed. Hattie tries to sort out how Adam can be someone with the needs of a child but the age of an adult, someone with unpredictable reactions but the caring of a friend.

Crash

Jerry Spinelli

New York: Dell Laurel-Leaf, 2004, ©1996
Grade Level: 5-8
Pages: 162
Themes: Respect for Elderly or Disabled,
    Bullying
Other: Audio

John "Crash" Coogan usually orders others around. However, his beloved grandfather's stroke changes Crash; and Penn Webb, a Quaker, challenges Crash's values.

Crazy Fish

Norma Fox Mazer

Orlando, FL: Harcourt, 2007, ©1980
Grade Level: 5-8
Pages: 184
Themes: Accepting Limitations and Gifts,
    Hurtful Words

Joyce lives with her uncle, Old Dad, who runs the city dump. Joyce's classmates are merciless in their teasing and name-calling. The school custodian Mrs. Fish befriends and loves Joyce and her uncle.

Crazy Lady

Jane Leslie Conly

New York: HarperTrophy, 1995, ©1993
Grade Level: 5-9
Pages: 180
Themes: Community Building, Empathy,
   Respect for Elderly or Disabled
Other: Audio

Vernon and his four siblings live with their widowed father. Through Miss Annie who tutors him, Vernon gets involved with Maxine Flooter and her son Ronald, who is developmentally disabled.

Crossing Jordan

Adrian Fogelin

Atlanta: Peachtree, 2002, ©2000
Grade Level: 4-7
Pages: 140
Themes: Friendship, Prejudice or Dislike
Other: Audio

When Cass Bodine's father hears that a black family is moving next door, he builds a fence. Jemmie Lewis's mother, the new neighbor, assumes that the fence is the work of a bigot. In spite of their parents' prejudices, the two 12-year-olds delight in their friendship, their love of running, and their fascination with Jane Eyre. By the end of summer the running team "Chocolate Milk" has broken several barriers. (*Iggie's House* by Judy Blume (New York: Dell Yearling, 2004, ©1970) also involves acceptance of new black neighbors after initial prejudice.)

The Crow and Mrs. Gaddy

Wilson Gage

Illustrated by: Marylin Hafner
New York: Scholastic, ©1984
Grade Level: 1-3
Pages: 47
Themes: Anger, Conflict Nature

Both the crow and Mrs. Gaddy spend so much time aggravating each other that they neglect their own lives.

Dare to Dream! 25 Extraordinary Lives

Sandra McLeod Humphrey

Amherst, NY: Prometheus Books, ©2005
   Paw Prints, 2008
Grade Level: 4-8
Pages: 121
Themes: Accepting Gifts and Limitations,
   Diversity of Individuals, Overcoming
   Obstacles

This is a collection of biographies, describing both the younger years and the adult years of twenty-five individuals from a variety of cultural and social backgrounds, spanning several periods of history. Each individual has endured hardship on the way to achievement.

Daring to be Abigail

Rachel Vail

New York: Puffin Books, 1997, ©1996
Grade Level: 4-6
Pages: 128
Themes: Friendship, Accepting Limitations
   and Gifts, Peer Pressure

Eleven-year-old Abigail "Abby," whose father is deceased, explores friendship and discovers her true self at summer camp.

Dawn and Dusk

Alice Mead

New York: Farrar, Straus and Giroux, ©2007
Grade Level: 5-9
Pages: 152
Themes: Diversity of Cultures, Oppression,
    Responsible Decision Making

The chemical warfare waged by Iraq on the Kurdish town of Sardasht, Iran, in 1987 is seen through the eyes of 13-year-old Azad. He learns how his mother's prevention of a 9-year-old girl's forced marriage, and his father's revelation under torture led to his parents' divorce. After a bombing attack involving poisonous gas, Azad, his mother, and other family members flee the country. After months, they settle in Maine to begin a new life in a strange land. (In *Swimming to America* (2005) eighth-graders Lindita Berati from Albania and Ramón Nieves from Cuba, and their families, struggle with their illegal status.)

The Day Joanie Frankenhauser Became a Boy

Frances Lantz

New York: Dutton, ©2005
Grade Level: 4-6
Pages: 151
Themes: Gender Roles, Empathy,
    Assertiveness

The school secretary at Joan Frankenhauser's new school lists Joan as "John," giving Joan an opportunity to play sports with the boys. So Joan goes undercover for a week but learns that boys have their own set of challenges. When Zane instigates some mean activities, Casey and Joan/"John" find it hard to resist the pressure. In the end, by standing up to Zane, Joan reveals her identity and continues being friends with Casey.

Deaf Child Crossing

Marlee Matlin

New York: Aladdin, 2004, ©2002
Grade Level: 4-6
Pages: 200
Themes: Friendship, Respect for Elderly or
    Disabled, Apologizing or Forgiving

Nine-year-old Megan Merrill is deaf. She is also stubborn and high-spirited. Cindy Calicchio moves to the neighborhood and becomes Megan's best friend, although Megan has difficulty when Cindy gives unsolicited help. Megan teaches Cindy to sign. Then the two girls go to camp, where Lizzie, who is also deaf, and Megan are excited to meet each other and leave Cindy behind. After a major conflict, Megan and Cindy are able to resolve their differences and again become best friends.

Dear Whiskers

Ann Whitehead Nagda

Illustrated by: Stephanie Roth
New York: Scholastic, 2002, ©2000
London: Frances Lincoln, 2006, ©2000
Grade Level: 2-4
Pages: 75
Themes: Empathy, Diversity of Cultures
Other: Audio

Each 4th grader, pretending to be a mouse living in a 2nd grader's desk, writes a letter to that 2nd grader. Jenny's mouse, Whiskers, writes to Sameera, a girl from Saudi Arabia who is learning English. After initially failing, Jenny successfully uses cookies shaped like mice to help Sameera learn.

Defiance

Valerie Hobbs

New York: Farrar, Straus and Giroux, ©2005
Grade Level: 5-7
Pages: 116
Themes: Friendship, Overcoming Obstacles,
  Respect for Elderly or Disabled
Eleven-year-old Toby Steiner has gone through chemo. During their summer vacation, he discovers a lump on his side and refuses to have any more treatments. 94-year-old Pearl Rhodes Richardson and her cow Blossom become Toby's friends. Blossom dies, and Pearl's faith in Toby gives him the courage to go on living.

Different Dragons

Jean Little

Illustrated by: Laura Fernandez
Toronto: Puffin Books, 2005, ©1986
Grade Level: 3-6
Pages: 123
Themes: Fear or Worry
Ben Tucker reluctantly stays with his Aunt Rose and learns to overcome some of his fears.

Dillon Dillon

Kate Banks

New York: Farrar, Straus and Giroux, 2005,
  ©2002
Grade Level: 4-6
Pages: 150
Themes: Accepting Limitations and Gifts
Other: Audio
When Dillon turns ten, he learns the secret of his name and discovers more about his identity.

Do Bananas Chew Gum?

Jamie Gilson

New York: Lothrop, Lee & Shepard, 1997,
  ©1980
Grade Level: 4-7
Pages: 158
Themes: Overcoming Obstacles
Sixth-grader Sam Mott has trouble reading. He is a good babysitter and loves archeology. Sam begins to get help from a learning-disability specialist and from his smart new friend Alicia.

Do Not Pass Go

Kirkpatrick Hill

New York: Margaret K. McElderry Books,
  ©2007
Grade Level: 6-9
Pages: 229
Themes: Anger, Coping, Responsible Decision
  Making, Stereotypes
Teenager Dietrich "Deet" Aafeldt is the responsible member of his family. Deet's father Charlie and his mother Patty are loving, though not fiscally wise. (Biologically, Charlie is Deet's stepfather, but their relationship is that of father and son.) After Charlie is arrested for possession of drugs which had been taken in order to keep awake during his second job, and Patty goes to work, Deet helps care for his young sisters Jamima Mae "Jam" and Patty Jane "P.J.". Deet balances his home and school responsibilities and time for visiting his father, worries about the disrespect of his classmates, and endures the harsh judgments of his father's parents. Along the way, Deet sees the diversity of the jail population, finds support from others who have loved ones in jail, and watches his parents find ways to improve their lives.

Dog Sense

Sneed B. Collard III

Atlanta: Peachtree, 2008, ©2005
Grade Level: 4-7
Pages: 176
Themes: Anger, Bullying, Nonviolent Response

Eighth-grader Guy Martinez and his mother have moved from California to Montana since Guy's father left them. When Brad Mullen bullies Guy, Grandpa encourages him to choose the "field of battle," and says, "The best victory is one where the other guy wins, too." With the help of his friend Luke Grant, Guy trains his border collie Streak to catch Frisbees. When they compete with Brad and his dog Shep, Guy manages to treat Brad decently.

Doing Time Online

Jan Siebold

Morton Grove, IL: Whitman, ©2002
Grade Level: 4-6
Pages: 88
Themes: Empathy, Respect for Elderly or
    Disabled, Responsible Decision Making

After Mitch Riley is involved in a prank that injures an elderly neighbor, he is assigned to regular online chats with Wootie, a spunky resident in Maple Grove Home. Mitch gains a friend and learns to take responsibility.

Don't You Dare Read This, Mrs. Dunphrey

Margaret Peterson Haddix

New York: Simon Pulse, 2004, ©1996
    Paw Prints, 2008, ©1996
Grade Level: 7-12
Pages: 125
Themes: Coping, Honesty, Responsible
    Decision Making
Other: Audio

Tish Bonner, 15, is more sensitive than she appears. Her assigned journal entries are not for Mrs. Dunphrey's reading, an option offered the students. The journal becomes Tish's therapy as she tries to care for her eight-year-old brother Matt after their abusive father has left for good and then their mother leaves. By April, when their resources are gone, Tish opens her journal to Mrs. Dunphrey, the only adult she trusts, and also finds help from her paternal grandparents for herself, Matt, and their mother.

The Double-Digit Club

Marion Dane Bauer

New York: Holiday House, ©2004
Grade Level: 3-5
Pages: 116
Themes: Friendship, Inclusion or Exclusion,
    Honesty

Sarah feels betrayed when her best friend Paige turns 10 and accepts Valerie's invitation to her exclusive club. As the weeks go on and Sarah is willing to deceive Miss Berglund her elderly blind friend in order to regain Paige's friendship, Sarah gains insight into her own bossiness.

An Early Winter

Marion Dane Bauer

New York: Dell Yearling, 2001, ©1999
Grade Level: 4-7
Pages: 120
Themes: Empathy, Respect for Elderly or
    Disabled
Other: Audio

Eleven-year-old Tim struggles with his grandfather's Alzheimer's disease and learns that his parents' intentions are different from what he had thought.

Eggs

Jerry Spinelli

New York: Little, Brown and Company, 2008,
    ©2007
Grade Level: 4-8
Pages: 220
Themes: Anger, Coping, Friendship, Hurtful
    Words
Other: Audio

David Limpert, nine, who is grieving the death of his mother in an accident caused by someone else's carelessness, becomes friends with Primrose Dufee, 13, who thinks she is not loved by her eccentric mother. The two each learn to care for the other's needs and then recognize that the adults in their lives really do love them.

Elijah of Buxton

Christopher Paul Curtis

Detroit: Thorndike Press, 2008, ©2007
Grade Level: 3-6
Pages: 341
Themes: Community in Action, Oppression,
    Responsible Decision Making
Other: Audio

In 1849, Reverend William King founded Buxton, a mission in Ontario for escaped slaves. This is an historic fiction based on the early days of that community, narrated by pre-teen Elijah "Eli" Freeman, the first child born in the settlement. Powerful scenes convey the strong sense of community nurtured by the Buxton residents as they care for each other and for the newly freed residents who make their way out of slavery. Elijah himself ends up encountering a group of captured slaves near Detroit and carries a baby, Hope, to freedom. An historical note tells about the founding of Buxton. (*The Watsons Go to Birmingham* – 1963 (2004, ©1995) describes more contemporary discrimination when 4th-grader Kenny Watson and his family go to Alabama and witness the bombing of the church.)

Emma Dilemma and the Two Nannies

Patricia Hermes

Tarrytown, NY: Marshall Cavendish Children,
    ©2007
Grade Level: 2-4
Pages: 117
Themes: Honesty

Emma O'Fallon, 3rd grade, and her siblings (Tim in 4th grade; McClain, almost 5; and Ira and Lizzie, almost 2) fear that Mrs. Potts will replace their nanny Annie when she goes to visit her family in Dublin. Emma covers up the accident when her pet ferret Marmaduke chews up a new book and Emma's classmate Jordan gets blamed. In addition, Emma and Tim make up a story to get Annie's family to come to the United States for a visit. In both cases, Emma finds relief after paying the price of revealing the truth.

Emma-Jean Lazarus Fell Out of a Tree

Lauren Tarshis

New York: Puffin Books, 2008, ©2003
Grade Level: 5-7
Pages: 199
Themes: Accepting Limitations and Gifts,
    Diversity of Individuals, Peer Pressure
Other: Audio

Emma-Jean Lazarus looks at life in very different ways from her 7th-grade classmates. Disliking imperfection in life and devoted to her loving father, a mathematics professor who died in a car accident two years earlier, Emma-Jean takes a logical approach to social situations. Assuming good will in others, she uses some unusual approaches in helping solve their problems. This leads to a friendship with Colleen Pomerentz, liberating Colleen from her fear of others' opinions and introducing Emma-Jean herself into the joys of social life, messy though it is.

Ever After

Rachel Vail

New York: HarperTrophy, 2005, ©1994
Grade Level: 7-9
Pages: 136
Themes: Friendship, Recognizing Emotions
Other: Audio

As she turns 14, Molly Garrett is caught between her two friends, Grace who is too sophisticated and Vicky who is very moody. Molly learns to be more true to herself and, by the end, is starting to spend time with Keiko who has more in common with her.

F Is for Fabuloso

Marie G. Lee

New York: Avon, ©1999
Grade Level: 6-8
Pages: 176
Themes: Honesty, Stereotypes

Two years after leaving Korea, junior high student Jin-Ha Kim and her family are trying to adjust to life in Minnesota. Jin-Ha learns the importance of honesty and discovers how hurtful stereotypes can be.

Fear Place

Phyllis Naylor

New York: Aladdin, ©1996
Grade Level: 5-8
Pages: 118
Themes: Fear or Worry
Other: Audio

In spite of a cougar and a narrow, high ledge in the mountains, Doug Grillo overcomes his fear in order to save his brother.

Feathers

Jacqueline Woodson

New York: Puffin Books, 2009, ©2007
Grade Level: 4-7
Pages: 118
Themes: Bullying, Diversity of Individuals,
    Respect for Elderly or Disabled
Other: Audio

Captivated by Emily Dickinson's poem about hope being "the thing with feathers," Abigail Francesca "Frannie" Wright-Barnes, 11, looks for signs of hope in the midst of bleakness. Frannie's mother is pregnant and not feeling well, which is a worry because her first child Lila died as a baby and she had two miscarriages after Sean and Frannie were born. Frannie's classmate Trevor who is biracial has much anger and bullies others, especially the new student who is called Jesus because of his white skin. Frannie finds support from her brother Sean who shares his deaf world through signing, and her friend Samantha whose father has a church. In the end, Trevor and Jesus fight about their dads (Jesus is adopted by black parents and Trevor's father is white). Trevor is the one who falls and cries, and both Jesus and Frannie go to his aid. Frannie's mother seems stronger, and hope seems to be something that is part of each day.

Ferret in the Bedroom, Lizards in the Fridge

Bill Wallace
New York: Aladdin, 2002, ©1986
Grade Level: 4-7
Pages: 132
Themes: Diversity of Individuals, Peer Pressure
Liz's family keeps animals from her dad's university research. However, the menagerie frightens her friends and jeopardizes her chances of winning class presidency. Finally, she realizes how many life lessons she has gotten from the pets.

The Field of the Dogs

Katherine Paterson
Illustrated by: Emily Arnold McCully
New York: HarperTrophy, 2002, ©2001
London: Fitzgerald Books, 2007, ©2001
Grade Level: 3-5
Pages: 89
Themes: Bullying
Other: Audio
Josh has an unusual ability; he is able to understand the language of dogs. Josh's pet dog Manch helps him deal with Wes Rockett's bullying.

Fire on Ice: Autobiography of a Champion Figure Skater

Sasha Cohen and Amanda Maciel
Photos by: Kathy Goedeken
New York: HarperCollins, ©2005
Grade Level: 4-8
Pages: 172
Themes: Competition, Accepting Limitations
   and Gifts, Coping
Sasha Cohen relates how her self-confidence has affected her skating performance, and how she has learned to cope with failures and accidents.

Fish Face

Patricia Reilly Giff
Illustrated by: Blanche Sims
New York: Scholastic, 2006, ©1984
Grade Level: 1-4
Pages: 75
Themes: Competition, Empathy
Other: Audio
Emily can run fast (when she has her unicorn) and can do her math, but she cannot spell. When Dawn, who is better at reading and running, arrives and steals Emily's unicorn, Emily discovers that Dawn is not as self-assured as she appears.

Flipped

Wendelin Van Draanen
New York: Scholastic, 2004, ©2001
Grade Level: 6-9
Pages: 212
Themes: Point of View, Diversity of Individuals
Other: Audio
In alternating chapters, Bryce Loski and Juli Baker tell how Juli grows wiser and Bryce learns to see beyond appearances.

For Your Eyes Only!

Joanne Rocklin
Illustrated by: Mark Todd
New York: Scholastic, ©1997
Grade Level: 4-7
Pages: 136
Themes: Diversity of Individuals
Lucy Keane's warm, humorous notebook and other class writings reveal how she learns to appreciate her irritating classmate Andy and to love the world as it is.

Freak

Marcella Pixley

New York: Farrar, Straus and Giroux, ©2007
Grade Level: 7-10
Pages: 131
Themes: Bullying, Inclusion or Exclusion,
   Nonviolent Response
Miriam Fisher, 12, is even shunned by her older sister Deborah, 14, who fears losing her friends if she acknowledges Miriam. Miriam's 7th-grade classmates harass Miriam who is infatuated with Artie Rosenberg, a high school senior staying with the Fisher family while his parents are in India. Although Miriam's prime attacker is Jenny Clarke, when several boys at a party get Jenny drunk and sexually attack her, Miriam is the one who goes to Jenny's aid.

Freak the Mighty

Rodman Philbrick

New York: Scholastic, 2005, ©1993
   Paw Prints, 2008, ©1993
Grade Level: 6-9
Pages: 169
Themes: Friendship, Accepting Limitations
   and Gifts, Empathy
Other: Audio, Video
In this poignant story, Max, who is physically strong but academically slow, and Kevin, who is extremely intelligent but has a skeletal disease that is life-threatening, develop a deep friendship.

A Friendship for Today

Patricia McKissack

New York: Scholastic Press, 2008, ©2007
Grade Level: 5-8
Pages: 172
Themes: Prejudice
Rosemary Patterson is the only African American student in her 6th-grade class. Although Rosemary experiences a range of hurtful acts based on prejudice, she and her classmates also learn to appreciate differences. This story is based on the author's own experience in Kirksville, MO.

From the Notebooks of Melanin Sun

Jacqueline Woodson

New York: Scholastic, ©1995
Grade Level: 7-11
Pages: 141
Themes: Gender Roles, Stereotypes
Melanin "Mel" Sun is a reflective 13-year-old who is concerned about endangered amphibians, wants to go out with Angie but is uncertain how to talk to her, and finds solace by journaling. His happy home life with his African American mother Encanta Cedar "EC" is disrupted when she falls in love with Kristin, a white lawyer whose family has disowned her because of her homosexuality. Mel and his friend Sean, 13, fight when Sean ridicules the situation, but Ralphael "Ralph" stays by Mel.

Funerals & Fly Fishing

Mary Bartek

New York: Henry Holt, ©2004
Grade Level: 4-7
Pages: 148
Themes: Accepting Limitations and Gifts,
   Respect for Elderly or Disabled
After completing 6th grade, Brad Stanislawski stays with his grandfather Stanley, an undertaker. Brad returns home with a new respect for himself and his family, and is better able to cope with the boys who had bullied him.

Games: A Tale of Two Bullies

Carol Gorman

New York: HarperCollins Publishers, ©2007
Grade Level: 4-6
Pages: 279
Themes: Bullying, Conflict Resolution,
   Nonviolent Response, Point of View
Mick Sullivan and Bart "Boot" Sullivan are notorious for their fights. Assigned by Mr. Maddox, their new principal, to daily game sessions, the 8th graders gradually learn to respect and even care about each other.

Gifted

Beth Evangelista

New York: Walker, 2007, ©2005
Grade Level: 4-7
Pages: 180
Themes: Friendship, Empathy, Diversity of
   Individuals

Thirteen-year-old George R. Clark is intellectually gifted. After a week at camp that ends with a hurricane, George discovers how self-centered he has been. He also realizes that he should appreciate Anita Newell's friendship and gains new respect for his teacher Mr. Zimmerman who risks his life to save George and his new friend Sam.

Gifted Hands: The Ben Carson Story

Ben Carson with Cecil Murphey

Grand Rapids, MI: Zondervan Publishing
   House, 2007, ©1990
Grade Level: 7-12
Pages: 232
Themes: Overcoming Obstacles, Hurtful
   Words, Responsible Decision Making
Other: Audio, Video

Ben Carson, a prominent neurosurgeon, tells of his beginnings in Detroit. Initially ridiculed because of his poor math scores, Ben went on to achieve high academic honors because of his mother's insistence that Ben and his brother begin reading extensively.

The Girl Who Knew It All

Patricia Reilly Giff

Illustrated by: Leslie Morrill
New York: Dell Yearling, 2000, ©1979
Grade Level: 4-7
Pages: 118
Themes: Accepting Limitations and Gifts,
   Hurtful Words

When Tracy Matson tries to hide her poor reading skills, she creates many problems for herself.

The Girls

Amy Goldman Koss

New York: Puffin Books, 2002, ©2000
Findaway World LLC, 2007, ©2000
Grade Level: 5-8
Pages: 121
Themes: Inclusion or Exclusion, Rumors or
   Suspicion
Other: Audio

When 7th-grader Maya Koptier is not invited to Darcy's sleepover, she learns that she is no longer in Candace Newman's group. In the end, Brianna, Renée, and Darcy herself find a new freedom in being outside the group.

Going for Great

Carolee Brockmann

Middleton, WI: American Girl, ©1999
Grade Level: 4-6
Pages: 119
Themes: Cooperation, Diversity of Individuals

Jenna Dowling, 6th grader, is a gifted flute player. When Heather Bardlow, who is not considered socially acceptable, collaborates with Jenna in a musical competition, Jenna overcomes her stage fright and learns to appreciate Heather.

The Gold Cadillac

Mildred D. Taylor

New York: Scholastic, 1999, ©1987
Grade Level: 2-3
Pages: 43
Themes: Discrimination
Other: Audio

In her story of a trip from Ohio to Mississippi, the author relates some personal memories of the humiliation caused by the Jim Crow laws. When her father drives the family in their brand new 1950 Cadillac to visit relatives in Mississippi, 'lois discovers the "WHITE ONLY, COLORED NOT ALLOWED" signs posted in the southern states. Then, after police accuse her father of stealing the car, he borrows Cousin Halton's car to continue the trip from Memphis. In the end, the new Cadillac is returned, leaving 'lois with a mixture of memories of the days when they rode in the fine car.

Gold-Threaded Dress

Carolyn Marsden
New York: Scholastic, 2006, ©2002
Grade Level: 3-5
Pages: 73
Themes: Friendship, Diversity of Cultures,
    Bullying
When Oy from Thailand tries to make friends with the girls in her class, she jeopardizes her prized Thai dress. In the end, she learns who her real friend is. (*The Quail Club* (2006) further explores Oy's relationship with Liliandra and develops Oy's search for her Asian-American identity.)

Goosed!

Bill Wallace
Illustrated by: Jacqueline Rogers
New York: Aladdin, 2004, ©2002
    Paw Prints, 2008, ©2002
Grade Level: 2-4
Pages: 125
Themes: Jealousy
The narrator, a birddog named T.P., is jealous of the attention his owner Jeff gives the new chocolate Lab who gets named Mocha. In the end, T.P. saves Mocha when the Lab tries to retrieve a large goose.

Gracie's Girl

Ellen Wittlinger
New York: Aladdin, 2002, ©2000
Grade Level: 4-6
Pages: 186
Themes: Accepting Limitations and Gifts,
    Stereotypes, Respect for Elderly or
    Disabled
Other: Audio
Because of Gracie Jarvis Butler, 6th-grader Bess Cunningham gets to know some people who are homeless. Bess's values are tested and she finds that she is coolest when she is true to herself.

Granny Torrelli Makes Soup

Sharon Creech
Illustrated by: Chris Raschka
New York: HarperCollins, 2005, ©2003
Findaway World LLC, 2008, ©2003
Grade Level: 4-7
Pages: 141
Themes: Anger, Jealousy, Respect for Elderly
    or Disabled
Other: Audio
Twelve-year-old Rosie, angry with her best friend Bailey, talks things over with her grandmother. Bailey had gotten upset when Rosie learned Braille, one thing that he could do and she could not. Then, when Janine moves into the neighborhood, Rosie needs to deal with her jealousy

The Great Gilly Hopkins

Katherine Paterson
New York: HarperTrophy, 2004, ©1978
London: Fitzgerald Books, 2008, ©1978
Grade Level: 5-9
Pages: 148
Themes: Community Building, Anger
Other: Audio, Video
Sixth-grader Galadriel "Gilly" Hopkins is now in the foster of Maime Trotter and William Ernest, her third foster home in less than three years. For most of her life, Gilly has waited for Courtney, her mother, to send for her.

A Group of One

Rachna Gilmore
New York: Henry Holt, ©2001
Markham, Ontario: Fitzhenry & Whiteside,
    2005, ©2001
Grade Level: 7-12
Pages: 184
Themes: Stereotypes, Diversity of Cultures
When her grandmother visits, 15-year-old Tara Mehta, who has lived in Ottawa all her life, learns about her Hindu roots. She struggles with the boundaries and labels imposed by others.

Hana's Suitcase: A True Story

Karen Levine

Morton Grove, IL: Whitman, 2007, ©2003
Grade Level: 4-7
Pages: 111
Themes: Community in Action, Oppression
Other: Audio

After Fumiko Ishioka secures Hana Brady's suitcase for her Holocaust museum in Tokyo, she discovers the poignant story of Hana, her brother George, and their family. "Small Wings," a group of young people from eight to 18, helps spread the story of Hana. This story tells parallel accounts of Hana's life and Fumiko's search.

Harold's Tail

John Bemelmans Marciano

New York: Viking, ©2003
Grade Level: 3-5
Pages: 130
Themes: Point of View, Stereotypes

Harold is a squirrel, content with his life in New York's tiny Straus Park, until a rat named Sidney challenges Harold to shave his tail and give it to Sidney. Harold complies, loses his begging privileges, and leaves Straus Park to live with two rats, King and Amelia. Harold changes many of his ideas about rats and they about him.

The Heart of a Chief

Joseph Bruchac

New York: Puffin Books, ©1998
Grade Level: 5-8
Pages: 153
Themes: Cooperation, Diversity of Cultures, Nonviolent Response, Responsible Decision Making, Stereotypes

Christopher "Nicola" Nicholas, 6th grader, has already had many life experiences. After his mother died, his grieving father left Chris and his younger sister Celeste in the care of Doda and Auntie who are like grandparents. Chris values his Native American heritage; he fears the building of a casino on a sacred island in the Penacook Reservation where he lives, and he finds himself increasingly offended by the name of the school football team, the Chiefs, and the associated cheers. Chris finds his voice for both issues and discovers that others are listening. He effectively engages others, including his father who is in alcoholic rehabilitation, in finding solutions.

The Heaven Shop

Deborah Ellis

Markham, Ontario: Fitzhenry & Whiteside, 2005, ©2004
Grade Level: 6-9
Pages: 186
Themes: Community Building, Coping, Problem Solving

Binti Phiri, 13, her sister Junie, 16, and their brother Kwasi, 14, of South Africa help their beloved father "Bambo" make coffins in The Heaven Shop. When Bambo dies of AIDS, the children are sent to live with uncles who take advantage of them. This is particularly difficult for Binti who had been a star in a radio show. Finally, they live with their grandmother "Gogo" who is taking care of a dozen children orphaned by AIDS. When Gogo dies, the young people continue to care for the orphans, supporting themselves by their own Heaven Shop. Notes by and about the author are included.

Here Today

Ann M. Martin

New York: Scholastic, 2005, ©2004
   Paw Prints, 2008, ©2004
Grade Level: 4-8
Pages: 308
Themes: Bullying, Responsible Decision
   Making
Other: Audio

In the fall of 1963, 6th-grader Eleanor Roosevelt "Ellie" Dingman feels her life is falling apart. On the bus and in school, Ellie and her best friend Holly Major are both ridiculed and shunned by classmates. At home Ellie has major responsibilities because her mother Doris Day Dingman is pursuing a stage life that takes her away from the family. In the end, Ellie finds peace with her life in Spectacular, NY.

The Hero of Third Grade

Alice DeLaCroix

Illustrated by: Cynthia Fisher
New York: Scholastic, 2004, ©2002
Grade Level: 2-3
Pages: 72
Themes: Community Building, Peacemaking

When Randall is afraid of not being accepted by his new school, he finds success by imitating the Scarlet Pimpernel and doing random acts of kindness.

Holly's Secret

Nancy Garden

New York: Farrar, Straus and Giroux, ©2000
Grade Level: 4-7
Pages: 132
Themes: Prejudice or Dislike, Gender Roles,
   Diversity of Individuals

When Holly starts 7th grade at a new school she tries to change her identity and hide the fact that her two moms are lesbians.

Hope Was Here

Joan Bauer

New York: Speak, 2005, ©2000
   Paw Prints, 2008, ©2000
Grade Level: 8-12
Pages: 186
Themes: Community Building, Coping,
   Responsible Decision Making
Other: Audio

Hope legally changed her name from Tulip at age 12, and became a waitress two years later. All her life she has longed to meet her father. Her mother has drifted in and out of her life, leaving bits of wisdom gleaned from waiting tables. Although they have moved frequently, Hope's Aunt Addie has been a steady presence in her life. They go to the Welcome Stairway diner in Mulhoney, WI, where Addie has been hired because G.T. Stoop the owner has leukemia. G.T. is not finished living; he is running for mayor and involves local teens in his fight to end corruption. During the campaign, Hope continues to learn life lessons from the food business and finds a father to surpass her dreams.

Horrible Harry and the Dragon War

Suzy Kline

Illustrated by: Frank Remkiewicz
New York: Puffin Books, 2003, ©2002
Grade Level: 2-3
Pages: 50
Themes: Conflict Escalator, Win-Win Solutions,
   Mediation or Negotiation
Other: Audio

Harry and Song Lee have a conflict over their dragon project. They resolve the conflict when they discover that Eastern and Western dragons are different. (*Horrible Harry in Room 2B* (New York: Puffin Books, 1998, ©1988) discusses friendship.)

Hot Issues, Cool Choices:
Facing Bullies, Peer Pressure, Popularity, and Put-Downs

Sandra McLeod Humphrey
Illustrated by: Brian Strassburg
Amherst, NY: Prometheus Books, ©2007
Grade Level: 4-7
Pages: 133
Themes: Bullying, Empathy, Peer Pressure,
    Responsible Decision Making
Twenty-five scenarios involving bullying, peer pressure, and other student dilemmas are posed, each containing a dilemma for one or more of the characters. The reader is then asked what he or she would do. Follow-up questions ask the reader to further analyze the situation. Additional information on responding to bullying is included. (*If You Had to Choose, What Would You Do?* (©1995), *More If You Had to Choose, What Would You Do?* (2003, ©1995) and *It's Up to You... What Do You Do?* (©1999) have additional stories with similar format.)

The House on Mango Street

Sandra Cisneros
New York: Knopf, 2007, ©1984
    Paw Prints, 2008, ©1984
Grade Level: 7-12
Pages: 134
Themes: Accepting Limitations and Gifts
This is a collection of short stories about growing up. "Four Skinny Trees" is the story of four trees that are misfits, with whom the narrator identifies. In "Eleven" the narrator feels like she is a combination of ages; she also tells of a teacher falsely accusing her of owning a ragged sweater.

How I Survived Being a Girl

Wendelin Van Draanen
New York: HarperCollins, 2007, ©1997
    Paw Prints, 2008, ©1997
Grade Level: 4-6
Pages: 163
Themes: Gender Roles
Sixth-grader Carolyn learns that she likes being a girl as long as she does not need to follow stereotyping.

How to Be Cool in the Third Grade

Betsy Duffey
Illustrated by: Janet Wilson
New York: Puffin Books, 1999, ©1993
Grade Level: 2-4
Pages: 69
Themes: Bullying, Peer Pressure, Responsible
    Decision Making
Other: Audio
Robbie York learns that being cool has more to do with who he is and how he treats others than with what he wears. He finds out that he can actually work with Bo Haney, the older boy who had bullied him, and Bo helps Robbie change his name to Rob. (*Good Grief Third Grade* by Colleen O'Shaughnessy McKenna (New York: Scholastic, ©1993) also features an unlikely team of 3rd graders who learns to work together. In *How to Survive Third Grade* by Laurie Lawlor (New York: Pocket Books, 1991, ©1988) a small boy who is bullied finds new life when he is befriended by a boy from Kenya.)

How to Steal a Dog

Barbara O'Connor

New York: Frances Foster Books, ©2007

Grade Level: 3-7

Pages: 170

Themes: Honesty, Point of View, Problem
    Solving, Responsible Decision Making

Since her father left, Georgina Hayes has been living in the car with her younger brother Toby and their mother. A poster offering $500 for a missing dog is the seed for a plot to steal and then "find" a missing dog. Although Georgina and Toby manage to take Carmella Whitmore's pet dog Willie, they do not bargain for the anguish of watching Carmella's pain, or for life lessons from Malcolm "Mookie" Greenbush who teaches them the importance of the trail they leave. While her mother manages to find housing, Georgina makes choices which reveal her growth in maturity.

The Hundred Dresses

Eleanor Estes

Illustrated by: Louis Slobodkin

Orlando, FL: Harcourt, 2006, ©1944

Grade Level: 4-7

Pages: 80

Themes: Inclusion or Exclusion, Empathy,
    Bullying

Other: Audio, Video

Wanda Petronski lives on the other side of town and is shunned by Maddie and Peggy. Too late, they appreciate Wanda's giftedness.

I Hadn't Meant to Tell You This

Jacqueline Woodson

New York: G. P. Putnam's Sons, 2006, ©1994

Grade Level: 7+

Pages: 114

Themes: Coping, Friendship, Hurtful Words,
    Prejudice

Other: Audio

Marie, an African American from Chauncey, OH, was 10 when her mother left Marie and her dad. When Elena "Lena" Cecelia Bright (whose mother had died) joins the eighth grade and Marie's old friend Sherry calls Lena "white trash," Marie stands by Lena and the two become close friends. Lena reveals her dad's sexual abuse and begs Marie not to call for help lest Lena and her sister Dion be sent to separate foster homes. Because of her friendship with Lena, Marie grows in acceptance and understanding of her own mother's departure.

I Hate Books!

Kate Walker

Illustrated by: David Cox

Chicago: Cricket Books, 2007, ©1995

Grade Level: 2-5

Pages: 79

Themes: Accepting Limitations and Gifts,
    Overcoming Obstacles

Hamish's gift as a storyteller hides his inability to read. In 3rd grade, when he is sent to Mr. Robinson for remediation, Hamish loses his confidence and decides he is "dumb." After his family convinces him that reading is a necessary skill, Hamish becomes motivated and his brother Nathan uses Hamish's own stories to help him finally learn to read.

Ida B... and Her Plans to Maximize Fun, Avoid Disaster, and (Possibly) Save the World

Katherine Hannigan

New York: HarperTrophy, 2007, ©2004
  Paw Prints, 2008, ©2004
Grade Level: 4-6
Pages: 246
Themes: Anger, Coping, Apologizing or
  Forgiving
Other: Audio
When Ida B Applewood's mother gets cancer, the family needs to sell some farmland, including Ida B's favorite trees, and Ida B has to leave home schooling to attend 4th grade at Ernest B. Lawson Elementary School. Feeling betrayed by her parents, Ida B withdraws and acts mean until the wisdom and understanding of others, especially her teacher Ms. Washington, helps Ida B live again.

Icy Sparks

Gwyn Hyman Rubio

New York: Penguin, 2001, ©1998
Findaway World LLC, 2006, ©1998
Grade Level: 7-12
Pages: 308
Themes: Empathy, Respect for Elderly or
  Disabled
Other: Audio
Icy Sparks has Tourette Syndrome, but it is not diagnosed until she is an adult. Mature Language.

If the Shoe Fits

Gary Soto

Illustrated by: Terry Widener
New York: Putnam, ©2002
Grade Level: 1-3
Pages: 32
Themes: Hurtful Words, Peer Pressure
When Rigo, who usually gets hand-me-downs, receives a brand new pair of shoes, he is thrilled, until Angel mocks them.

If the Shoe Fits: Voices from Cinderella

Laura Whipple

Illustrated by: Laura Beingessner
New York: Margaret K. McElderry, ©2002
Grade Level: 3-6
Pages: 67
Themes: Point of View
A series of poems tells the Cinderella story from the different characters' points of view.

I'm Somebody Too

Jeanne Gehret

Fairport, NY: Verbal Image Press, 1996, ©1992
Grade Level: 4-7
Pages: 159
Themes: Jealousy, Respect for Elderly or
  Disabled
Emily feels left out when her brother is diagnosed with ADHD.

I'm Sorry, Almira Ann

Jane Kurtz

Illustrated by: Susan Havice
Westport, CT: Libraries Unlimited, 2007,
  ©1999
New York: Scholastic, 2001
Grade Level: 2-4
Pages: 120
Themes: Jealousy, Apologizing or Forgiving
As they follow the Oregon Trail, Sarah Benton, in her jealousy, hurts her best friend Almira.

An Inconvenient Truth: The Crisis of Global Warming

Al Gore, adapted by Jane O'Connor
New York: Viking, ©2007
Grade Level: 5-8
Pages: 191
Themes: Community Building, Community in Action, Problem Solving
Other: Audio, Video

Al Gore's persuasive explanation of the urgency with which we need to confront climate change is made accessible for younger readers. *An Inconvenient Truth: The Planetary Emergency of Global Warming and What We Can Do About It* (2008, ©2006) has been reduced from 327 pages and adapted for middle school students. The new edition is divided into chapters, contains an index, and has a simpler layout with easier-to-read text. Some of the historical and political background has been removed. What remains is the essence of the original.

Indian Shoes

Cynthia Leitich Smith
Illustrated by: Jim Madsen
New York: HarperCollins, ©2002
Grade Level: 3-5
Pages: 66
Themes: Accepting Limitations and Gifts, Diversity of Cultures

Ray Halfmoon, Seminole-Cherokee, whose parents died in a tornado when he was a boy, now lives with his grandfather in Chicago. A series of stories relates the warm relationship between Ray and Grampa, a blending of their Native American and modern ways.

Indigo's Star

Hilary McKay
New York: Aladdin, 2006, ©2003
Grade Level: 5-8
Pages: 265
Themes: Friendship, Diversity of Individuals, Bullying
Other: Audio

Twelve-year-old Indigo Casson gets the support of his sisters Saffy and Rose when he and Tom Levin are bullied. Indigo and Tom form a friendship that will probably survive Tom's return to the U.S. after his year in England. (This is a companion book to *Saffy's Angel* (2006, ©2003) and *Permanent Rose* (2006, ©2005).)

The Invisible Rules of Zoe Lama

Tish Cohen
New York: Dutton Children's Books, ©2007
Grade Level: 4-7
Pages: 247
Themes: Diversity of Individuals, Friendship, Respect for Elderly or Disabled, Rumors or Suspicion

In this zany story, Zoë Monday Costello, 7th grader, has been called Zoë Lama since she met with Patrick "The Raptor" Hammens and helped calm him down. On the day when her peers no longer seek her advice or respect her unwritten rules, Zoë pursues her priorities: trying to care for her grandmother at home in spite of advancing Alzheimer's, and being a loyal friend even though it might destroy her reputation. In the end, she learns that Grandma's life is better in Shady Gardens, and she finds her friends rallying around her. Zoë decides that people should be allowed to be themselves rather than having to follow her unwritten rules.

Isabel and the Miracle Baby

Emily Smith Pearce

Honesdale, PA: Front Street of Boyds Mills
    Press, ©2007
Grade Level: 3-5
Pages: 125
Themes: Coping, Emotions, Inclusion or
    Exclusion, Peer Pressure

Eight-year-old Isabel Graham finds life very difficult. She worries about her mother's cancer; her four-month-old sister Rebekah, considered a miracle baby, gets most of the attention; and Isabel's classmates, especially Alicia, exclude her. Isabel's anger grows, climaxing in a fight at school that eventually leads to a new understanding between Isabel and her parents.

It's Test Day, Tiger Turcotte

Pansie Hart Flood

Illustrated by: Amy Wummer
Minneapolis: Carolrhoda Books, ©2004
Grade Level: 2-4
Pages: 72
Themes: Diversity of Cultures

In giving background information for a test, 7-year-old Tiger Turcotte does not know how to fill out the entry for race. Tiger does not want to label himself "Other" because his father is black and Meherrin Indian, and his mother is from Costa Rica. Tiger's father uses ice cream flavors to talk about diversity. The next day the class uses an updated test form which has "Multiracial" as a choice.

Izzy's Place

Marc Kornblatt

New York: Margaret K. McElderry, ©2003
Grade Level: 4-6
Pages: 118
Themes: Anger, Coping

While staying with his Grandma Martha the summer before 5th grade, Henry Stone learns to be at peace with his Grandpa Jay's death and the possibility of his parents' divorce.

The Jacket

Andrew Clements

Illustrated by: McDavid Henderson
New York: Aladdin, 2003, ©2002
Grade Level: 4-7
Pages: 89
Themes: Empathy, Prejudice or Dislike,
    Stereotypes
Other: Audio

Sixth-grader Philip discovers his own prejudice when he mistakenly accuses Daniel of having stolen the jacket of Philip's brother Jimmy.

Jackson Jones and Mission Greentop

Mary Quattlebaum

New York: Delacorte, ©2004
    Paw Prints, 2008, ©2004
Grade Level: 3-5
Pages: 101
Themes: Community in Action, Bullying,
    Responsible Decision Making

Fifth-grader Jackson Jones takes effective action to protect a 60-year-old community garden. He also deals well with Howard "Blood Green" who bullies Jackson.

Jacob Have I Loved

Katherine Paterson

New York: HarperTrophy, 2004, ©1981
Fitzgerald Books, 2007, ©1981
Grade Level: 5-9
Pages: 175
Themes: Accepting Limitations and Gifts,
    Anger, Jealousy
Other: Audio, Video

In 1941 Sara Louise "Wheeze" Bradshaw feels she has lived all her life in the shadow of her younger twin sister Caroline who is gifted with the best voice in Maryland. Through adolescence, Sara Louise thinks her family is forcing her to live on Rass, the Chesapeake island where she grew up. At last she becomes a midwife in Kentucky and gains new perspective on her life as a twin.

Jake Drake, Bully Buster

Andrew Clements

Illustrated by: Amanda Harvey
New York: Aladdin, 2007, ©2001
Grade Level: 2-5
Pages: 73
Themes: Bullying
Other: Audio

Fourth-grader Jake tells how he managed to understand and disarm Link Baxter when they were in 2nd grade.

Jakeman

Deborah Ellis

Illustrated by:
Brighton, MA: Fitzhenry & Whiteside, 2008
     ©2007
Grade Level: 4-7
Pages: 201
Themes: Coping, Cooperation, Discrimination,
     Stereotypes

Jacob "Jake" Tyronne DeShawn, 11, and his sister Shashona, 16, have been in a series of foster homes since their mother Shanice was incarcerated for possession of cocaine. Jake has learned to cope through his regular letters petitioning the governor to pardon their mother, and journaling a comic book which features Jakeman the Barbed Wire Boy who grows barbed wire on his skin when under attack. The novel shifts gears when Jake, Shashona, and others are taken ten hours from New York City to the upstate Wickham Penitentiary for Mother's Day. On the return trip, with their social workers hospitalized for food poisoning and the driver intoxicated, the youngsters take over the bus and end up meeting the governor. Although they return without hope of pardons, they each gain increased self-confidence in their own abilities.

Joey Pigza Swallowed the Key

Jack Gantos

New York: HarperTrophy, 2002, ©1998
     Paw Prints, 2008, ©1998
Grade Level: 4-8
Pages: 153
Themes: Empathy, Respect for Elderly or
     Disabled
Other: Audio

Joey is a good kid who is unable to control his behavior and is medicated sporadically and unsuccessfully for attention deficit disorder. Reactions to his behavior range from frustration to bullying. (*Joey Pigza Loses Control* (2002, ©2002) is a sequel.)

Joshua T. Bates Takes Charge

Susan Shreve

Illustrated by: Dan Andreasen
New York: Dell Yearling, 2000, ©1993
Grade Level: 3-6
Pages: 102
Themes: Fear or Worry, Bullying, Nonviolent
     Response
Other: Audio

In 4th grade Joshua Bates was so afraid of Tommy Wilhelm that he took a knife to school. Now Joshua is in 5th grade and the bullying has gotten worse, especially toward Sean O'Malley. Finally, Joshua rescues Sean and lets the adults know what is going on. (Two previous books, *The Flunking of Joshua T. Bates* (New York: Dell Yearling, 2000, ©1984) and *Joshua T. Bates in Trouble Again* (New York: Knopf, 1999, ©1997), cover Joshua's 3rd and 4th grades.)

The Jumping Tree

Rene Saldana, Jr.

New York: Random House, 2002, ©2001
Grade Level: 5-9
Pages: 181
Themes: Gender Roles

Rey Castaneda lives in a Texas border town. During his 6th through 8th grade years, Rey observes his friends, uncles, and most importantly, his father to see what it means to be a man. After watching his dad endure an insult without retaliating and weep when Roy's uncle dies, Roy realizes that there is more to being a man than acting tough.

Junebug and the Reverend

Alice Mead

New York: Dell Yearling, 2000, ©1998
Grade Level: 3-6
Pages: 185
Themes: Bullying, Responsible Decision
   Making
Other: Audio

In this sequel to *Junebug* (Bantam, 1997, ©1995) Reeve "Junebug" McClain, Jr., whose mother has divorced his father who is in prison, adjusts to a new home and school, where he is bullied. He learns the lessons of tai-chi and becomes a leader.

Junie B., First Grader Cheater Pants

Barbara Park

Illustrated by: Denise Brunkus
New York: Scholastic, 2004, ©2003
   London: Fitzgerald Books, 2007
Grade Level: 1-4
Pages: 86
Themes: Honesty, Responsible Decision
   Making
Other: Audio

Junie learns that copying May's homework gets her into trouble, and looking at Herb's spelling test leaves both her and Herb feeling terrible. (*Junie B. Jones is Not a Crook* (New York: Random House, 1997) also deals with honesty.)

Kickoff!

Tiki and Ronde Barber with Paul Mantell

New York: Simon & Schuster Books for Young
   Readers, ©2007
Grade Level: 4-6
Pages: 156
Themes: Community in Action, Cooperation,
   Overcoming Obstacles

Tiki and Ronde Barber, who later played for the New York Giants and the Tampa Bay Buccaneers, tell the story of their seventh grade when they began as third-string players for the Hidden Valley Eagles football team. As they learned the lessons of teamwork, they supported their mother Geraldine and Mrs. Pendergast, a neighbor, in a successful campaign to prevent the building of a factory that would pollute their air and water. A Glossary of Football Terms is included.

The Kids' Guide to Working Out Conflicts: How to Keep Cool, Stay Safe, and Get Along

Naomi Drew

Minneapolis: Free Spirit, ©2004
Grade Level: 6-10
Pages: 146
Themes: Recognizing Emotions, Bullying, Win-
   Win Solutions

This resource book has activities, discussions, surveys, and skits. It addresses a range of topics, including Listening, Managing Anger and Stress, Bullying, Conflict Solving, and Win-Win.

King of the Lost and Found

John Lekich

Vancouver, BC: Raincoast Books, ©2007
  Paw Prints, 2008, ©2007
Grade Level: 6-10
Pages: 308
Themes: Honesty, Inclusion or Exclusion
Raymond Jerome Dunne, grade 10, is prone to sneezing, nosebleeds, and fainting without warning. Not expecting to be popular through sports, Raymond creates a niche for himself in the Lost and Found room, which turns out to be the entrance to a hidden section of the school. Jack Alexander, a popular grade 12 student, enlists Raymond's help in creating a secret undercover club. While it lasts, the popular students and those on the fringe begin to know each other. When the "club" comes to an end, Raymond, Jack, and others move on with some positive changes in their lives.

Kira-Kira

Cynthia Kadohata

New York: Aladdin, 2006, ©2004
  Paw Prints, 2008, ©2004
Grade Level: 6-8
Pages: 244
Themes: Community Building, Coping,
  Discrimination
Other: Audio
Eleven-year-old Katie Takeshima tells the story of her sister Lynn, four years older than Katie, who died of lymphoma. The Japanese-American family encounters discrimination in the 1950s as they move from Iowa to Georgia, trying to make a living in a chicken factory.

The Kite Fighters

Linda Sue Park

Decorations by: Eung Won Park
New York: Dell Yearling, 2002, ©2000
  Paw Prints, 2008, ©2000
Grade Level: 4-7
Pages: 136
Themes: Honesty, Diversity of Cultures,
  Respect in General
Other: Audio
In 1473 Seoul, Korea Young-sup learns to use his gift for kite-flying and to respect his older brother Kee-sup, as they represent their young king in the New Year's Kite Festival.

The Last Holiday Concert

Andrew Clements

Detroit: Thorndike Press, 2007, ©2004
  Paw Prints, 2008, ©2004
Grade Level: 4-7
Pages: 166
Themes: Peacemaking, Peer Pressure,
  Responsible Decision Making
Other: Audio
Hart Evans is elected director of the Winter Concert when Mr. Meinert learns his job will be cut in January and gives up on the 6th-grade chorus. Hart learns leadership skills and finds help from Mr. Meinert, who is learning much about student motivation, as the 6th graders create "Winterhope," a moving concert about peace.

Laugh Till You Cry

Joan Lowery Nixon

New York: Yearling, 2006, ©2004
Grade Level: 4-7
Pages: 99
Themes: Bullying, Nonviolent Response
When Cody Carter and his mother move to Texas to take care of his grandmother, Cody's cousin Hayden bullies him. Using humor and quick thinking, Cory brings things to a satisfying conclusion.

Lefty Carmichael Has a Fit

Jon Trembath

Victoria, BC: Orca, 2000, ©1999
Grade Level: 8-12
Pages: 215
Themes: Overcoming Obstacles, Respect for
    Elderly or Disabled
Lefty Carmichael is an inner-city 15 year old
who has just been diagnosed with epilepsy. He
struggles with the disease.

Lenny's Space

Kate Banks

New York: Frances Foster Books, ©2007
Grade Level: 3-6
Pages: 152
Themes: Emotions, Friendship, Responsible
    Decision Making
Before he met Muriel, a counselor, 9-year-old
Lenny Brewster had become accustomed to
others avoiding him because of his unpredictable
behavior. Muriel helps Lenny use breathing to
help control his behavior, and she accompanies
him as he makes his first friend, Vander James,
and then loses Van to leukemia.

Let the Circle Be Unbroken

Mildred B. Taylor

New York: Puffin Books, 1995, ©1981
Grade Level: 5-9
Pages: 394
Themes: Community in Action, Discrimination,
    Nonviolent Response
Other: Audio
In this sequel to *Roll of Thunder, Hear My Cry*,
5th-grader Cassie Logan learns the harsh realities
of civil and social discrimination, including the
blatantly unfair trial and execution of Stacey's
friend T.J. Avery, the intolerance toward Cousin
Bud Rankin who had married a white woman,
the ruthless treatment Stacey meets in some
cane fields, and the unjust refusal to let Mrs. Lee
Annie Lees vote even though she could pass
the test. (See separate entries for *The Well* and
Roll of Thunder, Hear My Cry.)

The Liberation of Gabriel King

K. L. Going

New York: Scholastic, 2008, ©2005
Grade Level: 4-7
Pages: 151
Themes: Fear or Worry, Community in Action,
    Prejudice or Dislike, Nonviolent Response
Other: Audio
During the summer of 1976 Gabriel King's best
friend Frita Wilson helps him overcome his
worst fears. Most of all, Gabe is afraid of starting
5th grade, because Duke Evans and Frankie
Carmen will be in the same school. After Duke's
dad threatens Frita because she is black, both
Gabe and Frita enlist the help of their parents.
They learn important lessons about overcoming
fear and prejudice, and finding courage when
you are supported by people who love you.

Lizard Meets Ivana the Terrible

C. Anne Scott

Illustrated by: Stephanie Roth
New York: Scholastic, 2001, ©1999
Grade Level: 2-4
Pages: 117
Themes: Friendship, Assertiveness
Lizzie Gardener, 3rd grader, has moved from
Florida to Texas and, despite her fears, gets
new friends. She observes the sometimes
mean interactions among her classmates,
becomes friends with Ivana Romanov who can
be formidable, and even finds the courage to
defend Ivana.

Lizzie Bright and the Buckminster Boy

Gary D. Schmidt

New York: Laurel-Leaf Books, 2008, ©2004
Grade Level: 6-9
Pages: 219
Themes: Friendship, Discrimination, Diversity
    of Cultures, Bullying, Nonviolent Response
Other: Audio

Around 1910 in Maine, Turner Buckminster III, in his early teens, is lonely as he and his parents arrive for his father's call to minister in Phippsburg's First Congregational church. Turner finds a friend in Lizzie Bright Griffin, an African American girl from Malaga Island. The two befriend Mrs. Cobb. Turner is bullied by Willis Hurd but later befriends him. Turner's friendship with Lizzie is painful because of the way the townspeople evict her people in order to develop the island for tourism. Out of tragedy, Turner learns the beauty of relationships and the pain of human loss.

Lizzie Logan Wears Purple Sunglasses

Eileen Spinelli

Illustrated by: Melanie Hope Greenberg
New York: Aladdin, 1998, ©1995
Grade Level: 3-5
Pages: 95
Themes: Friendship, Diversity of Individuals

Although 3rd-grader Heather Wade cannot imagine being friends with bossy Lizzie, both girls grow through their unusual friendship.

Loser

Jerry Spinelli

New York: HarperCollins, 2008, ©2002
Grade Level: 4-6
Pages: 218
Themes: Empathy, Hurtful Words
Other: Audio

Donald Zinkoff is totally trusting and naïve, even when other kids pick on him. In the end he shows his faithfulness to young Claudia, and has hope of a new friendship.

Losers, Inc.

Claudia Mills

New York: Scholastic, 1999, ©1997
Grade Level: 4-6
Pages: 149
Themes: Inclusion or Exclusion, Accepting
    Limitations and Gifts, Diversity of
    Individuals
Other: Audio

After Ethan Winfield and his friend Julien form a Losers' Club, Ethan realizes they do not have to be losers.

Love that Dog

Sharon Creech

New York: HarperTrophy, 2008, ©2001
Grade Level: 4-7
Pages: 86
Themes: Recognizing Emotions
Other: Audio

At first Jack doesn't want to write poetry for his teacher because he thinks that it's something only girls write. Eventually, he finds his voice as a poet, and writes about his love for his dog and the grief he experiences after the dog's death.

Lucy Rose: Working Myself to Pieces and Bits

Katy Kelly

Illustrated by: Peter Ferguson

New York: Delacourt Press, ©2007

Grade Level: 3-5

Pages: 196

Themes: Community in Action, Hurtful Words, Respect for Elderly or Disabled

Lucy Rose Reilly, a loquacious 4th grader, and her second-best friend Jonique McBee are devoted to some women in a senior home. They are also part of the group helping the McBee family renovate the building where they will have a bakery. Meanwhile, classmate Ashley regularly insults Lucy Rose and publicly teases her about her best friend Adam "Melonhead" Melon. Lucy Rose decides their friendship is more important than the teasing; and she follows the advice of many adults in her life by acknowledging Ashley's sorrow at her parents' impending divorce, deciding to be mature, and not humiliating Ashley. This is a sequel to *Lucy Rose: Here's the Thing About Me* (2006, ©2004).

Macaroni Boy

Katherine Ayres

New York: Random House, 2004, ©2003

Grade Level: 4-7

Pages: 182

Themes: Bullying, Nonviolent Response, Problem Solving

Mike Costa, a 6th grader in 1933 Pittsburgh, and his friend Joseph Ryan stand up to the bullying of Andy Simms. When Andy and Mike's Grandpap have similar poisoning symptoms, Mike finds a way to help both of them.

Make Lemonade

Virginia Euwer Wolff

New York: H. Holt, 2006, ©1993
    Paw Prints, 2008, ©1993

Grade Level: 7-12

Pages: 200

Themes: Overcoming Obstacles, Responsible Decision Making

Other: Audio

Verna LaVaughn, 14, is saving for college in order to find a way out of public housing. So, she begins to baby-sit for 17-year-old Jolly who has 2-year-old Jeremy and baby Jilly. Although the job is frustrating and messy, LaVaughn loves the children and helps Jolly find the way to complete her GED after she is sexually harassed and loses her job. In the end, Jolly's life gains some order and she proves capable of acting under pressure. True Believer (2001) continues LaVaughn's story.

Makeovers by Marcia

Claudia Mills

New York: Farrar, Straus and Giroux, ©2005

Grade Level: 5-8

Pages: 149

Themes: Accepting Limitations and Gifts, Empathy, Respect for Elderly or Disabled

Marcia Faitak does not feel pretty as she enters 8th grade at West Creek Middle School with some extra pounds. Her exercise was curtailed because of a sprained ankle resulting from a prank by Alex Ryan the boy she likes. Through service learning at West Creek Manor, Marcia does makeovers for four women and discovers their inner beauty, which she captures in her portraits of them.

Mallory on Board

Laurie B. Friedman

Illustrated by: Barbara Pollak
Minneapolis: Carolrhoda Books, ©2007
Grade Level: 2-4
Pages: 175
Themes: Jealousy

Mallory McDonald, 9, resists celebrating the wedding of Colleen and Frank, the single parents of her best friends Mary Ann and Joey. Mallory's family is part of the five-day cruise on the "Sea Queen." Everyone is enjoying the trip except Mallory who feels left out when her friends are part of the formation of a new family. In the end, Mallory acknowledges her sorrow that she has found it so difficult to celebrate an event which is changing their friendship, and Mary Ann and Joey give special recognition to Mallory as a best friend of the family. (*Mallory on the Move* (2006, ©2004) involves friendship issues. *Mallory vs. Max* (2006, ©2005) involves Mallory's jealousy when Max's new dog gets too much attention.)

The Man with the Red Bag

Eve Bunting

New York: Johanna Cotler Books, ©2007
Grade Level: 5-8
Pages: 230
Themes: Rumors or Suspicion

While on a 10-day bus tour with his grandmother, 12-year-old Kevin "Kev" Saunders is wary of Charles Stavros, a fellow passenger who seems overly protective of his red Star Tours bag and resembles some of the men who bombed the World Trade Center. Enlisting the help of Geneva Jenson, 13, Kevin tries to apply what he has learned about writing mystery novels. The two are sure that Stavros is carrying a bomb which he will possibly detonate near Mount Rushmore. Their suspicions are laid to rest in a touching ending which reveals that often things are not as they first appear.

Maniac Magee

Jerry Spinelli

Boston: Little Brown, 2004, ©1990
Grade Level: 4-7
Pages: 184
Themes: Empathy, Prejudice or Dislike,
    Diversity of Individuals
Other: Audio, Video

Because he is without family or home, the talented Jeffrey "Maniac" Magee gets to know and understand a diverse group of people who are prejudiced against Maniac and each other—and he finally finds a home.

Martin Bridge Ready for Takeoff!

Jessica Scott Kerrin

Illustrated by: Joseph Kelly
Tonawanda, NY: Kids Can Press, ©2005
    Paw Prints, 2008, ©2005
Grade Level: 2-4
Pages: 120
Themes: Competition, Jealousy, Responsible
    Decision Making

In the first of three short stories, Martin and his friend Stuart decorate the school bus for Jenny, the substitute driver. However, the regular driver Mrs. Phips returns ahead of schedule; she is so pleased that she becomes more friendly to the students. In the second story, Martin cares for a hamster that dies. When the owners ask him to get a substitute so their daughter does not know of the death, Martin has to decide the right thing to do. In the third, Martin gives a rocket-decorating idea to his friend Alex, who gets credit for Martin's design. Martin gets jealous and needs to decide how important their friendship is.

Marvin and the Meanest Girl

Suzy Kline
Illustrated by: Blanche Sims
New York: Puffin Books, 2002, ©2000
Grade Level: 2-4
Pages: 70
Themes: Hurtful Words, Rumors or Suspicion
Other: Audio

Marvin draws several wrong conclusions about his new classmate Lucy Tinker. After he has caused trouble, Marvin discovers that Lucy has not stolen things; moreover, she is mourning her grandmother who recently died. So, he tries to make things right. (In *Marvin and the Mean Words* (1999, ©1997), after Marvin is hurt by his teacher's words he gains insights to the effect of his own words on others.)

The Meanest Girl

Debora Allie
New Milford, CT: Roaring Book Press, ©2005
Grade Level: 4-7
Pages: 120
Themes: Inclusion or Exclusion, Accepting
    Limitations and Gifts

Alyssa Fontana, a Brooklyn 6th grader, learns that life is not always as it appears. Her best friend Chelsea Gardner is so bossy that she is starting a new club, the Mona Lisas, so that she can be in charge. The new girl, Hayden Martin, is mean but others want to include her. Alyssa discovers that her own father left when Alyssa was a baby. She learns that no one's life is perfect, and that we can still find comfort and friendship from each other and from religion. In the end, Alyssa examines her own behavior and feels that she herself is the meanest girl in her group.

Milkweed

Jerry Spinelli
New York: Laurel Leaf Books, 2005, ©2003
Grade Level: 5-12
Pages: 208
Themes: Oppression, Hurtful Words
Other: Audio

An orphan in Nazi Warsaw befriends Janina Millgrom and becomes part of her family in the ghetto. He escapes the concentration camps and ends up in New Jersey. Having been called many names through his life, he finds his identity as grandfather of a little girl named for Janina.

Minnie and Moo: The Case of the Missing Jelly Donut

Denys Cazet
New York: HarperCollins, 2007, ©2005
Grade Level: 1-3
Pages: 45
Themes: Rumors or Suspicion
Other: Audio

When Minnie's jelly donut is gone, she and Moo (yes, two cows) see a blue feather and decide a blue chicken has stolen it.

The Misfits

James Howe
New York: Aladdin, 2003, ©2001
Grade Level: 4-8
Pages: 274
Themes: Inclusion or Exclusion, Diversity of
    Individuals, Gender Roles, Hurtful Words
Other: Audio

Seventh-grader Bobby Goodspeed, narrates the story of how he and his friends, Addison "Addie" Carle, Joe Bunch, and Schuyler "Skeezie" Tookis run for Student Council with the platform that students should not be called names. The group raises awareness, within themselves and within their school, of the deep hurt caused by name-calling as well as the richness of each person that is so much deeper than the names he or she is called. (*Totally Joe* (2005) is an alphabiography (a chapter for each letter of the alphabet), written by Joe during the same year.)

Missing May

Cynthia Rylant
New York: Scholastic. 2005, ©1992
Grade Level: 5-8
Pages: 89
Themes: Community Building, Coping,
    Diversity of Individuals
Other: Audio
May died suddenly and Summer's heart is breaking as she watches Ob grieve over his dear wife. Six year earlier Summer's mother died; Summer was passed among her Ohio aunts and uncles until May and Ob found her and took her back to West Virginia as their own daughter. Now Cletus Underwood, an eccentric character from Summer's school, appears and helps Ob and Summer find peace in a new sense of May's presence.

Molly Gets Mad

Suzy Kline
Illustrated by: Diana Cain Bluthenthal
New York: Putnam, ©2001
Grade Level: 1-3
Pages: 71
Themes: Competition, Anger
Third-grader Molly always wants to be the best and has a hard time when Florence turns out to be a star skater. After Molly hurts her friend in a race, both Morty and Florence help Molly learn to assist in hockey. Morty narrates this story.

Molly the Brave and Me

Jane O'Connor
Illustrated by: Sheila Hamanaka
New York: Random House, 2003, ©1990
Grade Level: 1-3
Pages: 48
Themes: Fear or Worry
Beth admires her 2nd-grade classmate Molly, who seems brave about everything. Then they go to the country and Molly is scared when they get lost in a corn field, but Beth helps them find the way home.

Molly's Pilgrim

Barbara Cohen
Illustrated by: Daniel Mark Duffy
New York: HarperTrophy, 2005, ©1983
Grade Level: K-3
Pages: 32
Themes: Diversity of Cultures
Other: Audio, Video
Molly and her mother fled Jewish persecution in Russia. For class Molly makes a Pilgrim that looks like her own mother. When her classmates make fun of her, Molly explains that her mother is a modern-day Pilgrim. Miss Stickley, Molly's teacher, affirms this and teaches the class that the first Pilgrims actually got their idea for Thanksgiving from the Jewish feast of Tabernacles, Sukkoth.

Morgy Makes His Move

Maggie Lewis
Illustrated by: Michael Chesworth
Boston: Houghton Mifflin, 2002, ©1999
Grade Level: 2-5
Pages: 74
Themes: Bullying
Other: Audio
Morgy MacDougel-MacDuff has moved from California to Puckett Corner, Massachusetts. While Byran Nooney befriends Morgy, Ferguson bullies him, until Morgy gains some confidence. In the end, Morgy feels at home.

The Most Beautiful Place in the World

Ann Cameron
Illustrated by: Thomas B. Allen
New York: Dell Yearling, 2000, ©1988
Grade Level: 2-5
Pages: 57
Themes: Overcoming Obstacles
Seven-year-old Juan's mother moves away, leaving him to live with his grandmother and other relatives in San Pablo, Guatemala. Juan "Pablo" works with his grandmother in the market and teaches himself to read, until his grandmother realizes Juan's age and enrolls him in school where he excels. In spite of all his hardships, Juan sees himself living in the most beautiful place in the world because he loves and is loved.

Mr. Cool

Jacqueline Wilson
Illustrated by: Stephen Lewis
Boston: Kingfisher, 2005, ©1996
Grade Level: 1-3
Pages: 48
Themes: Accepting Limitations and Gifts, Peer
    Pressure
Kevin does not have the singing or dancing talent of Ricky, Micky, or Nicky; nor does he look cool. But, Kevin is an integral part of their band, Mr. Cool.

Multiple Choice

Janet Tashjian
New York: Scholastic, 2001, ©1999
Square Fish, 2008, ©1999
Grade Level: 5-9
Pages: 186
Themes: Accepting Limitations and Gifts
In an effort to be perfect, Monica Devon devises a game that she applies to life. She learns that life cannot be controlled, and it can involve high stakes.

My Dog, Cat

Marty Crisp
Illustrated by: True Kelley
New York: Scholastic, 2002, ©2000
Grade Level: 2-4
Pages: 106
Themes: Accepting Limitations and Gifts,
    Bullying
Fourth grader Abbie Williamson, small for his age, takes care of a small Yorkie. He manages to stand up to Pete Street's bullying.

My Friend the Enemy

J. B. Cheaney
New York: Yearling, 2007, ©2005
Grade Level: 5-8
Pages: 266
Themes: Friendship, Rumors or Suspicion
Hazel Anderson, whose ninth birthday coincided with Pearl Harbor, lives in Oregon where many Japanese people have been interred. Hazel, on the lookout for spies, meets Sogoji, an orphan who is being hidden by neighbors, the Lanskis. Hazel overcomes her suspicions and finds in Sogoji a friend. (In *The Eternal Spring of Mr. Ito* by Sheila Garrigue (New York: Aladdin, 1994, ©1985) a young girl from England becomes friends with a Japanese man who goes into hiding after his family is imprisoned.)

My Mother the Cheerleader

Robert Sharenow
New York: Harperteen, 2009, ©2007
Grade Level: 8-10
Pages: 289
Themes: Discrimination, Point of View, Racism
When Ruby Bridges entered William Frantz Elementary (located in the Ninth Ward of New Orleans) in November, 1960, 13-year-old Louise Collins's mother Pauline was one of the "cheerleaders" who heckled Ruby each morning. Louise narrates the story of a turning point which occurred when a New York reporter, Morgan Miller, stayed at their boarding house and broke open their ways of viewing segregation before becoming the victim of the Ku Klux Klan. [This book contains a rape scene which is integral to the story.]

My Name is María Isabel

Alma Flor Ada

Illustrated by: K. Dyble Thompson
Translated by: Ana M. Cerro
New York: Aladdin, 1996, ©1993
Grade Level: 3-4
Pages: 57
Themes: Assertiveness

Because there are two other Marias in her new class, María Isabel Salazar López is called Mary Lopez by her teacher. María is no longer proud of her name and often does not even know when she has been called on. In the end, María finds her voice, her teacher listens, and María participates in the class.

My Nights at the Improv

Jan Siebold

Morton Grove, IL: Whitman, ©2005
Grade Level: 4-8
Pages: 98
Themes: Recognizing Emotions, Empathy

Eighth-grader Lizzie Marino is having a hard time making friends at her new school. Lizzie's widowed mother refuses to talk about Lizzie's dad, and classmate Vanessa makes fun of her. Then, while Lizzie's mother teaches her weekly Community Education class, Lizzie waits for her in a projection booth, allowing her to eavesdrop on an improvisation class attended by Vanessa. Lizzie learns many life lessons and gains empathy for Vanessa.

Ninjas, Piranhas, and Galileo

Greg Leitich Smith

New York: Little, Brown, ©2003
   Paw Prints, 2008, ©2003
Grade Level: 6-8
Pages: 179
Themes: Cooperation, Honesty, Point of View
Other: Audio

Elias, Shohei, and Honoria from the Peshtigo School in Chicago are best friends who take turns narrating their story. They grow and learn through their experiences: a romantic triangle (Eli-likes-Honoria-likes-Shohei), Shohei's adoptive parents trying too hard to nurture his Japanese roots, and a science project with unpredicted results. [At one point they blackmail a teacher; this could be a drawback, or it could lead to a discussion of better alternatives.]

No Laughter Here

Rita Williams-Garcia

New York: Tempest, 2007, ©2004
Grade Level: 5-9
Pages: 133
Themes: Overcoming Obstacles, Diversity of
   Cultures, Conflict Nature

In the summer before 5th grade, Akilah Hunter's best friend Victoria Ojike returns from Nigeria a changed person. Reluctantly Victoria tells Akilah of her female genital circumcision and swears Akilah to silence. Akilah's mother, a social worker, discovers Victoria's problem and gets help for her. In the end, Akilah helps Victoria plan to contribute her story to a website on female genital mutilation (FMG).

No More Dead Dogs

Gordon Korman

New York: Hyperion, 2002, ©2000
   Paw Prints, 2008, ©2000
Grade Level: 5-8
Pages: 180
Themes: Honesty, Point of View, Stereotypes
Other: Audio

Wallace Wallace's compulsive honesty does not allow him to write a favorable review of "Old Shep, My Pal." So, the 8th-grade football star gets a long-term detention to be served with the Drama Club, practicing for the Old Shep play. Wallace's creative suggestions are taken seriously, the play becomes a hit, and Wallace learns to admire the hard work of the drama students, especially their outspoken president, Rachel Turner.

No Talking

Andrew Clements

Illustrated by: Mark Elliott
New York: Scholastic, 2008, ©2007
Grade Level: 3-6
Pages: 146
Themes: Competition, Gender Roles
Other: Audio

The 5th graders of Laketon Elementary, known as "the Unshushables," love to talk. When Dave Packer decides to imitate Gandhi who was silent a day a week, his experiment spreads to a two-day boy-girl contest to see which group says the fewest illegal words. Dave and Lynsey Burgess lead their teams in a contest that leaves both students and teachers more appreciative of words.

Nory Ryan's Song

Patricia Reilly Giff

New York: Dell Yearling, 2008, ©2000
Grade Level: 5-8
Pages: 148
Themes: Overcoming Obstacles, Responsible
   Decision Making
Other: Audio

During the Irish Potato Famine in 1845, 12-year-old Nory cares for her family and for Anna, an old lady who teaches herbal remedies to Nory. In the end, Nory prepares to join the rest of her family in the United States.

Not-So-Perfect Rosie

Patricia Reilly Giff

Illustrated by: Julie Durrell
New York: Puffin Books, 1998, ©1997
Grade Level: 2-4
Pages: 73
Themes: Accepting Limitations and Gifts,
   Cooperation, Competition

Rosie tries to produce the perfect ballet. She learns to work with 14-year-old Julie instead of against her. They both help awkward Stephanie take the lead. Book #4 of the Ballet Slippers Series.

Notes from the Midnight Driver

Jordan Sonnenblick

New York: Scholastic Press, 2007, ©2006
   Paw Prints, 2008, ©2006
Grade Level: 8+
Pages: 265
Themes: Anger, Cooperation, Point of
   View, Respect for Elderly or Disabled,
   Responsible Decision Making

Alex Peter Gregory, 16, angry at his parents who are getting divorced, drives drunk and crashes his mother's car. Although Alex's goal was crashing into his father's house, he lands in someone else's yard and decapitates a lawn gnome. His community service involves time with Solomon "Sol" Lewis, an elderly man who is as colorful as Alex. From a love-hate relationship, the two become friends, enrich each other, and affect the community around them. Among other lessons, Alex learns about second chances and begins to see his parents differently. (*Zen and the Art of Faking it* (©2007) involves another teen who has issues with anger and honesty. *The Losers' Club* by John Lekich (London: Macmillan Children's, 2004, ©2002) features a group of sophomores who challenge the limits of stereotypes.)

Nothing's Fair in Fifth Grade

Barthe DeClements
New York: Puffin Books, 2008, ©1981
Grade Level: 4-7
Pages: 137
Themes: Empathy, Stereotypes, Hurtful Words
Other: Audio
As Jenny gets to know Elsie Edwards, she learns that Elsie is more than a fat girl who steals. Their classmates, who are mean to Elsie in the beginning, end up supporting her so she can stay at their school.

Oh No, It's Robert

Barbara Seuling
Illustrated by: Paul Brewer
New York: Scholastic, 2001, ©1999
Grade Level: 2-3
Pages: 118
Themes: Friendship, Empathy, Bullying
Robert Dorfman struggles with reading and math but excels in caring about others and working hard. He and his best friend Paul Felcher survive some tests to their friendship. Robert's attention to Lester, who had bullied him, helps Lester achieve and be a friend.

Old People, Frogs, and Albert

Nancy Hope Wilson
Illustrated by: Marcy D. Ramsey
New York: Farrar, Straus and Giroux, 1999, ©1997
Grade Level: 2-4
Pages: 58
Themes: Respect for Elderly or Disabled
Fourth-grader Albert learns to read when his friend Mr. Spear tutors him, using a book on frogs. Albert is afraid of the people in the nursing home until Mr. Spear moves there.

Olive's Ocean

Kevin Henkes
New York: HarperTrophy, 2005, ©2003
Grade Level: 5-8
Pages: 217
Themes: Inclusion or Exclusion, Empathy
Other: Audio
Twelve-year-old Martha Boyle learns that Olive Barstow, a lonely classmate recently killed in an accident, wanted to be a writer, to see an ocean, and to be Martha's friend. During the summer at her grandmother "Godbee" Boyle's Cape Cod home, Martha, who also wants to write, thinks about Olive and wishes she had been Olive's friend.

Oliver and Albert, Friends Forever

Jean Van Leeuwen
Illustrated by: Ann Schweninger
New York: Puffin Books, 2002, ©2000
    Paw Prints, 2008, ©2000
Grade Level: P-2
Pages: 48
Themes: Friendship
Other: Audio
Two young pigs are best friends who enjoy sports and insect hunting together, even though Albert is more studious and Oliver is a better athlete and they have an occasional conflict.

On My Honor

Marion Dane Bauer
New York: Yearling, 1997, ©1986
Grade Level: 4-6
Pages: 90
Themes: Peer Pressure, Responsible Decision Making
Other: Audio
Joel learns to deal with consequences when his best friend Tony drowns as a result of a tragically poor choice.

One-Handed Catch

M. J. Auch

New York: Henry Holt, ©2006
Findaway World LLC, 2008, ©2006
Grade Level: 4-6
Pages: 248
Themes: Friendship, Overcoming Obstacles
Other: Audio

During the summer before 6th grade, Norm Schmidt loses his left hand in a meat-grinder accident. Norm learns to develop his artistic talent and to become an outstanding baseball player. Set during World War II, this story was inspired by the experience of the author's husband.

Our Kansas Home, Book Three of the Prairie Skies Series

Deborah Hopkinson

Illustrated by: Patrick Faricy
New York: Aladdin, ©2003
    Paw Prints, 2008, ©2003
Grade Level: 2-4
Pages: 69
Themes: Community in Action, Oppression

During the summer of 1856, Charlie Keller and his family hide Lizzie, a runaway slave, until she can safely go to Canada. In Books One and Two, *Pioneer Summer* (2007, ©2002) and *Cabin in the Snow* (2007, ©2002), the Keller family travels from Massachusetts in order to vote against slavery for the new state of Kansas.

Our Sixth-Grade Sugar Babies

Eve Bunting

New York: HarperTrophy, 1993, ©1990
Grade Level: 4-7
Pages: 147
Themes: Friendship, Respect for Elderly or
    Disabled, Responsible Decision Making
Other: Audio

Vicki Charlip learns the importance of responsibility when she tries to take care of a five-pound bag of sugar as if it were a real baby. She also learns that her classmate Harry Hogan is a better friend than the new boy across the street, and that she really cares about Mr. Ambrose who has dementia.

Our Stories, Our Songs:
African Children Talk About AIDS

Deborah Ellis

Allston, MA: Fitzhenry & Whiteside, 2006,
    ©2005
Grade Level: 6-12
Pages: 104
Themes: Recognizing Emotions, Coping,
    Community in Action

Over fifty children from Zambia and Malawi, ages seven to 19, and some of their caregivers are interviewed. They tell how they have coped with AIDS in their lives. They share their wisdom, hopes, dreams, and fears, and they describe local organizations that give them hope. Facts on poverty and AIDS and resources are included.

Out of the Dust

Karen Hesse
New York: Scholastic, 2005, ©1997
Grade Level: 5-10
Pages: 227
Themes: Accepting Limitations and Gifts,
    Overcoming Obstacles, Apologizing or
    Forgiving
Other: Audio

Billie Jo Kelby, 14, writes in free verse of her experiences during 1934 and 1935 in the Oklahoma dust bowl. Billie Jo suffers deeply when she loses her mother and newborn brother and when she is burned because her father left kerosene near a fire. Yet she manages to heal and return to the piano playing that gives her joy. She finally forgives her father and learns that her real home is where she has grown up. She expresses gratitude for all that has made her who she is.

The Outsiders

S. E. Hinton
New York: Viking, 2007, ©1967
Grade Level: 5-12
Pages: 180
Themes: Anger, Conflict Escalator, Fear or
    Worry, Stereotypes
Other: Audio, Video

Fourteen-year-old Ponyboy Curtis and his older brothers Sodapop, 16, and Darry, 20, live by themselves since their parents' fatal accident. As an East-Side "Greaser," Ponyboy gets beat up by some West-Side Socials "Socs," which begins a series of conflicts that results in three deaths during the span of a week. In the meantime, Ponyboy gets acquainted with Sherry "Cherry" Valance from the West Side. Both discover that people from the other side of town do not fit stereotypes, and they painfully learn the futility of violence.

Owen Foote, Mighty Scientist

Stephanie Greene
Illustrated by: Cat Bowman Smith
New York: Clarion, 2006, ©2004
Grade Level: 2-4
Pages: 90
Themes: Cooperation, Honesty

When Owen and Joseph's tadpole experiment backfires, they learn the importance of being honest with each other throughout the project.

Pay Attention, Slosh!

Mark Smith
Illustrated by: Gail Piazza
Morton Grove, IL: Whitman, ©1997
Grade Level: 2-3
Pages: 54
Themes: Respect for Elderly or Disabled,
    Hurtful Words

When Josh and his parents discover that he has ADHD, a sticker plan and then medicine help Josh focus. Eventually, his classmate Alex, who had previously called Josh "Slosh," defends Josh against that hated nickname.

Pearl and Wagner: Two Good Friends

Kate McMullan
Illustrated by: R. W. Alley
New York: Dial, ©2003
Grade Level: K-3
Pages: 48
Themes: Cooperation, Friendship, Conflict
    Nature

Pearl, a rabbit, and Wagner, a mouse, cooperate in making a science project. Then they have a conflict when Wagner tells Pearl he does not like her new shoes.

Perfect

Natasha Friend

New York: Scholastic, 2006, ©2004
Grade Level: 6-9
Pages: 172
Themes: Recognizing Emotions, Responsible
    Decision Making
Other: Audio

Thirteen-year-old Isabelle Lee began bingeing and purging when her dad died. Now, in an eating disorder group, Isabelle is shocked to see her 8th-grade classmate Ashley Barnum, who seems perfect in every way. For the first time since her dad's death two years ago, Isabelle becomes able to talk about him with her sister April and their mother. Also, after becoming friends with Ashley, Isabelle gets insight into how harmful her own behavior is, and, with the help of her group counselor Trish, begins to make progress with her addiction.

Petey

Ben Mikaelsen

New York: Hyperion, 2000, ©1998
    Paw Prints, 2008, ©1998
Grade Level: 7-12
Pages: 280
Themes: Friendship, Respect for Elderly or
    Disabled, Nonviolent Response
Other: Audio

Petey Corbin was born with cerebral palsy in 1920, a time when such a condition was misunderstood. At age two he was placed in an insane asylum and lived in institutions all his life. Occasionally a caregiver would recognize his intelligence and spend time with him and eventually leave. When Petey was 12 years old, nine-year-old Calvin Anders who was mildly retarded came into the ward and eventually helped Petey develop his own language. The best friends were parted in 1977 when Calvin was transferred. Then, in 1990, Trevor Ladd protected Petey from some bullying and the two became friends until Petey's death, a year and some months later. This is based on the author's 13-year friendship with Clyde Cothern.

Pieces of Georgia

Jennifer Bryant

New York: Yearling, 2007, ©2006
Grade Level: 5+
Pages: 166
Themes: Emotions, Friendship, Diversity of
    Individuals

Thanks to the journal given to her by her counselor, 13-year-old Georgia McCoy renews her memories of her deceased mother and is able to discuss her grieving father and her friend Tiffany, who is using uppers to keep up with parental demands. As the year unfolds, Georgia develops her gift of art, finds a new relationship with her father, and supports Tiffany in a new stage of life.

Pickle Puss

Patricia Reilly Giff

Illustrated by: Blanche Sims
New York: Young Lions, 1988, ©1986
Grade Level: 1-4
Pages: 69
Themes: Sharing, Honesty
Other: Audio

Emily Arrow tries to win the reading contest so she can have the cat that she and Dawn Bosco found. Instead she teaches her sister Stacy to write her name and tells the truth about her reading score.

The Pigman

Paul Zindel

New York: HarperTrophy, 2005, ©1968
Grade Level: 5-9
Pages: 158
Themes: Empathy, Respect for Elderly or
    Disabled, Peer Pressure, Responsible
    Decision Making
Other: Audio

Lorraine Jensen and John Conlan meet Angelo Pignati in a random prank phone call. The two high school sophomores brighten the life of the lonely old man whom they call the Pigman because of his collection of ceramic pigs, and Mr. Pignati is a caring adult in the lives of the two teenagers. When Mr. Pignati is hospitalized after a heart attack, he gives his house key to Lorraine and John; they have a party that gets out of control and that seems like a betrayal of trust to Mr. Pignati. Days later he has another heart attack and dies when all three are together. Through Mr. Pignati's friendship, Lorraine and John, who had blamed their families for some of their problems, grow to accept responsibility for their own lives. They write their story in alternating chapters.

Pinky and Rex and the Bully

James Howe

Illustrated by: Melissa Sweet
New York: Aladdin, 2006, ©1996
Grade Level: 1-3
Pages: 40
Themes: Gender Roles, Bullying
Other: Audio

Pinky learns to be true to himself, after he gets support from Mrs. Morgan and his friend Rex in standing up to Kevin's bullying. (In *Pinky and Rex and the Spelling Bee* (2006, ©1991), Rex supports Pinky in an embarrassing situation.)

The Power of One: Daisy Bates and the Little Rock Nine

Judith Bloom Fradin and Dennis Brindell Fradin

New York: Clarion, ©2004
Grade Level: 6-9
Pages: 178
Themes: Overcoming Obstacles,
    Discrimination, Conflict Escalator

The life of Daisy Lee Gatson Bates (circa 1913–1999) is told: her childhood in Huttig, Arkansas, when her mother was killed and her father fled for safety; her adoption by a loving couple; early experiences of racism; marriage to journalist L. C. Bates; Presidency of the Arkansas NAACP; mentoring the Little Rock Nine who, in 1957, were the first black students to attend a white school in Arkansas; and her later years when she continued to work for civil rights. The threats, harassment, and danger endured by Daisy, L. C., and the students are described in vivid detail, as are their courage and fears.

Preacher's Boy

Katherine Paterson

New York: HarperTrophy, ©1999
    Paw Prints, 2008, ©1999
London: Fitzgerald Books, 2007, ©1999
Oxford University Press, 2003, ©1999
Grade Level: 5-8
Pages: 186
Themes: Honesty, Respect for Elderly or
    Disabled, Responsible Decision Making
Other: Audio

The year is 1899 and Robbie Hewitt's father is the Congregational minister in Leonardstown, VT. Robbie has to defend his retarded brother Elliot from bullying and he is dealing with his own doubts about faith and God. Robbie's concern for himself and for Violet Finch and her alcoholic father, as well as Robbie's claim of being kidnapped lead him to a painful lesson on honesty.

A Pride of African Tales

Donna L. Washington

Illustrated by: James Ransome
New York: HarperCollins, ©2004
Grade Level: 1-5
Pages: 70
Themes: Anger, Problem Solving, Apologizing
    or Forgiving

This is a collection of six stories from different regions in Africa. In "The Roof of Leaves: A Tale of Anger and Forgiveness," a man and his wife get angry with each other. The husband begins removing leaves from their roof before he remembers that this is an indication of intention to divorce. His wife finds a way to save face for both of them and mends their relationship.

Probably Still Nick Swansen

Virginia Euwer Wolff

New York: Simon Pulse, 2002, ©1988
Pages: 151
Grade Level: 6-10
Themes: Accepting Limitations and Gifts,
    Respect for Elderly or Disabled, Rumors or
    Suspicion

Nick Swansen, 16, blames himself (because he probably did not think fast enough) for his sister Dianne drowning when she was ten and he was seven. After Shana Kerby "goes UP" from their Special Ed room, Nick carefully plans their date to the prom, only to have things go awry because of an unfortunate sequence of events. In the end, Nick has gained a friend and a new level of self-acceptance.

Project Mulberry

Linda Sue Park

New York: Yearling, 2007, ©2005
Grade Level: 4-7
Pages: 225
Themes: Cooperation, Prejudice or Dislike,
    Diversity of Cultures
Other: Audio

Julia Song and her friend Patrick do a silkworm project for the Wiggle Club (Work-Grow-Give-Love). In the process Julia learns about sustainable farming and the pain of taking life, new aspects of her Korean heritage, the subtleties of racism, friendship, how to be a team member, and how to get along with her seven-year-old brother Kenny.

The Pushcart War

Jean Merrill

Illustrated by: Ronni Solbert
New York: Yearling, 2001, ©1964
Grade Level: 6-10
Pages: 222
Themes: Respect in General, Conflict
    Escalator, Win-Win Solutions
Other: Audio

Set in 1986, this is the story of a New York City conflict between three large trucking companies and the people with pushcarts.

Queen of the Toilet Bowl

Frieda Wishinsky

Custer, WA: Orca, ©2005
Grade Level: 7-9
Pages: 104
Themes: Assertiveness, Stereotypes, Bullying,
    Nonviolent Response

Ninth-grader Renata Nunes, her little brother Lucas, and her widowed mother originally lived in Sao Paolo, Brazil. Mrs. Nunes supports the family by cleaning homes. When Renata gets the lead in "The Sound of Music," Karin, her understudy, tries to undermine Renata by an unsuccessful accusation of theft and then with a picture on the internet of Mrs. Nunes cleaning a toilet. Renata's friend Liz never wavers in her support, and Renata makes a public stand for her mother without lashing out at Karin.

Queen Sophie Hartley

Stephanie Greene

New York: Clarion, ©2005
Grade Level: 3-5
Pages: 136
Themes: Feelings, Accepting Limitations and
    Gifts, Feelings, Inclusion or Exclusion, Social
    Skills

Sophie Hartley, the middle of five children, has learned she is not good at several things, including ballet. Now, following her mother's advice, Sophie is trying to be kind. When she helps grumpy Dr. Hoyt plant her garden, the elderly history professor teaches Sophie to curtsy and act with dignity. Sophie learns some hard lessons about friendship when she befriends Heather, her new elementary school classmate who harshly rates everyone. By the end of the story, Sophie has greater appreciation of her family and herself. [Some of Sophie's actions toward the end may warrant critical class discussion.]

The Rachel Resistance

Molly Levite Griffis

Austin, TX: Eakin Press, ©2001
Grade Level: 4-7
Pages: 232
Themes: Rumors or Suspicion

In the fall of 1940, Rachel Dalton and her best friend Paul Griggs, avid fans of Captain Midnight, suspect several people of being traitors. Their 5th-grade classmate John Alan Feester is one of the wrongly accused suspects.

Racing the Past

Sis Deans

New York: Puffin Books, 2005, ©2001
    Paw Prints, 2008, ©2001
Grade Level: 6-8
Pages: 151
Themes: Bullying, Rumors or Suspicion,
    Nonviolent Response

Ricky Gordon is trying to overcome the bad reputation of his father who has died. In order to stay out of trouble with Bugsie McCarthy, Ricky walks to and from school, eventually outrunning the bus in order to avoid the ridicule.

Rain of Fire

Marion Dane Bauer

New York: Clarion Books, ©1983
Grade Level: 5-9
Pages: 153
Themes: Conflict Escalator, Honesty,
    Nonviolent Response, Peer Pressure

It is 1946, the war is over, and Steve Pulaski, 12, feels estranged from his brother Matthew who returned from the military a distraught person. Trying to impress 14-year-old Ray Celestino, whose father was wounded in the war, Steve makes up a story about Matthew's heroism. Hurt by name-calling, Steve gets involved in a sequence of events that culminates in an unintended explosion which injures both Steve and Ray. In the process, Steve discovers the consequences of his lies, gains an understanding of Matthew's experience with victims of Hiroshima, realizes that Ray is living in a painful home situation, and learns that retaliation only makes situations worse.

Randall's Wall

Carol Fenner

New York: Aladdin, 2000, ©1991
Grade Level: 4-6
Pages: 85
Themes: Friendship, Coping
Other: Audio

Randall Lord is a defensive 5th grader and a gifted artist, whose abusive father is in prison. He lives with his mother and siblings in a house with little food and no running water. Jean Neary's friendship breaks through Randall's wall and changes his life.

The Real Slam Dunk

Charisse K. Richardson

Illustrated by: Kadir Nelson
New York: Scholastic, 2006, ©2001
Grade Level: 3-5
Pages: 68
Themes: Cooperation, Responsible Decision Making

Marcus Robinson and his twin sister Mia are excited that they will get to meet basketball star Jason Carter. Jason encourages them to go to college so they have options in addition to athletics. (In *The Real Lucky Charm* (©2005) Mia learns the value of practice and hard work.)

Really, Truly, Everything's Fine

Linda Leopold Strauss

New York: Marshall Cavendish, ©2004
Grade Level: 4-7
Pages: 149
Themes: Accepting Limitations and Gifts, Coping, Hurtful Words, Peer Pressure

Jill Rider, her little brother Mark, and their mother all suffer when Mr. Rider is sentenced to jail for theft. In addition to her struggle to clarify her role in the family struggles, Jill deals with name-calling and peer pressure.

Red Glass

Laura Resau

New York: Delacorte Press of Random House, ©2007
Grade Level: 8+
Pages: 275
Themes: Diversity of Cultures, Fear

Sophie Gutiérrez, 16, finds her world changed when her stepfather Juan brings home 5-year-old Pablo, the sole survivor of his family's attempt to cross over the border from Mexico. A year later, Sophie, her great-aunt Dika from Bosnia, Dika's friend Mr. Lorenzo, and his son Ángel travel to Mexico and Guatemala where Pablo is reunited with his extended family, Ángel and his dad find peace after the death of Mrs. Lorenzo, and Sophie finds new strength and overcomes old fears.

Reflections of a Peacemaker:
A Portrait Through Heartsongs

Mattie J. T. Stepanek

Introduced and edited by: Jennifer Smith Stepanek
Illustrations by: Mattie J. T. Stepanek
Kansas City, MO: Andrews McMeel, ©2005
Grade Level: 2-5
Pages: 222
Themes: Accepting Limitations and Gifts, Coping, Peacemaking, Respect for Elderly or Disabled

Poet and Peacemaker Mattie Stepanek (1990–2004) began writing at age three. After losing his three older siblings, Katie, Stevie, and Jamie, to dysautonomic mitochondrial myopathy, Mattie lived with that disease most of his life and died a month before his 14th birthday. He celebrated the wonders of everyday sensations, expressed gratitude for the gifts of life and nature, and ardently worked for peace. The book has a Foreword by Oprah Winfrey.

Remember as You Pass Me By

L. King Pérez

Minneapolis: Milkweed Editions, ©2007
Grade Level: 5-8
Pages: 184
Themes: Discrimination, Racism, Responsible
    Decision Making

Growing up in Hughes Springs, TX, Silvan "Silvy" enters 7th grade immediately after the 1953 court decision to integrate schools. Pained by the growing separation from her best friend Mabalee, an African American, and distressed by the prejudicial attitudes of her family and classmates, Silvy negotiates the challenges of family feuds and the growing intolerance in her town. In the end, she gains insight into her family background and the person she is becoming.

Remembering Mrs. Rossi

Amy Hest

Illustrated by: Heather Malone
Cambridge, MA: Candlewick Press, ©2007
Grade Level: 3-5
Pages: 184
Themes: Emotions

After her mother's death following a short illness, eight-year-old Annie Rossi and her dad cope with their profound loss. As the year goes by, Mrs. Rossi's 6th-grade class creates a book in honor of their teacher and Mr. Rossi also writes memories. Feelings of anger and sadness and gratitude sweep over Annie and her dad as they work out their grief and realize how precious they are to each other.

Remembering Raquel

Vivian Vande Velde

Orlando, FL: Harcourt Children's, ©2007
Grade Level: 7-10
Pages: 137
Themes: Diversity of Individuals, Inclusion or
    Exclusion, Point of View

When freshman Raquel Falcone is hit by a car and killed, her classmates and other acquaintances pay more attention to her than they had during her life. Their reflections range from grief or guilt to new appreciation of the heavy girl who was clever, humorous, and kind, and who was overlooked by most people.

Replay

Sharon Creech

New York: HarperTrophy, ©2005
Grade Level: 6-8
Pages: 180
Themes: Accepting Limitations and Gifts,
    Recognizing Emotions, Empathy
Other: Audio

Twelve-year-old Leonardo gains insight through several converging pieces. He secretly finds his father's autobiography from age 13. He has the part of Old Crone in a school play and reflects on life and family. He is pained to find his siblings (Contesta, 15; Pietro, 11; and Nunzio, 8) growing away from him at the same time his family is becoming more precious to him. Finally, he discovers the importance of talking about feelings and loss.

The Revealers

Doug Wilhelm

New York: Farrar, Straus and Giroux, 2005, ©2003
    Paw Prints, 2008, ©2003
Grade Level: 5-7
Pages: 207
Themes: Prejudice or Dislike, Bullying,
    Nonviolent Response

Russell Trainor narrates the story of how he, Elliot Gekewicz, and Catalina Aarons talked with each other about being bullied, and then shared with the whole school via the e-mail network. Their truth-telling changed Parkland Middle School. [Some discussion may be needed regarding those members of the administration who behave unfavorably.]

REVOLUTION Is Not a Dinner Party

Ying Chang Compestine

New York: Henry Holt, ©2007
Grade Level: 4-6
Pages: 248
Themes: Nonviolent Response, Oppression

From the time Ling Chang is nine until she is 13, (1972–1976) her family lives under the oppression of the Cultural Revolution in Wuhan, China. Ling's beloved father, a surgeon, is arrested and, when called upon, ministers to his oppressors. Meanwhile, Ling endures bullying by her classmates as she and her mother eke out a living until Chairman Mao dies and Dr. Chang is freed.

Rickshaw Girl

Mitali Perkins

Illustrated by: Jamie Hogan
Watertown, MA: Charlesbridge, 2008, ©2007
Grade Level: 2-5
Pages: 91
Themes: Community Building, Gender Roles
Other: Glossary and Background Notes

Naima, a young girl in Bangladesh who is artistically gifted, yearns to go on in school or help earn wages to supplement her father's faltering rickshaw business. After attempting to drive the rickshaw and crashing it, Naima discovers Hassan's Rickshaw Repair Shop, run by Hassan's widow and microfinanced by the women's bank. The story ends with Naima looking forward to becoming an employee of the repair shop.

The Right–Under Club

Christine DeRiso

New York: Delacorte Press, ©2007
Grade Level: 5-8
Pages: 208
Themes: Friendship, Problem Solving,
    Responsible Decision Making, Rumors or
    Suspicion

During the summer, 8th-graders Tricia, Hope, Mei, and Leighton; and 6th-grader Elizabeth form the Right-Under Club. Meeting in Tricia's tree house and using a talking stick, the girls identify their common experience of being invisible members of their blended families even though they are "right under" their parents' noses. The diverse group of girls grows in trust, friendship, and respect as each calls on the others to help her with a family dilemma. (In *I Smell Like Ham* by Betty Hicks (Brookfield, CT: Roaring Book Press, ©2002) a boy tries to adapt to his stepmother and a precocious stepbrother.)

Rinehart Lifts

R. R. Knudson

New York: Farrar, Straus and Giroux, 1989,
 ©1980
Grade Level: 4-7
Pages: 88
Themes: Accepting Limitations and Gifts,
 Diversity of Individuals

Fifth-grader Arthur Rinehart's best friend Zan Hagen helps him discover the one sport he can master, lifting.

Robert and the Happy Endings

Barbara Seuling

Illustrated by: Paul Brewer
Chicago: Cricket Books, ©2007
Grade Level: 2-4
Pages: 147
Themes: Cooperation, Inclusion or Exclusion,
 Respect for Elderly or Disabled

Robert Dorfman learns about hearing impairment when Taylor James joins the class. After Susanne Lee Rodgers publicly invites only part of the class to her birthday party, Robert and his best friend Paul Felcher create a party in the park for the remaining elementary school classmates. In the end, Susanne Lee and Robert actually enjoy working together as science partners. (Robert deals with peer pressure in *Robert and the Sneaker Snobs* (©2002), and he makes a new friend in *Robert Goes to Camp* (2007, ©2005).)

Roll of Thunder, Hear My Cry

Mildred B. Taylor

New York: Puffin Books, 2005, ©1976
Grade Level: 5-9
Pages: 288
Themes: Community in Action, Racism,
 Conflict Nature
Other: Audio

This book introduces 9-year-old Cassie Logan's family saga. Living in Mississippi during the Depression, Mary and David Logan, Cassie, and her brothers Stacey, Christopher-John, and Clayton Chester "Little Man," (12, 7, and 6, respectively), are a loving family with a supportive extended family and community. Each year, the Logans' struggle to keep their land is made more difficult because of growing discrimination. Stacey's classmate T. J. Avery is framed for a crime and fears for his life. (See separate entries for *The Well* and *Let the Circle Be Unbroken*.)

Room in the Heart

Sonia Levitin

New York: Speak, 2008, ©2005
Grade Level: 6-10
Pages: 290
Themes: Community in Action, Oppression

The setting for this story is Denmark under German occupation, 1940–1943, when over 7,000 of the 8,000 Jewish people were safely taken to Sweden. Teenagers Julie Weinstein and Niels Nelson and their families are featured.

Roughing

Lorna Schultz Nicholson
Custer, WA: Orca, 2005, ©2004
Grade Level: 4-6
Pages: 108
Themes: Respect for Elderly or Disabled,
    Bullying, Nonviolent Response
Josh Watson attends an Elite Hockey Camp and rooms with Peter Kuiksak from the Northwest Territories. As Josh struggles to care for his Type 1 Diabetes, his friends Sam and Peter (whose mother died of the disease) are supportive. When Peter, who is talented and appears aloof, is targeted by Kevin Jennings and others for some dangerous hazing, Josh and Sam prevent the plan from being carried out.

Ruby Lu, Brave and True

Lenore Look

Illustrated by: Anne Wilsdorf
New York: Aladdin, 2006, ©2004
    London: Fitzgerald Books, 2007, ©2004
Grade Level: 1-3
Pages: 105
Themes: Sharing, Competition, Bullying
Seven-year-old Ruby Lu and Emma and their little brothers Oscar and Sam compete in several areas. Ruby learns to treat with kindness Christina who bullies. She also discovers the benefits of sharing with her Chinese cousin who comes to stay with the Lu family.

Rules

Cynthia Lord
New York: Scholastic, ©2006
Grade Level: 4-7
Pages: 200
Themes: Friendship, Empathy, Respect for
    Elderly or Disabled
Twelve-year-old Catherine is conflicted in her love of her eight-year-old brother David who has autism. "Everyone expects a tiny bit from him and a huge lot from me." (p. 61) Fear of embarrassment when friends visit and outrage over some of the ways her peers treat David cause Catherine to examine the nature of friendship. She finds a friend in Jason who is a few years older than she and attends the same occupational therapy clinic as David. Catherine's empathy for Jason enables her to contribute to the collection of word cards he uses for communication and to grow in appreciation of David.

Running on Eggs

Anna Levine
Chicago: Front Street, ©1999
Grade Level: 5-9
Pages: 128
Themes: Empathy, Prejudice or Dislike
Karen from a kibbutz and Yasmine from an Arab village find their friendship growing in spite of their backgrounds and the tensions between their communities. Through their running, they begin a process of healing.

The Same Stuff as Stars

Katherine Paterson

New York: HarperTrophy, 2004, ©2002
    Paw Prints, 2008, ©2002
London: Fitgerald Books, 2007, ©2002
Grade Level: 5-8
Pages: 242
Themes: Accepting Limitations and Gifts,
    Assertiveness
Other: Audio

Eleven-year-old Angel Morgan, with her alcoholic mother Verna and her father Wayne in prison, feels responsible for her nine-year-old brother Bernie. While the children live on the Morgan farm in Vermont with their great-grandmother Erma, a star-gazing man and Liza Irwin the town librarian teach Angel about the stars. Angel finally finds her place as a child with dignity who is able to call the adults in her life to accountability.

Sara Summer

Mary Downing Hahn

New York: Avon Books, 1995, ©1979
Grade Level: 4-7
Pages: 135
Themes: Friendship, Accepting Limitations
    and Gifts

Twelve-year-old Emily's best friends are ignoring her and she is self-conscious about her height. Sara, who is taller, moves in from New York with an attitude and values that conflict with Sara's, but they become friends.

Sarah and the Naked Truth

Elisa Lynn Carbone

Cassville, NJ: Cloonfad Press, 2006, ©2000
Grade Level: 4-6
Pages: 144
Themes: Accepting Limitations and Gifts,
    Honesty, Peer Pressure

Sarah, a 5th grader, and her friends grow in several ways. Sarah is willing to give up playing on a boy's basketball team, and she has a lesson in honesty. Olivia from Trinidad accepts her artificial leg. Christina from El Salvador claims her heritage. (Discussion may be needed regarding the teacher who is defied and some situations that are solved in ways that may be too simple.)

Saying Good-bye to Grandma

Jane Resh Thomas

Illustrated by: Marcia Sewall
New York: Clarion Books, ©1988
Grade Level: K-3
Pages: 48
Themes: Recognizing Emotions, Coping

Suzie, seven years old, travels with her parents to her grandmother's funeral. Suzie tells of trying to help her grandfather. She describes the family gathering with its rituals and meals. In the end she is surprised at the presence of laughter as well as tears, and she is looking forward to future visits with her grandfather.

School Trouble for Andy Russell

David A. Adler

Illustrated by: Will Hillenbrand
San Diego: Harcourt Brace, 2005, ©1999
    Paw Prints, 2008, ©1999
Grade Level: 2-4
Pages: 118
Themes: Point of View, Apologizing or
    Forgiving
Other: Audio

Although 4th-grader Andy Russell has trouble paying attention in class, his substitute teacher Ms. Salmon blames Andy for more than he has done. In the end, both teacher and students apologize and get a new start.

Second Grade — Friends Again!

Miriam Cohen

Illustrated by: Diane Palmisciano
New York: Scholastic, ©1994
Grade Level: 2-5
Pages: 78
Themes: Friendship, Hurtful Words

When Jacob calls Honey a name, he loses her friendship and that of his best friend Gregory.

The Secret Circle

Dona Schenker

New York: Knopf, 2000, ©1998
Grade Level: 4-7
Pages: 154
Themes: Inclusion or Exclusion, Accepting
    Limitations and Gifts

As Jamie McClure overcomes the consequences of belonging to a group of friends, she realizes that she is not being true to herself.

Seedfolks

Paul Fleischman

Illustrated by: Judy Pederson
New York: HarperTrophy, 2004, ©1997
Findaway World LLC, 2008, ©1997
Grade Level: 5-10
Pages: 69
Themes: Community Building, Point of View,
    Diversity of Cultures
Other: Audio

Thirteen stories are told by an ethnically diverse group of neighbors who grow a garden in a vacant lot, thus creating community.

Sees Behind Trees

Michael Dorris

Orlando, FL: Harcourt, 2005, ©1996
Grade Level: 4-8
Pages: 104
Themes: Listening, Diversity of Cultures,
    Responsible Decision Making
Other: Audio

Walnut is a Native American living in the 1500s. Though he has very poor eyesight, Walnut's hearing is so acute that he can "see" what others cannot. He comes of age in the Native ritual where he receives the name "Sees Behind Trees." Gray Fire, an elder, requests help in finding a place hidden to him since his youth. So, Sees Behind Trees continues his journey into manhood, learning life lessons and acquiring new responsibilities.

Shark Girl

Kelly Bingham

Cambridge, MA: Candlewick Press, ©2007
Grade Level: 6-10
Pages: 276
Themes: Emotions, Overcoming Obstacles,
    Peer Pressure

Fifteen-year-old Jane Arrowood's dream of becoming a professional artist seems shattered when she is attacked by a shark off the coast of California and loses her right arm. Jane narrates her first year in free verse, frankly telling the struggle to accept her new limitations and relate with others. With the friendship of Justin, a young boy who lost his leg in a car accident, the counseling of Mel, a hospital therapist, and the constant support of her older brother Michael and their mother, Jane again tries to develop her artistic talent and begins to consider a medical profession where she can help others.

Shiloh Season

Phyllis Naylor

New York: Aladdin, 2000, ©1991
Grade Level: 3-5
Pages: 137
Themes: Peacemaking
Other: Audio, Video

In this second book of the Shiloh Trilogy, Marty Preston makes peace with Judd Travers through persistent kindness. The other books in the trilogy are: *Shiloh* (2003, ©1991) where Marty makes some hard moral choices when he rescues Judd Travers' abused beagle, Shiloh; and *Saving Shiloh* (2006, ©1997) where Judd is suspected of murder but the Preston family rightly stands by him.

The Shortest Kid in the World

Corinne Demas Bliss

Illustrated by: Nancy Poydar
New York: Random House, 1995, ©1994
Grade Level: 1-3
Pages: 48
Themes: Accepting Limitations and Gifts

Emily hates being the shortest kid until Marietta comes along and has a whole different attitude about her short stature.

The Show–Off

Stephanie Greene

Illustrated by: Joe Mathieu
Tarrytown, NY: Marshall Cavendish
    Corporation, ©2007
Grade Level: 1-3
Pages: 53
Themes: Listening, Social Skills

Hildy, a pig, hosts her cousin Winston for a few days. Hildy and her friend Moose find great difficulty with Winston's overbearing sense of being an expert on practically everything. After they teach Winston that others appreciate his interest in them rather than his expertise, he becomes a welcome house guest who is invited back.

Silent to the Bone

E. L. Konigsburg

New York: Simon Pulse, 2004, ©2000
Grade Level: 6-9
Pages: 261
Themes: Listening, Empathy
Other: Audio

Thirteen-year-old Connor Kane describes the weeks when his best friend Branwell Zamborska is unable to speak. Branwell's half-sister Nikki has a head injury that Vivian, the British au pair, blames on Branwell. As they wait for Nikki to recover, Branwell is in a juvenile behavioral center. Connor communicates with him, trying to figure out what really happened.

Sixth-Grade: Glommers, Norks, and Me

Lisa Papademetriou

New York: Hyperion, 2006, ©2005
Grade Level: 5-7
Pages: 217
Themes: Inclusion or Exclusion, Accepting
    Limitations and Gifts, Diversity of
    Individuals

Allie Kimball and her best friend Tamara "Tam" Thompson begin Grover Cleveland Middle School where their former friend Renee Anderson becomes Tam's best friend. Although Allie feels the pain of being excluded, she learns to appreciate her brother Lionel, her bookish lab partner Orren Kendall, and her old friend Justin Thyme; and she discovers that she has soccer talent.

Skin Deep

Lois Ruby

New York: Scholastic, ©1994
Grade Level: 8-12
Pages: 280
Themes: Anger, Racism

Laurel O'Grady's boyfriend Dan Penner, upset by the hiring consequences of equal opportunity, joins the Skinheads in Boulder, CO.

The Skin I'm In

Sharon G. Flake

New York: Hyperion, 2007, ©1998
    Paw Prints, 2008, ©1998
Grade Level: 5-9
Pages: 176
Themes: Accepting Limitations and Gifts,
    Empathy, Prejudice or Dislike, Bullying
Other: Audio

Maleeka Madison is a gifted writer in 7th grade who is struggling to accept her dark skin and to deal with the bullying of Charlese and the teasing of John-John. Miss Saunders who has had to deal with her blotched face, sees Maleeka's potential and befriends her. [Mature language is used.]

Sky Memories

Pat Brisson

Illustrated by: Wendell Minor
New York: Bantam, 2000, ©1999
Grade Level: 3-6
Pages: 71
Themes: Coping

Ten-year-old Emily and her mother "click" sky memories during the year before her mother's death of cancer.

A Small Boat at the Bottom of the Sea

John Thomson

Minneapolis: Milkweed Editions, ©2005
Grade Level: 5-7
Pages: 148
Themes: Prejudice or Dislike, Responsible
    Decision Making, Apologizing or Forgiving

Twelve-year-old Donovan is sent to stay in Puget Sound with Bix and Hattie Sanger. Donovan's father Ray had separated from his older brother Bix when Bix started getting into trouble at a young age and went to prison. Now Hattie is dying of lung cancer. Donovan helps his uncle retrieve a sunken boat, Prometheus, and fix its engine, a project that delights Hattie. Over the summer Donovan watches Bix grow from prejudice to informing the police of racial crimes committed by someone to whom he had been too indebted. Hattie dies and Donovan's family is reconciled with Bix.

Snap: A Novel

Alison McGhee

Cambridge, MA: Candlewick Press, 2006,
    ©2004
Grade Level: 5-8
Pages: 129
Themes: Accepting Limitations and Gifts,
    Coping
Other: Audio

During the summer after 6th grade, Edwina
"Eddie" Beckey loves lists, and she snaps the
colored rubber bands on her wrist in order to
change her habits. As Eddie and her best friend
Sally Hobart grieve the serious illness of Willie,
Sally's grandmother, Eddie learns that rubber
bands and lists cannot control life.

Snowboard Champ

Paul Mantell and Matt Christopher

Boston: Little, Brown, ©2004
Grade Level: 4-8
Pages: 146
Themes: Anger, Bullying, Rumors or Suspicion,
    Nonviolent Response

Thirteen-year-old Matt Harper makes the most of
his school year in Dragon Valley. Riley Hammett
spreads rumors that Matt has brought gang
activity from Chicago, but Matt's Uncle Clayton
tutors Matt and helps him become Snowboard
Champ, able to use his own ways of dealing with
students who are being harassed.

Snowboarding on Monster Mountain

Eve Bunting

Illustrated by: Karen Ritz
Chicago: Cricket Books, ©2003
Grade Level: 4-7
Pages: 91
Themes: Inclusion or Exclusion, Fear or Worry

Callie Druger's best friend is Jen Webster, and
Callie is worried that Isabela "Izzy" Garcia will
come between them. When Jen invites Callie for
a snowboarding weekend, Callie wrestles with her
fear of heights and gains insight into her own failings
as she observes two others excluding someone.

Snowed in with Grandmother Silk

Carol Fenner

Illustrated by: Amanda Harvey
New York: Puffin Books, 2005, ©2003
    Paw Prints, 2008, ©2003
Grade Level: 2-3
Pages: 75
Themes: Coping, Respect for Elderly or
    Disabled

Eight-year-old Ruddy "Rudford" Silk feels
stranded when his parents take a cruise and
leave him with his very proper Grandmother
Silk. A snow storm on the day before Halloween
leaves them without electricity, water, or heat.
As Ruddy and Grandmother cope, they find
companionship and even fun.

Some Friend

Marie Bradby

New York: Scholastic, 2007, ©2004
Grade Level: 5-7
Pages: 245
Themes: Bullying, Peer Pressure

Eleven-year-old Pearl Jordan is so intent on
being accepted by the popular Lenore that she
stands by when Artemesia is bullied by Lenore
and her friends.

Some Friend!

Carol Carrick

Illustrated by: Donald Carrick
Boston: Houghton Mifflin, ©1979
Grade Level: 4-7
Pages: 112
Themes: Friendship

Even though Mike's best friend Rob usually tries
to have his own way, Mike puts up with a lot in
order to preserve their friendship. Then Rob
goes too far and Mike fights him.

Something About America

Maria Testa

Cambridge, MA: Candlewick Press, 2007,
 ©2005
Grade Level: 6-8
Pages: 84
Themes: Coping, Assertiveness, Community in
 Action, Nonviolent Response

A 13-year-old girl tells in blank verse of the war in Kosova, Yugoslavia, when, at age three, she was trapped in their burning house. Her family came to America for medical attention, but her father resents many aspects of America. When a hate group organizes against the people in their Maine town who are from Somalia, her father leads a protest rally. "If you can't find the welcome mat when you arrive, put one out yourself."

Something Very Sorry

Arno Bohlmeijer

New York: Putnam & Grosset, 1997, ©1996
Grade Level: 5-8
Pages: 175
Themes: Recognizing Emotions

Nine-year-old Rosemyn and her family were injured in the fatal accident that killed her mother. This true story describes the time when she, her father, and her six-year-old sister Phoebe were in the hospital together, sharing their stages of grief.

Song Lee and the "I Hate You" Notes

Suzy Kline

Illustrated by: Frank Remkiewicz
New York: Puffin Books, 2001, ©1999
Grade Level: 2-5
Pages: 50
Themes: Hurtful Words
Other: Audio

Song Lee teaches Mary what it is like to receive a hate note.

Sparks

Graham McNamee

New York: Dell Yearling, 2003, ©2002
Grade Level: 4-6
Pages: 119
Themes: Inclusion or Exclusion, Hurtful Words,
 Peer Pressure

Todd Foster, in a regular 5th-grade class after being in Special Needs, is struggling to learn. In addition, he is being called names and is trying to dodge his former best friend Eva from the Needs class. With the help of his teacher Mr. Baylock, Todd successfully completes a class project. He also learns to deal with the name calling and once again claims Eva as his friend.

The Spying Game

Pat Moon

London: Orchard, 2003, ©1993
Grade Level: 5-8
Pages: 200
Themes: Empathy, Apologizing or Forgiving

Joe Harris wants revenge for his father's death. After stalking the man who killed his father in a car accident, Joe meets the man's son, Alex Moss, and learns how hard the accident has been on the Moss family as well.

Stanford Wong Flunks Big-Time

Lisa Yee

New York: Scholastic, 2007, ©2005
Grade Level: 5-7
Pages: 296
Themes: Diversity of Individuals, Point of View, Responsible Decision Making

To avoid flunking 6th grade, Stanford Wong (the only potential 7th grader to make the Basketball A-Team) loses out on summer basketball camp. Instead, he must take Mr. Glick's summer school English class with Millicent Min as his tutor. Throughout the summer, while he worries about his parents fighting and his grandmother Yee-Yee's adjustment to Vacation Village, Stanford tries to keep his academic secret from his best friends and from his new love Emily Ebers. Stanford grows in his appreciation of Millicent, and gains a better relationship with his parents. He realizes that he does have intelligence and plays an important part on others' "teams," just as they do on his. (*Millicent Min, Girl Genius* (2004, ©2003) and *So Totally Emily Ebers* (2008, ©2007) tell the same story from other points of view. Entries in all three books are dated, making parallel reading convenient.)

Starting School with an Enemy

Elisa Lynn Carbone

Cassville, NJ: Cloonfad Press, 2005, ©1998
Grade Level: 4-6
Pages: 103
Themes: Anger, Bullying, Nonviolent Response
Other: Audio

Sarah spends so much time reacting to Eric Bardo's bullying that her friend Christina feels left out. Then Sarah's brother teaches her how to react like a pillow and Sarah learns to treat Eric's actions like a riptide.

Starting with Alice

Phyllis Reynolds Naylor

New York: Simon & Schuster, 2004, ©2002
Grade Level: 3-6
Pages: 181
Themes: Social Skills, Inclusion or Exclusion

Eight-year-old Alice McKinley (whose mother died a few years earlier), her brother Lester, and their father have moved from Chicago to Takoma Park, MD. Alice and her best friend Rosalind help Sara improve her social skills and personal hygiene; then the three of them break the pattern of being enemies with the "Terrible Triplets" (Megan, Jody, and Dawn) and invite them to Alice's birthday party.

Stealing Home

Paul Mantell

Boston: Little, Brown, ©2004
Grade Level: 3-6
Pages: 135
Themes: Jealousy, Empathy
Other: Audio

Just as Joey Gallagher is becoming recognized as a strong pitcher for the Marlins, Jesus Rodriguez arrives from Mexico to spend the year with Joey's family. Eventually Joey manages to overcome jealousy and the two boys become friends.

Sticks and Stones

Beth Goobie

Custer, WA: Orca, 2006, ©1994
Grade Level: 7-12
Pages: 86
Themes: Hurtful Words, Rumors or Suspicion

When Jujube Gelb is unjustly accused of being easy with boys, she confronts the students who are spreading lies about her. [Mature language is used.]

Stink Bomb

Lynn Cullen
New York: Avon, 1999, ©1998
Grade Level: 4-6
Pages: 120
Themes: Hurtful Words, Responsible Decision
    Making, Apologizing or Forgiving
Kenny Peek falsely blames Alice Flowers for passing gas in gym class. After several miserable weeks he decides to apologize.

Stinky Stern Forever

Michelle Edwards
Orlando, FL: Harcourt, 2007, ©2005
Grade Level: 1-3
Pages: 49
Themes: Recognizing Emotions, Hurtful Words
Although Pa Lia is mad at Matthew "Stinky" Stern because he tried to ruin her snowflake, she actually improves it when she fixes it. Then, on the way home, Stinky runs into traffic and is fatally hurt. The next day, Mrs. Fennessey's 2nd grade class talks about Stinky; they realize that his death hurts more than anything he said or did. Pa Lia tells the snowflake story and puts her flake on his desk. The classmates follow, saying "Stinky Stern Forever." (In *Pa Lia's First Day* (2005, ©1999), 1st-grader Pa Lia chooses honesty and a nonviolent response. Both are Jackson Friends Books.)

Stone Fox

John Reynolds Gardiner
Illustrated by: Greg Hargreaves
New York: HarperTrophy, 2005, ©1980
Findaway World LLC, 2008, ©1980
Grade Level: 4-7
Pages: 83
Themes: Mediation or Negotiation
Other: Audio, Video
Little Willie saves his grandfather's farm by entering a race with his dog Searchlight. The story involves mediation with the tax man Clifford Snyder, and the banker Mr. Foster.

Stop, Look & Listen: Using Your Senses from Head to Toe

Sarah A. Williamson
Illustrated by: Loretta Trezzo Braren
Charlotte, VT: Williamson Publishing, ©1996
Grade Level: P-3
Pages: 141
Themes: Recognizing Emotions, Listening
Fifty-five activities engage children, ages three and older, in using their senses.

The Stories Huey Tells

Ann Cameron
Illustrated by: Roberta Smith
New York: Random House, 2006, ©1995
Grade Level: 2-5
Pages: 102
Themes: Fear or Worry, Respect in General
In "Blue Light, Green Light," Huey has bad dreams and is afraid of the dark. In "Tracks," Huey plays a trick on his brother Julian who is treating him like he is little and helpless. In "My Trip to Africa," Huey tells Julian that he is the one who tricked him.

The Stranger Next Door

Peg Kehret and Pete the Cat
New York: Puffin Books, 2008, ©2002
Grade Level: 4-8
Pages: 162
Themes: Anger, Bullying, Rumors or Suspicion
Sixth-grader Alex Kendrill, new to Valley View Estates, is bullied by Duke Brainard and his friend Henry who are angry because the new housing development has usurped their dirt bike trail. Rocky Morris whose family is in the Witness Security Program, is also new to school. After a fire threatens Alex's life, Alex and Rocky become friends, thanks to the persistent care of Alex's cat Pete who helps write the story.

Strike Three! Take Your Base

Frosty Wooldridge

Illustrated by: Pietri Freeman
Sterling, VA: The Brookfield Reader, ©2001
Grade Level: 5-9
Pages: 160
Themes: Anger, Coping, Responsible Decision
 Making

Narrator Bob Whitman, 17, and his 15-year-old brother Rex inherit their love of baseball from their father Howard. When Howard has a fatal heart attack, Bob takes on more responsibility (helping his mother with six-year-old Linda and eight-month-old Carrie) and Rex shuts down. Eventually the brothers carry on and live up to their father's pride in them.

Sugar Plum Ballerinas: Plum Fantastic

Whoopi Goldberg with Deborah Underwood

Illustrated by: Maryn Roos
New York: Disney: Jump at the Sun Books,
 2008
Grade Level: 3-7
Pages: 155
Themes: Cooperation, Diversity of Cultures,
 Gender Roles, Overcoming Obstacles

Although nine-year-old Alexandrea "Al" Petrakova Johnson's idol is speed skater Phoebe Fitz, her mother's dream is that Al become a ballerina. Having recently moved to Harlem from Atlanta, Mrs. Johnson enrolls Al in the Nutcracker School of Ballet where Al is chosen by lot to be the Sugar Plum Fairy. Al finds friends who help her learn her role and then, in a masterful strategy of cooperation, see her through her performance.

Surviving Brick Johnson

Laurie Myers

Illustrated by: Dan Yaccarino
New York: Clarion, ©2000
Grade Level: 3-5
Pages: 74
Themes: Friendship, Point of View, Respect in
 General
Other: Audio

After imitating his 5th-grade classmate "Brick" Johnson, Alex is scared that Brick will maim him. Alex is surprised that his 1st-grade brother Bob loves Brick, who reads to the class. When Alex lands in the same karate class as Brick, he learns that respect is essential, and the two boys, both avid baseball-card fans, become friends.

Surviving the Applewhites

Stephanie S. Tolan

New York: HarperTrophy, 2004, ©2002
 Paw Prints, 2008, ©2002
Findaway World LLC, 2008, ©2002
Grade Level: 5-8
Pages: 216
Themes: Community Building, Diversity of
 Individuals
Other: Audio

After being expelled from a series of schools, Jake Semple joins the Applewhite's home school, Creative Academy. He learns what it means to be a part of an eccentric family who is passionate about learning and creating.

Take Two, They're Small

Elizabeth Levy

Illustrated by: Mark Elliott
New York: HarperCollins, 2003, ©1981
Grade Level: 2-4
Pages: 86
Themes: Cooperation

As her twin sisters Amy and May enter kindergarten, 4th-grader Eve Kirby thinks they will get all the attention. The twin Miss Shermans teach the two classes and create a buddy system that matches Eve and her new friend Adam with May and Amy. Through their Zodiac project (the Kirby girls are all Geminis) Eve learns to appreciate her siblings and to work well on a group project.

Taking Care of Terrific

Lois Lowry

Santa Barbara, CA: Cornerstone Books, 1989,
    ©1983
Grade Level: 5-9
Pages: 168
Themes: Accepting Limitations and Gifts,
    Diversity of Individuals
Other: Video
Enid Crowley, a 14-year-old girl, takes a summer job babysitting Joshua Cameron IV. Joshua has been overprotected by his mother as much as Enid has been ignored by hers. However, this summer, Enid has decided that it is time for a change. Enid and Joshua spend each day at the Boston Public Garden, where they make new friends, including an old bag lady, a hawk, and a saxophonist.

Taking Sides

Gary Soto

San Diego: Harcourt Brace, 2003, ©1991
Grade Level: 5-7
Pages: 138
Themes: Competition, Friendship, Diversity of
    Cultures
Other: Audio
Eighth-grader Lincoln Mendoza is pulled by friends and teammates at his former junior high school, Franklin, and his new basketball team at Columbus, a mostly white school. He manages to keep his old friend Tony even though their friendship has changed. Lincoln also finds a way to play on the Columbus team and still respect Franklin, a way to live in his new world and still identify with his Hispanic background.

Tank Talbott's Guide to Girls

Dori Hillestad Butler

Morton Grove, IL: Whitman, ©2006
Grade Level: 4-6
Pages: 177
Themes: Nonviolent Response, Empathy,
    Stereotypes, Gender Roles, Diversity of
    Individuals
In danger of flunking 5th grade, Thomas "Tank" Talbott tries to hide his secret from his stepsister Mollie and his best friend Jason. Tank spends the summer doing extra math and writing, hence, the Guide to Girls. His older brother Zack teaches Tank the painful consequences of violent reactions, and Mollie leads Tank to greater understanding and empathy. (*Trading Places with Tank Talbott* (2005, ©2003), is the story of Jason dispelling a stereotype when he discovers that Tank, who bullies others, can be a friend.)

Tarantula Power

Ann Whitehead Nagda

Illustrated by: Stephanie Roth
New York: Holiday House, ©2007
Grade Level: 2-4
Pages: 93
Themes: Bullying, Cooperation
Fourth-grader Richard helps 2nd-grader Sam to stand up to Kevin's bullying. Richard also successfully cooperates with his classmate Kevin after Kevin steals Richard's idea for their 4th-grade "Invent a Cereal" project.

The Thing about Georgie

Lisa Graff

New York: HarperTrophy, 2008, ©2006
Grade Level: 4-7
Pages: 220
Themes: Apologizing or Forgiving, Point
of View, Respect for Elderly or Disabled,
Stereotypes

George "Georgie" Washington Bishop, a dwarf, is worried that he is losing his best friend Andrea "Andy" Moretti because Andy is hanging out with their new 5th-grade classmate Russ Wilkins. He is also dreading the birth of his new sibling who will soon be taller than Georgie is. He discovers that his annoying project partner, Jeanette "Jeanie the Meanie" Wallace, is actually an advocate and friend. (Throughout the book the reader is asked to engage in activities which give insight into Georgie's everyday experiences. A clever twist at the end of the story reveals the author of these exercises.)

Third Grade Bullies

Elizabeth Levy

Illustrated by: Tim Barnes
New York: Hyperion, ©1998
Grade Level: 2-4
Pages: 57
Themes: Conflict Nature, Bullying, Nonviolent
Response

Jake is known for his bullying. Sally, new to the class, is much smaller than Jake. They constantly insult each other. Meanwhile, Tina always gives in to the demands of her 4th-grade cousin Darcy. In the end, the 3rd graders listen to their teacher Ms. Garrick and try to "be something different."

This Is Just to Say: Poems of Apology & Forgiveness

Joyce Sidman

Illustrated by: Pamela Zagarenski
Boston, MA: Houghton Mifflin, ©2007
Grade Level: 4-7
Pages: 45
Themes: Apologizing or Forgiving,
Cooperation, Point of View

Inspired by the poem "This is Just to Say" by William Carlos Williams, Mrs. Merz's 6th-grade class writes eighteen poems of apology, each with a poem in response. The fictitious class, with 6th-grader Anthony K. as editor and Bao Vang as illustrator, might serve as a model for a real class who can collect their poems and produce a book.

Three Cups of Tea: One Man's Journey to Change the World ... One Child at a Time

Greg Mortenson and David Oliver Relin, Adapted by Sarah Thomson

New York: Dial Books for Young Readers, 2009, ©2009
Grade Level: 3-7
Pages: 240
Themes: Community Building, Diversity of Cultures, Gender Roles, Nonviolent Response, Peacemaking

This is the true story of Greg Mortenson who began building schools in Pakistan after the people in the village of Korphe nursed him back to health in 1992 when he was separated from his mountaineering party. Greg was supported in his selfless efforts by many donors, including school children in the United States, Dr. Jean Hoerni and other donors, and his family. By listening to the people of Pakistan and Afghanistan, Greg gained their respect and collaboration, eventually establishing the Central Asia Institute (CAI) and building over 50 schools in those countries. Greg's efforts, especially when juxtaposed with activities after 9/11, demonstrate the power of peaceful relations with other countries. The Young Reader's Edition is a simplified version of the adult version (Viking, 2008, ©2006) with several added features: an introduction by Jane Goodall, an interview with Greg's 12-year-old daughter Amira, expanded photo sections in color, a timeline, a list of Who's Who, and a glossary. Endpapers explain Pennies for Peace and give website information. (The picture book *Listen to the Wind* (Mortenson and Roth, 2009) tells the beginning of this story.)

Three Wishes: Palestinian and Israeli Children Speak

Deborah Ellis

Toronto: Groundwood Books, ©2004
London: Frances Lincoln Children's, 2007, ©2004
Grade Level: 5-8
Pages: 110
Themes: Point of View, Diversity of Cultures, Conflict Nature

Palestinian and Israeli youth, ages eight to 18, tell of their hopes and dreams, their daily frustrations, and their feelings about war and the children in the country at war with them.

Through My Eyes

Ruby Bridges

New York: Scholastic, 2001, ©1999
Grade Level: 4-7
Pages: 63
Themes: Coping, Discrimination, Responsible Decision Making
Other: Audio; Video: "The Ruby Bridges Story"

Ruby Bridges tells her story of entering 1st grade in 1960 as the only black child at William Frantz Public School in New Orleans.

Tiger Turcotte Takes on the Know-It-All

Pansie Hart Flood

Illustrated by: Amy Wummer
Minneapolis: Carolrhoda, ©2005
Grade Level: 2-4
Pages: 71
Themes: Conflict Escalator, Hurtful Words

Second-grader Tiger gets into an escalating conflict with Donna Overton. They quarrel about art supplies and then put down each other's names. After spending detention time together, they become friends. (*Meet M & M* by Pat Ross (New York: Puffin Books, 1997, ©1980) relates the escalating conflict between two girls who are best friends.)

To Kill a Mockingbird

Harper Lee

New York: HarperPerennial, 2006, ©1960
London: Heinemann, 2007, ©1960
Grade Level: 5-9
Pages: 323
Themes: Honesty, Empathy, Stereotypes,
   Diversity of Individuals, Responsible
   Decision Making
Other: Audio, Video

In the 1935 Southern town of Maycomb, AL, Atticus Finch is appointed to defend Tom Robinson who is black, accused of raping Mayella Ewell who is white. The widowed Atticus is closely watched by his 2nd-grade daughter Jean Louise "Scout" who narrates the story and his 6th-grade son Jeremy "Jem." They learn about prejudice and integrity as the case is carried out amidst injustice and threats.

Toad Away

Morris Gleitzman

New York: Yearling, 2007, ©2003
Grade Level: 3-6
Pages: 194
Themes: Nonviolent Response

Limpy, a cane toad, wants to make friends with humans so that their bulldozers will not continue flattening his relatives. Limpy, his peacemaking sister Charm, and his war-loving cousin Goliath go to the Amazon to learn their ancestors' secrets for living in harmony with humans. Although the secret is bizarre, the journey features the absurdity of violence and the power of nonviolence.

Touching Spirit Bear

Ben Mikaelsen

New York: HarperTrophy, 2005, ©2001
Grade Level: 7-12
Pages: 241
Themes: Anger, Empathy, Apologizing or
   Forgiving
Other: Audio

Fifteen-year-old Cole Matthews is sentenced to an Alaskan island because he attacked 9th-grader Peter Driscal. Cole is angry and turns away from everyone until he almost dies. All along, Garvey his parole officer and Edwin a Tlingit elder support Cole and eventually find a way that he and Peter can be reconciled.

Tripping over the Lunch Lady and Other School Stories

Nancy E. Mercado, Editor

New York: Puffin Books, 2006, ©2004
Grade Level: 5-7
Pages: 178
Themes: Cooperation, Point of View, Diversity
   of Individuals

This is a collection of 10 short stories about students. "Science Friction" by David Lubar relates how four randomly selected students create a clever science project, but only after much conflict. In "The Girls' Room" by Susan Shreve, 4th-grader Zale finds out that she is not the only one having trouble reading, and she decides she has not been trying hard enough. *Tied to Zelda* by David Rice is the story of Alfonso Flores, who is randomly paired with Zelda Fuerte in a three-legged race and an egg-throwing contest. After overcoming his initial resistance, Alfonso cooperates and then negotiates a satisfying victory for all the finalists.

26 Fairmount Avenue

Tomie DePaola
New York: Puffin Books, 2001, ©1999
Grade Level: K-4
Pages: 56
Themes: Overcoming Obstacles, Community in Action
Other: Audio

While Tomie's family is building their house, there are many obstacles, including a hurricane and new city streets, that leave the house standing on a muddy hill.

Unbroken

Jessie Haas
New York: HarperTrophy, 2001, ©1999
Grade Level: 5-8
Pages: 185
Themes: Anger, Empathy
Other: Audio

It is 1910 on a Vermont farm where Harriet "Harry" Gibson is sent to live with her deceased father's sister Aunt Sally after Harry's mother Ellen dies in an accident that also kills her mare. While 13-year-old Harry and her two-year-old colt both grieve for their mothers, they teach their caregivers that harsh discipline is ineffective, but they also learn that love can be hidden in that discipline. Harry heals and grows in her love of family as she learns more about her family history.

Understanding Buddy

Marc Kornblatt
New York: Margaret K. McElderry, ©2001
Grade Level: 4-7
Pages: 113
Themes: Empathy

Fifth-grader Sam Keeperman knows the secret of Buddy White's sadness, because Buddy's late mother Laura was a friend to Sam.

Up Country

Alden R. Carter
New York: Speak, 2004, ©1989
Grade Level: 8-12
Pages: 256
Themes: Anger, Responsible Decision Making

Sixteen-year-old Carl Staggers is sent to relatives north of Milwaukee while his mother is in alcohol treatment. Although his previous electronics work for a car stereo theft ring threatens his future, Carl finds a new life.

The Upstairs Room

Johanna Reiss
Los Angeles, CA: LRS, 2002, ©1970
    Paw Prints, 2008, ©1970
Grade Level: 7+
Pages: 196
Themes: Anger, Community in Action, Oppression
Other: Audio Book

During the Nazi oppression of Jewish people in Holland, Annie de Leeuw spends over two of her preteen years hiding with her older sister Sini on the farm of Johan and Dientje Oosterveld and Johann's mother Opoe The Oosterveld's, knowing they are risking their lives by hiding the girls, continue to find ways to conceal their guests, even when the German soldiers take up residence in one part of the house. Meanwhile, Anne grows weaker and Sini more impatient during their confinement, until their release at the end of the war. While not an historical novel, this grew from the author's own experience.

The Very Ordered Existence of Merilee Marvelous

Suzanne Crowley

New York: HarperCollins Children's Books, ©2007
Findaway World LIC, 2008, ©2007
Grade Level: 5-8
Pages: 380
Themes: Accepting Limitations and Gifts, Bullying, Respect for Elderly or Disabled
Other: Audio

Merilee Monroe, 13, who has Asperger's Syndrome, manages to cope by deep breathing, journaling, keeping a strict routine, and ignoring the classmates who bully her. She narrates the story, set in Jumbo, TX, of Biswick O'Connor, 8, who has Fetal Alcohol Syndrome, and Veraleen Holliday, who has endured sorrow in her past. Although Merilee is loved by her family and Uncle Dal, she has insulated herself from others. Biswick and Veraleen, and classmate Gideon Beaurogard (who helps fend off the bullying), all help Merilee rely on the love of those around her.

Vive La Paris

Esmé Raji Codell

New York: Hyperion, 2007, ©2006
London: Hodder Children's, 2008, ©2006
Grade Level: 4-6
Pages: 210
Themes: Bullying, Nonviolent Response, Responsible Decision Making, Point of View
Other: Audio

Paris McCray learns why her classmate Tanaeja bullies Paris's younger brother Michael, and his nonviolent responses lead to peace among the three. Because of her piano teacher, Mrs. Rosen, who is a survivor of the Holocaust, Paris also discovers how people have hurt one another.

The Voice that Challenged a Nation: Marian Anderson and the Struggle for Equal Rights

Russell Freedman

New York: Scholastic, 2005, ©2004
Grade Level: 4-7
Pages: 114
Themes: Overcoming Obstacles, Discrimination, Nonviolent Response
Other: Audio

This documented story tells Marian Anderson's (1897–1993) struggle to be accepted on equal terms with other performers in the United States. Although widely acclaimed by Europeans, Marian faced discrimination in the U.S. On Easter, 1939, she performed before 75,000 people at the Lincoln Memorial after not being allowed to perform at Constitution Hall. Eleanor Roosevelt was a strong supporter for Marian, who kept her dignity as she continued to strive for excellence and for equal rights.

Waiting for the Rain

Sheila Gordon

New York: Dell Laurel-Leaf, 1997, ©1987
Grade Level: 7-12
Pages: 214
Themes: Anger, Oppression, Nonviolent Response
Other: Audio

Although they grow up under the Apartheid in South Africa, Tengo and Frikkie are good friends. Frikkie knows he will inherit, from his aunt and uncle, the farm he loves. Tengo, whose family works on the farm, becomes aware of the education and privileges Frikkie takes for granted. When Tengo is finally able to study in Johannesburg, his education is disrupted by the revolution, and he is torn between completing his education in a foreign country and fighting with his people for their rights. In a dramatic sequence of events, Tengo and Frikkie meet each other as adults, acknowledging their old friendship and their painful differences, and Tengo's choice about his future is clarified.

Walking to the Bus-Rider Blues

Harriette Gillem Robinet

New York: Aladdin Paperbacks, 2002, ©2000
  Paw Prints, 2008, ©2000
Grade Level: 3-7
Pages: 146
Themes: Community Building, Discrimination, Nonviolent Response

During the 1956 Montgomery, AL bus boycott, while 12-year-old Alpha "Alfa" Merryfield worries about rent money that keeps disappearing and about the false accusation that he and his family have been stealing, he tries to respond nonviolently to racial attacks and unjust accusations. Alfa and his sister Zinnia, 15, are supported by their great-grandmother Lydia "Big Mama" Merryfield, a local heroine who delivered many of the Montgomery residents and a longtime bus rider who gets lost when she walks. As the trio manages to help each other, Alpha retains his dream of someday becoming a doctor.

The War with Grandpa

Robert Kimmel Smith

Illustrated by: Richard Lauter
New York: Random House, 1996, ©1984
Tandem Library Books, 1999, ©1984
Grade Level: 4-7
Pages: 140
Themes: Conflict Escalator, Win-Win Solutions
Other: Audio, Video

Peter Stokes loves his grandpa but declares war when his grandpa moves into Peter's room. Through the conflict, both Peter and his grandpa learn more about the ways of war and manage to find a solution.

The Warriors

Joseph Bruchac

Plain City, OH: Darby Creek, ©2003
  Paw Prints, 2008, ©2003
Grade Level: 5-8
Pages: 117
Themes: Stereotypes, Diversity of Cultures, Win-Win Solutions

Lacrosse is more than a game for 12-year-old Jake Forrest, it is part of his Iroquois heritage. When Jake reluctantly leaves the reservation to live with his widowed mother and then boards at Weltimore Academy, he is sad to see how Coach Scott's views perpetuate warlike images of Native Americans. After Coach Scott is shot in a store robbery, Jake initiates a healing game of lacrosse, a collaboration that honors the spirit of the game.

Warriors Don't Cry: A Searing Memoir of the Battle to Integrate Little Rock's Central High

Melba Pattillo Beals

New York: Simon Pulse, 2007, ©1995
  Paw Prints, 2008, ©1995
Grade Level: 4-9
Pages: 226
Themes: Fear or Worry, Overcoming Obstacles, Discrimination
Other: Abridged Edition

This is a first-hand account of Melba Pattillo Beals's junior high school year as one of the Little Rock Nine.

The Way a Door Closes

Hope Anita Smith

Illustrated by: Shane W. Evans
New York: Henry Holt, ©2003
Grade Level: 4-8
Pages: 52
Themes: Coping, Responsible Decision
    Making
Through poems 13-year-old C. J. tells about life before his father lost his job and left home, about his growing care of his mother and siblings, and about his father's return.

Weedflower

Cynthia Kadohata

New York: Aladdin Paperbacks, 2009, ©2006
Pages: 260
Grade Level: 5-8
Themes: Coping, Friendship, Diversity of
    Cultures, Oppression,
Other: Audio
Sumiko Yamaguchi, 12, her brother Takao "Tak-Tak," almost 6, her cousins Ichiro and Bull, and their mother are all sent to the Japanese internment camp on a Mohave reservation in Poston, AZ. Although Sumiko initially sees this as the end of her dream to have her own florist shop, she helps create a prize-winning garden in the desert. Sumiko also becomes a friend of Huulas "Frank" Butler, who encourages her to begin a new life when she, Tak-Tak, and her aunt have a chance to move to Chicago. An endnote gives historical background.

A Week in the Woods

Andrew Clements

New York: Aladdin, 2004, ©2002
Grade Level: 4-6
Pages: 190
Themes: Fear or Worry, Stereotypes, Problem
    Solving
Other: Audio
Mark Chemsley moves from Scarsdale, NY, to Whitson, NH, where he begins to appreciate the outdoor life. His teacher, Bill Maxwell, learns that Mark does not fit the stereotype of a wealthy only child. During the highpoint of 5th grade, a week in the woods, Mark is falsely accused of having a knife. This leads both Mark and Mr. Maxwell to an experience which results in their mutual appreciation.

The Well: David's Story

Mildred D. Taylor

New York: Scholastic, 1999, ©1995
Grade Level: 4-7
Pages: 92
Themes: Anger, Racism, Conflict Escalator
The Well, by Mildred Taylor, is a prequel to *Roll of Thunder, Hear My Cry*. It is set in the South during a time when daily life is dominated by white men's rules. The Logans, a black family, are landowners, living among white neighbors, many of whom are sharecroppers. One of the sharecropper families, the Simms, is particularly resentful of the Logan's prosperity, and an ongoing feud exists between the two families. When the story begins, the characters are coping with a drought. The Logan's well provides the only source of water in the area. Mama Logan shares her water with everyone, black and white alike. Her son, Hammer, cannot understand how Mama can share with the Simms, who have been particularly cruel to his family. Hammer is especially resentful of Charlie Simms, who degrades Hammer for being black. (See separate entries for *Roll of Thunder, Hear My Cry* and *Let the Circle be Unbroken*.)

What I Believe: A Novel

Norma Fox Mazer

Orlando, FL: Harcourt Brace, 2007, ©2005
Grade Level: 5-8
Pages: 169
Themes: Accepting Limitations and Gifts,
    Honesty, Apologizing or Forgiving

Victory "Vicki" Marnet uses several poetry forms to reflect on her experiences. Her dad loses his job and, suffering a depression, leaves his family for a period of time after they have sold their home and moved to an apartment in a lower class neighborhood. To save face in language arts class, Vicki steals money to pay for book club and then struggles with her guilt even after returning the money. In the end, Vicki finds that her new friend Sara accepts her as she is, and Vicki grows to accept her family as they are.

What I Call Life

Jill Wolfson

New York: Henry Holt, ©2005
Grade Level: 5-8
Pages: 270
Themes: Accepting Limitations and Gifts,
    Recognizing Emotions, Empathy
Other: Audio

Cal Lavender's mother Betty has an "episode" in public. Betty is sent to get help and 11-year-old Cal is taken to a group home where "the Knitting Lady" cares for Cal and four other girls. Although Cal initially denies the reality of her situation, through living with the others and listening to the Knitting Lady's stories, Cal learns to accept her life, to express some emotions, and to recognize the common bonds she has with others.

What If They Knew?

Patricia Hermes

New York: Dell, 1989, ©1980
Grade Level: 5-9
Pages: 121
Themes: Inclusion or Exclusion, Accepting
    Limitations and Gifts, Respect for Elderly or
    Disabled

Jeremy Martin is afraid her friends will leave her when they learn that she has epilepsy. Along the way she learns about her capacity to be mean to others, and she discovers that she is still accepted after having a seizure.

The Wheel on the School

Meindert DeJong

Illustrated by: Maurice Sendak
New York: Trumpet Club, 1988, ©1954
Grade Level: 3-6
Pages: 298
Themes: Community Building, Cooperation,
    Respect for Elderly or Disabled
Other: Audio, Video (1972)

Lina, the only girl in school, writes an essay on storks that inspires her teacher and the five boys in school. They search for a wagon wheel to perch on the steep school roof, so that storks will once again come to Shora, Holland. Soon the entire fishing village is engaged. New relationships develop among the older and younger residents, and community spirit grows.

When the Circus Came to Town

Polly Horvath

New York: Farrar, Straus and Giroux, 1999,
    ©1996
London: Scholastic Children's, 2003, ©1996
Grade Level: 4-6
Pages: 138
Themes: Prejudice or Dislike

Ten-year-old Ivy makes a new friend when Alfred Halibut and his family from the circus move next door. However, when other circus people move to town, they are not accepted.

When the Emperor Was Divine

Julie Otsuka

New York: Knopf, 2003, ©2002
   Paw Prints, 2008, ©2002
London: Penguin, 2004, ©2002
Grade Level: 7-12
Pages: 143
Themes: Point of View, Oppression
Other: Audio

After Pearl Harbor the father of a nameless Japanese family is arrested and sent away for over four years. During that time his wife, son, and daughter are interred and then go home to await his return. Multiple points of view are used in telling the story. The encampment experience is a painful disruption of their former lives, and when they return they are no longer accepted in their community. They themselves have been changed, especially the father whose spirit seems broken and suspicious. The lack of names gives a sense of how many people were involved in this tragic time.

When My Name Was Keoko

Linda Sue Park

New York: Dell Yearling, 2004, ©2002
   Paw Prints, 2008, ©2002
Grade Level: 6-9
Pages: 199
Themes: Oppression, Gender Roles, Diversity
   of Cultures
Other: Audio

During World War II, Sun-hee and her brother Tae-yul watch their elders try to preserve their Korean heritage under Japanese oppression. Their uncle, who has resisted, leaves the family so that his actions do not harm them. Eventually each member of the family resists in his or her own way. Each chapter is narrated by either Sun-hee or Tae-yul.

While No One Was Watching

Jane Leslie Conly

New York: HarperTrophy, 2000, ©1998
Grade Level: 5-8
Pages: 233
Themes: Honesty, Empathy
Other: Audio

After Franklin helps steal a rabbit and two bikes from Addie who lives in an exclusive neighborhood, the children meet.

While You Were Out

J. Irvin Kuns

New York: Puffin Books, 2006, ©2004
Grade Level: 4-6
Pages: 132
Themes: Friendship, Recognizing Emotions,
   Coping, Empathy

Fifth-grader Penelope Grant, whose best friend Tim Daniels died of bone cancer at the end of 4th grade, is struggling with the loss of Tim in her life, her father's position as school custodian, and her neighbor Diane who wants to be her new best friend. Penelope copes by using Poetry Therapy to name her feelings and by writing memos to Tim. Eventually, she finds understanding from Diane, unexpected friendship with classmate Russell who also misses Tim, and appreciation for her creative dad.

Whirligig

Paul Fleischman

New York: Dell Laurel-Leaf, 1999, ©1998
Findaway World LLC, ©1998
Grade Level: 7-12
Pages: 133
Themes: Point of View, Responsible Decision
   Making
Other: Audio

Sixteen-year-old Brent Bishop takes a journey to pay tribute to Lea, the young girl he killed in an auto accident when he was trying to end his own life. He creates four whirligigs, each in honor of Lea.

Whitewater Scrubs

Jamie McEwan

Illustrated by: John Margeson
Plain City, OH: Darby Creek, ©2005
Grade Level: 1-3
Pages: 63
Themes: Competition, Fear or Worry, Peer Pressure

Clara finds kayaking more difficult than other sports and almost quits out of fear after she capsizes. She is also embarrassed to be outclassed by Willy, Dan, and Rufus who were "scrubs" on the football team. In the end, Laura helps Willy and learns that it's not necessary to be the best or to be one of the cool kids in order to have fun.

Who Moved My Cheese? for Teens: An A-Mazing Way to Change and Win!

Spencer Johnson

Illustrated by: Steve Pileggi
New York: Putnam, ©2002
London: Vermillion, 2003, ©2002
Grade Level: 5-12
Pages: 96
Themes: Fear or Worry, Responsible Decision Making

Seven high school friends discuss scheduling changes. Chris tells his six friends the story of four mice, Sniff and Scurry, Hem and Haw, who learn life lessons on their daily search for cheese in a maze. After the story, the students apply it to various aspects of their lives.

Willow Run

Patricia Reilly Giff

New York: Yearling, 2007, ©2005
Grade Level: 4-7
Pages: 149
Themes: Honesty, Rumors or Suspicion
Other: Audio

During World War II, Margaret "Meggie" Dillon, 11, and her parents move from Rockaway, NY, to Willow Run, MI, so that her father can work in a B-24 bomber factory. Her brother Eddie has already gone to Europe on military duty and her German grandfather, who has been accused of being a Nazi, stays behind. During their time in Willow Run, Meggie grows in courage and learns some lessons about honesty and suspicion.

The Witch of Blackbird Pond

Elizabeth George Speare

Boston: Houghton Mifflin, 2001, ©1958
London: Collins, 2003, ©1958
Grade Level: 5-9
Pages: 223
Themes: Friendship, Rumors or Suspicion
Other: Audio

Kit Taylor is suspected of being a witch when she befriends Hannah Tupper, a Quaker, in 1687 Connecticut.

With Courage and Cloth: Winning the Fight for a Woman's Right to Vote

Ann Bausum

Washington, DC: National Geographic, ©2004
Grade Level: 7-12
Pages: 111
Themes: Community in Action, Discrimination, Gender Roles

This documentary chronicles the struggle for women's suffrage from 1848 until 1920, describing the nonviolent protests, hunger fasts, and arrests, as well as the political strategies which were needed in this 72-year campaign. Photographs, a chronology, resources, bibliography, and an afterword with a brief history of Susan Paul's work on the Equal Rights Amendment are included.

Witness

Karen Hesse

New York: Scholastic, 2005, ©2001
    Paw Prints, 2008, ©2001
Grade Level: 5-9
Pages: 161
Themes: Point of View, Racism
Other: Audio

In 1924 the KKK is moving into a small Vermont town. Key characters give their points of view through monologues in free verse. They include Leonora Sutter, a 12-year-old African American girl; Esther Hirsch, a 6-year-old Jewish girl; and townspeople on both sides of the conflict.

Wolf Shadows

Mary Casanova

New York: Hyperion, 1999, ©1997
Grade Level: 5-8
Pages: 127
Themes: Friendship, Empathy, Apologizing or
    Forgiving
Other: Audio

In this story set in Minnesota, Seth Jacobson's friendship with Matt Schultz is threatened when Matt shoots a wolf. However, the boys grow in their appreciation of each other.

Woodsie, Again

Bruce Brooks

New York: HarperTrophy, ©1999
Grade Level: 4-7
Pages: 100
Themes: Cooperation, Problem Solving

Dixon "Woodsie" Woods and his hockey team struggle when some of the members use marijuana. Woodsie discovers that Ernie uses the weed to calm his nerves before tense games. (This is a sequel to Woodsie (©1997).)

Words of Stone

Kevin Henkes

New York: HarperTrophy, 2005, ©1992
Grade Level: 5-9
Pages: 152
Themes: Friendship, Recognizing Emotions,
    Apologizing or Forgiving
Other: Audio

Words of Stone is the story of Blaze and Joselle, two troubled students who face many challenges, including their new friendship. Blaze, still coping with his mother's death, invents imaginary friends. Each year, the imaginary friend is unable to fulfill Blaze's needs and he buries his friend on top of a hill, marking his grave with a stone. Joselle, abandoned by her mother, who is supposedly traveling across the country with her new boyfriend, is so miserable that she wants to know that someone else's life is worse than hers. Finding out about Blaze's secret, she rearranges Blaze's stone graves to spell Rena, the name of his deceased mother. Joselle wasn't bargaining for the fact that she and Blaze, two very different students, would become friends. Both students feel mixed emotions about one another and the conditions of their lives.

The World According to Humphrey

Betty G. Birney

New York: Puffin Books, 2005, ©2004
Grade Level: 2-4
Pages: 124
Themes: Point of View, Diversity of Individuals

During a year in Room 26, Humphrey, a hamster, gains insight as he learns about the lives of Mrs. Brisbane and her students. (In *Friendship According to Humphrey* (2006, ©2005), the new class frog Og teaches Humphrey about friendship. In *Trouble According to Humphrey* (2008, ©2007), Humphrey shows his growing concern for the students when he sacrifices the freedom allowed by his lock-that-doesn't-lock in order to clear the reputation of one of the students. *Surprises According to Humphrey* (©2008) includes lessons on listening and conflict resolution.)

Worlds Apart

Lindsey Lee Johnson

Asheville, NC: Front Street, ©2005

Grade Level: 5-8

Pages: 166

Themes: Diversity of Individuals, Inclusion or Exclusion, Rumors or Suspicions, Stereotypes

The year is 1959. Eighth-grader Winona "Winnie" May feels exiled when her physician father is banned from his practice in Chicago and takes a position at a mental institution in Bridgewater, MN. Winnie is ridiculed for living on the grounds of the institution; her mother is depressed; and when Winnie asks to live with one of her old Chicago friends, she learns that her former in-group, the Starlings, want nothing to do with her because of her father's situation. Winnie finds a friend in Justice Goodwater and gets personally acquainted with some of the institutional residents; some stereotypes are shattered. As she grows in empathy, Winnie gains some understanding of her father's dilemma; she also reflects on the way she had treated a Chicago classmate who had polio and makes amends.

Wringer

Jerry Spinelli

New York: HarperTrophy, 2004, ©1997

Grade Level: 4-7

Pages: 228

Themes: Fear or Worry, Gender Roles, Peer Pressure

Other: Audio

Palmer LaRue does not want to become ten, the age when boys become wringers at the annual Pigeon Day shooting.

Yang the Third and Her Impossible Family

Lensey Namioka

Illustrated by: Kees de Kiefte

New York: Bantam, 1996, ©1995

Grade Level: 4-6

Pages: 143

Themes: Friendship, Accepting Limitations and Gifts, Diversity of Cultures

Other: Audio, Limited

Yingmei "Mary" Yang is worried that her family, who recently moved to Seattle, will not be accepted. She learns that it's best when each person is true to who he or she is.

Theme Clusters

Making Connections

    Community Building

    Social Skills

    Cooperation, Sharing, Dealing with Competition

    Friendship, Inclusion and Exclusion

    Alike and Different

Emotional Literacy

    Satisfying Basic Emotional Needs

    Accepting Limitations and Gifts

    Recognizing and Identifying Emotions in Self and Others, Anger, Fear or Worry, Jealousy

    Anger (as a subtheme of Recognizing and Identifying Emotions)

    Overcoming Obstacles, Coping

Caring and Effective Communication

    Listening

    Honesty

    Mean vs. Strong Words: Assertiveness, I-Messages

    Empathy

    Point of View

Cultural Competence and Social Responsibility

    Appreciating Cultural Diversity

    Community in Action

    Prejudice and Dislike, Stereotypes, Oppression, Racism, Discrimination

    Gender Roles

    Peacemaking

    Diversity of Cultures

    Diversity of Individuals

    Respect for Elderly and Disabled

    Respect in General

Conflict Management and Responsible Decision Making

    Exploring Conflict: Conflict Nature, Conflict Escalator

    Relational Conflict: Bullying, Hurtful Words, Peer Pressure, Rumors or Suspicion

    Responsible Decision Making

    Solving Conflicts: Problem Solving, Win-Win Solutions

    Solving Conflicts: Mediation or Negotiation, Nonviolent Response

Theme List

Accepting Limitations and Gifts
Alike and Different
Anger
Apologizing or Forgiving
Appreciating Cultural Diversity
Assertiveness

Basic Emotional Needs
Bullying

Community Building
Community in Action
Competition, Dealing with
Conflict Escalator
Conflict Nature
Cooperation
Coping

Discrimination
Diversity of Cultures
Diversity of Individuals

Emotions in Self and Others
Empathy

Fear or Worry
Friendship

Gender Roles

Honesty
Hurtful Words

I-Messages
Inclusion or Exclusion

Jealousy

Listening

Mediation or Negotiation

Nonviolent Response

Oppression
Overcoming Obstacles

Peacemaking
Peer Pressure
Point of View
Prejudice or Dislike
Problem Solving

Racism
Respect for Elderly or Disabled
Respect in General
Responsible Decision Making
Rumors or Suspicion

Sharing
Social Skills
Stereotypes

Win-Win Solutions

Index of Book Themes

A

Accepting limitations and gifts

Anger

Chapter books

E

Elderly, respect for. *See also* **Respect for elderly and disabled**

Chapter books

Empathy
  Chapter books

Friendship, inclusion and exclusion

Chapter books

G

Gender roles

Gifts, accepting. *See* **Accepting limitations and gifts**

H

Honesty

Hurtful words. *See also* **Bullying; Peer pressure; Rumors**

S

T

Teasing. *See* **Bullying**; **Hurtful words**; **Rumors**

W

Women, roles of. *See* **Gender roles**
Worry or fear. *See* **Fear and/or worry**

Index of Authors and Illustrators

Note: Following each name is an A, an I, or an A/I in parentheses. The A is an indication that the individual is the writer of the listed books. The I is an indication that the individual is the illustrator of the listed books. The A/I indicates that the individual is both an author and illustrator.

K

Theme List

Accepting Limitations and Gifts
Alike and Different
Anger
Apologizing or Forgiving
Appreciating Cultural Diversity
Assertiveness

Basic Emotional Needs
Bullying

Community Building
Community in Action
Competition, Dealing with
Conflict Escalator
Conflict Nature
Cooperation
Coping

Discrimination
Diversity of Cultures
Diversity of Individuals

Emotions in Self and Others
Empathy

Fear or Worry
Friendship

Gender Roles

Honesty
Hurtful Words

I-Messages
Inclusion or Exclusion

Jealousy

Listening

Mediation or Negotiation

Nonviolent Response

Oppression
Overcoming Obstacles

Peacemaking
Peer Pressure
Point of View
Prejudice or Dislike
Problem Solving

Racism
Respect for Elderly or Disabled
Respect in General
Responsible Decision Making
Rumors or Suspicion

Sharing
Social Skills
Stereotypes

Win-Win Solutions